A New Engagement?

A New Engagement?

Political Participation,

Civic Life,

and the Changing

American Citizen

Cliff Zukin, Scott Keeter,

Molly Andolina, Krista Jenkins,

and Michael X. Delli Carpini

OXFORD
UNIVERSITY PRESS

2006

OXFORD
UNIVERSITY PRESS

Oxford University Press, Inc., publishes works that further
Oxford University's objective of excellence
in research, scholarship, and education.

Oxford   New York
Auckland   Cape Town   Dar es Salaam   Hong Kong   Karachi
Kuala Lumpur   Madrid   Melbourne   Mexico City   Nairobi
New Delhi   Shanghai   Taipei   Toronto

With offices in
Argentina   Austria   Brazil   Chile   Czech Republic   France   Greece
Guatemala   Hungary   Italy   Japan   Poland   Portugal   Singapore
South Korea   Switzerland   Thailand   Turkey   Ukraine   Vietnam

Published by Oxford University Press, Inc.
198 Madison Avenue, New York, New York 10016

www.oup.com

Oxford is a registered trademark of Oxford University Press

Library of Congress Cataloging-in-Publication Data
A new engagement? political participation, civic life, and the changing American citizen /
Cliff Zukin . . . [et al.].
p. cm.
Includes bibliographical references and index.
ISBN-13 978-0-19-518316-0; 978-0-19-518317-7 (pbk.)

1. Political participation — United States. 2. Citizenship — United States. 3. Civil
society — United States. I. Zukin, Cliff.
JK1764.N488   2006
323'.042'08420973 — dc22   2005025374

Printed in the United States of America
on acid-free paper

To my ladies: Debbie, Hannah, and Rachel
CZ

To four fine GenXers: Brad, Ethan, Eric, and Hunter
SK

To my mother, Sandra Sonner
MA

To Sean, and the newest citizen in my life, Zoe Claire
KJ

To my father, Domenick
MXDC

Preface

A New Engagement? is about the intersection of two important highways of American political life. The first is the nature of citizen engagement — its amount, quality, and health; the second is the nature of political and societal change through generational differences and population replacement. Our goal in writing this book is to tell a generational tale of citizen engagement at the millennium, focusing largely on those under 40 years of age, using their elders for contrast. We offer a first look at a new generation of citizens, aged 15 to 27, whom we call the DotNets. And we offer the first systematic, comprehensive look at political participation in the post 9/11 era.

Let us state a clear bias at the outset: we believe *citizen engagement matters.* We believe it is better to be involved than not, and that the transmission of the value of engagement from one generation to the next is the responsibility of all of us. After all, no one spends such time, energy, and money studying a problem they believe to be unimportant. We were motivated to better understand, explain, and hopefully contribute to the reversal of the disconnection of young people from the political process. But while the choice of a research problem is not value-free, the means of studying it must be. In addition to being citizens and teachers, we aspire to be counted as scholars. Though the authors have different backgrounds, we all worship at the altar of empiricism. We strive to make our observations dispassionately, and without regard for what we would like to find.

A main story avenue is that the generational chain of engagement has been broken, at least in the electoral realm. In this case the new-comers look very much like their predecessors, Generation X. They are quite removed from the arena of traditional political participation, and the finding that sizable portions of two successive generations have now opted out of electoral political life portends a less attentive citizenry and potentially dire consequences for the quality of our democracy.

However, we believe another important contribution of the book is to distinguish *political* from *civic* engagement. And in the more private, civic sphere of activity–volunteering, being active in one's community, and using the economic muscle of consumerism–these younger citizens are quite active. Indeed, when viewed through this prism even Genera-tion X, often held up as the poster child for poor citizenship, hasn't turned out to be as detached as widely believed. And, we find some evidence that the DotNets may be reversing the generational slide into political indifference. In the end, we're not sure if the glass is half-empty or half-full. In some measure, it depends whether one is pouring or drinking. We will let our readers judge for themselves.

Almost all of the data presented in *A New Engagement?* were col-lected by the authors in the course of the National Youth Civic En-gagement Index project, funded by The Pew Charitable Trusts. Ours has been a four year journey, beginning in January 2001 and finishing with a completed manuscript in the summer of 2005. We started by convening two panels of experts, many of whom worked with politically active youth on a daily basis, in March and April of 2001. We felt it important to start *tabula rasa*: we knew little about how young people were active in the civic and political life of the country, and wished to be blinded by no presumptions. Taking what we learned from these discussions, we con-ducted 13 focus groups during May and June of 2001 in four different regions of the country — the Midwest, Northeast, South, and West. Most groups were conducted with people from a single generation, with a greater number of groups conducted with DotNets and GenXers. But we talked with others as well. With the assistance of Knowledge Networks we then conducted a web-based probability survey of 1,200 15- to 25-year-olds in January and February of 2002. Our questionnaire focused on volunteerism, assorted civic and political behaviors, attitudes toward pol-itics, and high school and college experiences.

With a greater sensitivity to the experiences of both young and old, as well as the nuances of question wording, we launched our primary data collection activity, the National Civic Engagement Survey—a nationwide telephone survey of 3,200 respondents ages 15 and older in April and May of 2002, fielded by Schulman, Ronca and Bucuvalas, Inc. (SRBI). To gauge the reliability of our results and to explore some unexpected findings from the initial survey, we subsequently conducted a second national telephone survey shortly after the 2002 national elections, interviewing a random sample of 1,400 adults (this time 18 and over) between November 14–20 of 2002. Half of this was fielded by SRBI and half by Princeton Survey Research Associates International (PSRAI) to test various methodological issues. We also made use of a variety of other national and statewide surveys to augment our primary data collection activities, as appropriate.

A New Engagement? has five owners. The idea was initially developed by Cliff Zukin and Scott Keeter, longtime collaborators, with the encouragement of Michael X. Delli Carpini. At the time Delli Carpini was director of the Public Policy program at The Pew Charitable Trusts. Molly Andolina joined Zukin and Keeter as one of the three co-principal investigators on the grant, and Krista Jenkins later joined as the project manager. Delli Carpini joined the author group in time for the writing of this manuscript upon his move from Pew back to an academic perch. We've listed the authors in the order of joining the research team; all five of us were intimately involved in writing the book.

Acknowledgments

We have an unabashedly long list of acknowledgments. It would be impossible for the five of us to have come on such a long journey without incurring heavy debts along the way. We first want to thank The Pew Charitable Trusts, who awarded us a grant to explore civic engagement through a generational prism. Tabitha (Tobi) Walker, our program officer, was a delight to work with. Subsequent to awarding us this grant, Pew funded CIRCLE, the Center for Information and Research on Civic Learning and Engagement, and we've reaped benefits through contact, feedback, and encouragement from Carrie Donovan, Bill Galston, Emily

Kirby, Peter Levine, Mark Hugo Lopez, and Demetria Sapienza, among others at the Center.

Second, we want to recognize our institutions. Both George Mason University, where Keeter began the project, and Rutgers spent copious time on grant and contract administration, and we're especially indebted to the Edward J. Bloustein School of Planning and Public Policy, as well as to the Eagleton Institute of Politics at Rutgers. We're also appreciative of the support of DePaul University, its political science faculty, staff and students, Fairleigh Dickinson University, and the Annenberg School for Communication of the University of Pennsylvania.

Third, we are indebted to a number of professional colleagues who are scattered about, including Liz Beaumont, Lance Bennett, Deborah Both, Harry Boyte, Henry Brady, Richard Brody, David Campbell, Beth Donovan, Tom Ehrlich, Ivan Frishberg, Cassandra Harper, Sheilah Mann, David Moore, Linda Sax, Kay Lehman Schlozman, Merrill Shanks, David Skaggs, Judith Torney-Purta, and Lori Vogelgesang. At Rutgers, valued colleagues included Jocelyn Crowley, Jane Junn, Rick Lau, and especially Alan Rosenthal. And, the biggest thank you to Michele Horgan! At the Pew Research Center for the People and the Press, Peyton Craighill, Michael Dimock, Andrew Kohut, and Nilanthi Samaranayake lent their keen eyes to the enterprise.

Fourth, we had some of the best minds in survey research to bounce ideas off of and oversee our data collection activities. Thanks to Mark Schulman and Chintan Turakhia of SRBI, G. Evans Witt and Jonathan Best of PSRA, Mike Dennis, Michael Dender, and Bill McCready of Knowledge Networks.

The graduate research assistants who have touched the project while passing through Rutgers have been a privilege to teach and learn from. With very deep gratitude for contributions more than they probably know, a heartfelt bow to Rachel Askew, Dana Birnberg, P. Markley Craighill III, Allison Kopicki, Rebecca Moore, Kelly Sand, Rob Suls, and Tiffany Turner.

At Oxford, we had the good fortune to be guided by Dedi Felman, Laura Lewis, and Linda Donnelly. We thank them for their substantive suggestions and for getting the book out in a timely way.

At most, we owe our respondents more than we can say. All told, we interviewed about 5,800 people in our three major data collection activities, and probably upwards of 7,000 including our pilot testing on statewide surveys in New Jersey and Virginia, not including the hundred-plus who sat around focus group tables to help us figure out the genes and experiences that lead to civic engagement. Thanks to each of these individuals for giving us more than 2,500 hours of collective time, answers, and insights, without which these pages would be blank.

At last, we acknowledge each other. The book has truly been a collaborative project, and a joyful one at that. In addition to our seven chapters, this period produced four new jobs, four new houses, four (obviously new) babies, and five very close friends along the way. We share with pride whatever contribution *A New Engagement?* makes along with whatever errors may be between the covers. The final word of thanks goes to our spouses, families, friends, and pets. It's been a long time.

All data gathered by the authors for this research (NCES1, NCES2, and NYS) are available on the web site of the Center for Information and Research on Civic Learning and Engagement (CIRCLE) at http://civic youth.org

—Cliff Zukin
New Brunswick, October 22, 2005

Contents

A New Engagement?

1

Introduction

The nature of citizen engagement in public life in the United States is changing. Citizen participation both determines who will hold positions of government power and communicates the public's values and opinions to these officials. Consequently, changes in the nature and scope of participation affect the quality of our democracy. A consistent theme of social and political analysis over the past four decades has been the gradual disengagement of the American citizenry from public life, and especially from traditional political participation. This apparent decline has been greatest among the youngest Americans, who have historically been the least engaged. But we believe these generalizations may be misleading.

In this book we describe levels and patterns of political and civic participation, and the variety of ways people make their voices heard in the political arena. We conduct our examination through the prism of generational differences among those living in the United States today. We argue that citizens are participating in a different *mix* of activities from in the past, and that this is due largely to the process of generational replacement. We believe the volume of citizen engagement has not declined so much as it has spread to a wider variety of channels. And this may require different listening skills among political and social analysts to correctly measure the decibel level and fully understand the messages being sent.

The 2004 election notwithstanding, voter turnout among young citizens has been declining over the past three decades while remaining stable among older people. In contrast, however, younger Americans are relatively active in the *civic* arena, and there is evidence that this participation is growing. Aided in part by the Internet, young people are matching their elders in the public expression of their civic voices. And their participation involves an intriguing combination of continuity with the past mixed with a variety of new perspectives.

What is driving these changes in participation? The last 40 years have been marked by a series of political events and trends that have had a profound impact on the way American politics and government are perceived by citizens. High-level government scandals and unpopular wars have eroded public trust in the honesty and sagacity of leaders. Antigovernment and antipolitical rhetoric has dampened Americans' belief in the relevance of government for solving problems. National elections still matter—some would say more than ever—but gerrymandering at the state and local level has rendered most legislative districts uncompetitive, relegating real competition to the intraparty struggles for nomination when incumbents retire or are perceived as straying from party orthodoxy. Government and politics increasingly seem, to paraphrase Schattschneider (1942), a song sung by and to elites and special interests. At the same time, a growing shift in power and responsibility to the private and nonprofit sectors from government has further dampened the resonance of traditional politics.

We are not arguing that this new version of participation substitutes seamlessly for the old. Indeed, we believe that active participation in elections remains one of the most important venues for citizen input, and in this arena younger Americans still lag behind. Nonetheless, the changes we document in this book are consequential, and paint a very different picture from either the usual laments of a disengaged, apathetic public or the static posture that little if anything has changed. Many Americans are now engaged in a range of public activities that go beyond participation in traditional electoral politics. About as many people undertake civic activities as electoral ones, and the collective amount of time spent in civic work probably greatly exceeds the time devoted to purely political activity. A significant segment of the public eschews voting and campaigning and concentrates on civic activities such as volunteering and community problem solving with others. Just as organized interest groups are increasingly doing, many Americans also engage in public affairs by giving voice to their opinions through the media, through direct contacts with other citizens, through contact with public officials and policy makers, and even through their choices as consumers. In short, we argue that, for better or worse, we are witnessing the emergence of new patterns of public engagement that are already affecting the nature of politics in contemporary America and that, absent direct intervention or unforeseen events, promise to continue to do so well into the future.

Of course none of this is written in stone, and the full story of trends in participation is a complicated narrative. Consider, for example, participation in American national elections. Despite the uptick in 2004, voter turnout has been at best stagnant over the past 30 years, despite growing levels of education and greater citizen access to news and information (McDonald 2001). Turnout among young people dropped after 1972, declining nearly 15 percentage points between 1972 and 2000, resulting in a larger gap between younger and older citizens (Levine and Lopez 2002).

This pattern was interrupted in 2004. The presidential contest that year was marked by sharply higher citizen engagement, driven by divisive but important issues, as well as an unusually high degree of personal and partisan bitterness and rancor. Accompanying the strong emotions of the campaign were new and broader efforts to mobilize voters by both sides. And there was a special focus on turning out younger voters. Perhaps in response to both the general uptick in mobilization and the specific efforts aimed at them, turnout among younger citizens increased more than among older ones (see fig. 1.1). More younger citizens were active in the election in other ways as well. It is hard to know at this juncture if 2004 was an anomaly or a harbinger of further positive change. At the least, it demonstrated that youth may be willing to participate if the effort is made to draw out that participation.

The Civic-Political Divide

While there are numerous ways to categorize the various kinds of citizen involvement in public life, in this book we identify and focus on what we believe is a potentially important fault line in citizen engagement:

the distinction between political and civic participation. Following Verba, Schlozman, and Brady, we define political engagement as "activity that has the intent or effect of influencing government action — either directly by affecting the making or implementation of public policy or indirectly by influencing the selection of people who make those policies" (Verba, Schlozman, and Brady 1995: 38). Voting is the most important activity within this domain, but it also includes activities such as working for a candidate or party, trying to convince someone how to vote, or working (individually or collectively) to affect the making or implementation of public policies by officials. Political engagement has long been marked by significant age differences, with younger citizens much less active. Figure 1.2 shows the scope of age differences in voting and general attention to government and public affairs.

The lower level of youth engagement in the political world has consequences. Currently, the youngest cohort of citizens is more liberal and Democratic than the rest of the electorate. As a result, the 2004 election would have been even closer had younger voters turned out at the same rate as older ones. And if young people had come out to vote at the same rate as their older counterparts, we believe Al Gore would have defeated George W. Bush in the 2000 election for president.[1]

FIGURE 1.1
Trends in voter turnout.

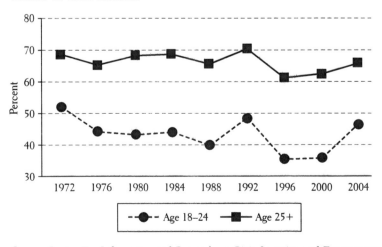

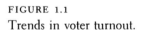

Source: Center For Information and Research on Civic Learning and Engagement.

In contrast to political engagement, civic engagement is defined as organized voluntary activity focused on problem solving and helping others. It includes a wide range of work undertaken alone or in concert with others to effect change. Unlike the situation with political engagement, young people match their elders in many aspects of civic engagement, an avenue of participation increasingly encouraged by the schools and facilitated by parents and community organizations. As figure 1.3 shows, the percentage of young Americans engaged in regular volunteer activity nearly equals that of their Baby Boomer parents. And our qualitative evidence provides many examples of volunteering and other civic activities in which youth are taking part. In focus groups we conducted across the country we found some of those young people who eschew voting were nevertheless involved in an impressive variety of activities that speak in a different voice.

- We met "Larry," 20, living in Chicago. Although eligible to vote, he did not do so in 2000. But confronted with the problem of a driver who repeatedly sped at "eighty miles per hour" down his neighborhood street filled with children, he worked through local government filling out forms and getting neighbors to sign a petition in order to get authorization for "Chil-

FIGURE 1.2
Political engagement by age.

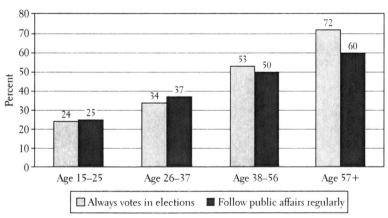

Source: NCES1 Survey.

dren at Play, Slow Down" signs to be put up. When the signs didn't slow down the driver, he went to his local police to convince them to stake out the area at the appropriate time. They caught the driver, who, Larry said, had alcohol on his breath and drugs in his car.

- In California we met "Alex," who described himself as one of "a lot of us who aren't getting into the political arena." But he went on tell us how he exercised his lone, unorganized voice as a consumer in everyday life: "You just don't buy it. I don't like the way Nike does business. I don't buy Nikes . . . I don't buy Exxon gas, unless I'm out of gas and it's the only gas station around. . . . because of the way they handled the cleanup [of the Exxon Valdez] and everything they did up there" [in Alaska].

- In North Carolina it was "Erin," 28. Although she did not vote in 2000, she was very active in an organization of breast cancer survivors, "Save Our Sisters." She got involved, as she noted in our African American focus group, because "even though Caucasian females have a higher rate of breast cancer, the mortality rate among black women is greater because a lot of [our] people don't go and get mammograms and checkups."

FIGURE 1.3
Volunteerism by age.

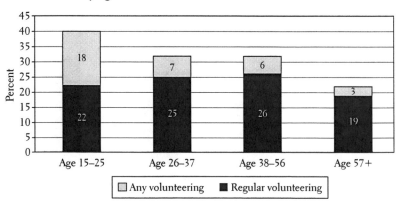

Source: NCES1 Survey.

The changes we are seeing in how and how much citizens engage in the public sphere raise two sets of questions that guided our research. The first revolves around the nature of citizen engagement itself. What does "citizen engagement" entail in twenty-first-century democracies such as the United States? This is a question that has no simple answer — as is attested by the myriad of existing and often competing theories of democracy and empirical measures of participation (Brady 1999; Dahl 1989; Hanson 1985; Morone 1990; Pateman 1970). We do our best to capture as wide a range of civic and political activities as possible — from consumer boycotting to voting in presidential elections.

A second and more normative question regarding the nature of citizen engagement is "What kinds of participation are 'best,' both for individuals and for the polity more broadly?" Two polar stances might be considered. First, rather than assuming that a particular kind of participation (for example voting) is inherently more important than others (such as nonpolitical volunteering) or that citizens *must* engage in certain kinds of activities to fulfill their civic obligations, why not start from the premise that there are many ways citizens can and do participate in the democratic life of a nation? We are a very pluralistic society, after all, and few would disagree that different types of participation may be more appropriate for and/or accessible to different individuals and groups, for different purposes, and at different times in the life of a person or a nation. From this perspective, the trend in declining turnout among the young (2004 aside) can be interpreted as not a rejection of public life but a shift in the types of participation in which these citizens are engaging.

An alternative view is that certain kinds of engagement are individually or collectively superior to others. For example, many theorists and practitioners see campaigns and elections as the sine qua non of a representative democracy, providing accountability while also assuring stability. Others are as or more vehement in their disdain for privileging this kind of "thin democracy," arguing for the superiority of more local and direct forms of democratic involvement.

In this book we try to walk a middle ground between these two views. We acknowledge the necessity and value of diverse participation, while remaining cognizant that civic engagement can not substitute for political engagement or vice versa. The "gold standard" for a democratic polity would be equitable and substantial participation in both the civic and political spheres, and the "gold standard" for a democratic citizen would be someone who is facile in both types of engagement.

Generational Replacement and the Changing Nature of Citizen Engagement

Given the emphasis we place on the implications of longer term trends in the mix of civic and political engagement for the health of American democracy, the impact of generational replacement is of particular relevance. We have already noted the generation gap in voter turnout over the past 30-plus years. There is additional, if mixed and debated, evidence that the growing generational divide in the public's psychological and behavioral engagement in public life goes far beyond voting (National Commission on Civic Renewal 1998; Putnam 2000; Skocpol 2003). This includes, among other things, electoral activity such as working for parties and candidates, choosing public service careers, and following public affairs in the news. And it extends to certain kinds of engagement in civil society, such as organizational membership, social interactions with friends and neighbors, and trust in fellow citizens (National Commission on Civic Renewal 1998; Putnam 2000; Rahn 1998; Skocpol 2003). Political scientist Robert Putnam has decried this apparent erosion of the public sphere, carefully documenting a 30-year trend in declining political and civic engagement and the impact of this decline on the quality of our individual and collective personal and public lives (Putnam 2000).

While numerous "suspects" have been identified as the potential source of this political and civic decay—for example, changes in family structure, the decline of political parties, the increased pressures of limited time, the need/desire for money, suburbanization, immigration, politicians' scandalous behaviors, television and other electronic media— according to Putnam the most important cause has been the replacement of older, more engaged cohorts with younger, less engaged ones, accounting for fully half of the downward spiral in engagement. But identifying generational replacement as a cause begs the question of why the younger cohort arrives with a diminished commitment to participation. Generational replacement is one of the most fundamental issues any polity faces, since over time it literally involves the placing of its future into the hands of an entirely new and untested public. At the heart of this process is the generational transfer of a society's collective norms, values, beliefs, and knowledge. To say that younger Americans are less committed to the value of engagement than their predecessors raises the obvious question of why this has happened.

Not surprisingly, given its complexity, the way in which new generations come to reflect, reject, or *remix* the civic and political patterns of their elders is much studied but only partially understood. Simplifying a bit, the core assumption is that each new cohort has the potential to develop its own worldview, which in turn affects its members' more specific opinions and behaviors. This generational perspective is a product of many influences, being based (1) in part upon what it has learned through the informal and formal education and socialization that takes place daily through families, friends, schools, the media, and other social, cultural and political institutions, (2) in part on key events that occur while one is coming of age (for example a war or economic depression), and (3) in part on more long-term trends that lead new generations to reach adulthood in social, cultural, economic, and political circumstances significantly different from prior ones (for example, major changes in the communications environment brought on by the development of television or the Internet). The period of adolescence through young adulthood (approximately the mid-teens through early twenties) is viewed as particularly important in this process, as both individual and generational identities are most likely to crystallize during this time (Delli Carpini 1989; Jennings 1981; Mannheim 1952). In short, generations, much like individuals, can develop their own distinct "personalities."

But people also change as they grow older because of age-specific experiences. Different stages of the life cycle bring different politically relevant events, for example, paying income taxes for the first time, choosing a school for a child, or helping an elderly parent deal with Medicare and other health care choices. In addition, habits such as voting take time to build. It is natural that certain behaviors will become more frequent with practice.

The fact that both generational and life cycle effects operate simultaneously makes it difficult to draw conclusions about age-related differences in attitudes and behavior at any single point in time. Life cycle perspectives assume that these differences are mostly tied to cohort members' specific place on a developmental continuum, and thus will change in predictable ways as these members age. Generational perspectives assume that age differences will mostly persist through time. For example, a generational interpretation of the greater support for gay marriage among today's young adults would argue that these views will persist as this cohort ages, while a life cycle interpretation would argue these attitudes are characteristic of the relatively more open views young people have about sexuality in any era, and so support for gay marriage will decline as this cohort grows older. And, of course, the picture becomes even more complicated when one considers that both generational and life cycle influences can occur at the same time, and that they can sometimes work in opposite directions. Undoubtedly, both life cycle and generational effects are at play in explaining differences in the amount and type of engagement across age cohorts, and we will try to tease out these distinct forces as we go.

Plan of the Book

Our generationally driven tale of the changing nature of citizen engagement unfolds in the following six chapters. We begin in chapter 2 by presenting a brief social and political history of the past 40 years. Although this history was largely made by the two oldest cohorts, its consequences play out in the attitudes and behavior of the two younger cohorts. We explore the cultural and political conditions in which GenXers and DotNets have grown up.

Chapter 3 describes the broad panoply of current citizen engagement by presenting a lay-of-the-land exposition of what people do across a wide variety of behavioral and cognitive indicators. We then use these indicators to develop a summary typology of citizen engagement that distills these 28 indicators into four dimensions — what we call political engagement, civic engagement, cognitive engagement, and public voice. This chapter also describes patterns of involvement among our four cohorts, finding sharp differences in political and cognitive engagement, but greater similarity in civic work and the expression of public voice.

In chapter 4 we present an in-depth look at the attitudes and values of the public that are relevant to citizen engagement — most closely examining the two youngest cohorts who are still forming their political habits. The chapter begins with a examination of the reasons young people give for not participating in the electoral arena. We then present data on how they view themselves and the role and responsibilities of citizenship, along with their attitudes about politics, government, and their fellow citizens.

Chapter 5 examines the various pathways to civic and political participation, teasing out the factors—from parental socialization to values, norms and attitudes—that lead citizens to engage in public life and/or to privilege certain kinds of participation over others. We also explore generational differences in this process and address ways engagement among young people might be encouraged and facilitated.

Chapter 6 turns to the question of how the changing nature of citizen engagement is likely to affect the substance of politics and governance. From a generational perspective, we examine where our cohorts stand on the broad indicators of partisanship and ideology, and on the substantive issues of the day. Beyond its relevance for politics today, this analysis may tell us something about the politics of tomorrow, when the younger cohorts will be in positions of greater responsibility. As with the question of participation itself, we ask—and try to answer—whether cohort differences in political attitudes will persist or diminish as younger cohorts age and pass through the life cycle.

Our final chapter has three goals. First, we take stock of what we have found, summarizing our argument, evidence, and conclusions regarding the remixing of citizen engagement in America. Second, we look ahead to the implications of our findings—what it means if current trends continue and how things might be different if a larger group and variety of citizens were to become engaged, or become engaged in a different way. Finally, we modestly offer a few prescriptions. Although our work has been largely descriptive and analytical, it does yield some clear implications for practice on the part of those seeking and holding public office, the schools, parents, and the media.

The Cast of Characters

Much of the book focuses on the experiences, attitudes, and activities of four distinct age cohorts that constitute the U.S. population at the start of the twenty-first century. These cohorts are offered as potential generations, but we recognize that drawing boundaries between generations is a risky activity, one informed as much by a general sense of how the social and political environment has differed across time as by empirical data about individual differences across age groups. In drawing such boundaries we consulted a mix of scholarly and popular analyses of generations, as well as our own examination of history and survey data. The next chapter will look in detail at the historical experiences of the past 40 years and how different cohorts may have been affected by these events.

The four cohorts are as follows.

"Dutifuls," born before 1946, are about 52 million strong in the country today. They arrived before the explosion of the first nuclear weapon. Driven by duty and sculpted by sacrifice, this generation was forged by the experiences of the Depression and World War II, even though many experienced them indirectly through their parents while growing up. The terrorist attacks of September 11, 2001, are often compared to Japan's surprise attack on Pearl Harbor of December 7, 1941. The call to arms in 1941 was met by what has been called the "greatest generation" in the popular press (Brokaw 1998). However, this generation is now mainly a romantic memory—most are long buried, along with their immigrant histories and values. We are now close to being four times removed from the World War II generation that is said to have represented the gold standard of political and civic participation. What is left in this category is the last remnant of that generation, along with the following cohort, often called the Silent Generation, who paid their dues by working hard for a better life and upholding the responsibilities and privileges of citizenship. We group them together, as there are too few of those in the greatest generation remaining for independent statistical analysis, and we believe the participative natures of both groups to be similar.

"Baby Boomers," born between 1946 and 1964, constitute the largest age cohort—about 71 million. Perhaps the best known of the generations, this group was parented by prosperity. Formative political experiences were the civil rights movement, Vietnam, and Watergate, not to mention drugs and the sexual revolution. Their rebellion against the norms of the generation that preceded them has marked Baby Boomers as a reference point for most contemporary generational analysis. The Boomer cohort has always been big enough to force the culture to adapt to them. For years they have dictated politics and culture by their sheer numbers in a market-driven economy, and policy to the degree they have had a coherent outlook. But they are no monolith politically, as is dramatically illustrated by the successive presidencies of Bill Clinton and George W. Bush.

"Generation X," "GenXers," or "Xers," born between 1965 and 1976, are slightly smaller than the Dutifuls (40 million), and the two generations have many differences. This group's formative experiences were framed by familial and financial insecurity. They grew up amid rising rates of divorce and recession (Zukin 1997). Where the sexual revolution of the Boomers brought free expression and experimentation, the threat of AIDS brought Xers fear and caution. During adolescence and early adulthood, their political worldview was shaped by perceived government economic and foreign policy failures during the late 1970s, Ronald Reagan's "Morning in America" followed by the embarrassment of the Iran-Contra scandal, all ladled with big doses of antipolitical rhetoric. This generation's youngest members came of age around the time of the Persian Gulf War, which ended quickly and without many American casualties, with computer-aimed smart bombs falling on targets as in a video arcade game. Little has been asked of them in the way of sacrifice, and they have responded in kind. Indeed, Generation X has been the poster child for poor citizenship. Described as "slackers," and scorned for a worldview that begins and ends with themselves, even their moniker is about something that never happened.

"DotNets" are the new kids in town—the 50 million young adults now between 15 and 28 years of age, at the writing of this book—born after 1976. They go by many labels—Millennials, Generation NeXt, Generation Y—but calling them a true generation remains premature. Generations are shaped by shared experiences and are clear only in history's rear-view mirror. We call them the DotNets because we think one of their defining characteristics will be having come of age along with the Internet. Information has always been virtually costless and universally available to them; technology cheap and easily mastered; community as much a digital place of common interest as a shared physical space. The oldest in this cohort grew up in the simultaneous prosperity and scandal of the Clinton era and amid a renewed focus on the family. As we began our research, little was known about DotNets; indeed, this was a principal motivation for our project.

In the next chapter we devote considerable attention to the social, political, and economic cultures in which GenXers and DotNets grew up, speculating on how these different socialization experiences may lead to differences in political outlook and participation.

Coming of Age
in a Post-Boomer World

On March 19, 2003, the United States attacked Iraq. The devastating aerial bombardment of Baghdad and other major cities, described by military leaders as a campaign of "shock and awe," involved thousands of sorties flown by U.S. fighter planes, bombers, and helicopters. Several days later, over 150,000 troops entered Iraq from Kuwait and began their trek north, battling Iraqi soldiers and paramilitary fighters along the way. Within three weeks they reached Baghdad, and Saddam Hussein's regime collapsed. Each day hundreds of millions of television viewers around the world watched live broadcasts as the events unfolded.

In the United States, practically every American was transfixed by the military light shows, edited video, and debriefings being transmitted daily into their homes. What was the impact of these images? There is of

SELECTED EVENTS AND TRENDS
1965

Los Angeles race riots	Malcolm X assassinated	New York City blackout	U.S. combat troops sent to Vietnam	1.6% inflation rate

AGE RANGE: Dutifuls = 20+   Boomers = 1–19   GenXers = <1

course no simple answer to this question, as each individual was undoubtedly affected by a host of personal experiences that influenced the way he or she attempted to make sense of the flood of images and commentary. But personal experiences are not completely unique. They are influenced by larger economic, cultural, political, and technological trends, and by the resulting events that capture the attention and imagination of whole communities, societies, and, as the Iraq War itself demonstrates, even the world.

The combination of personal and collective experiences can lead to generational differences in political attitudes, opinions and behaviors. Consider, for example, the ages of the four cohorts we defined in chapter 1 as the Iraq War began. In 2003 Dutifuls (those born during or before 1945) were 58 years old or older, with a median age of approximately 70. As this age cohort viewed the unfolding events, they could draw on personal memories, feelings, and attitudes shaped by collective experiences reaching back as far as World War II. Baby Boomers (those born between 1946 and 1964) were between the ages of 39 and 57, with a median age of approximately 47. For most of this age cohort, Vietnam (and for some, Korea) marked the outer limits of their collective memories of war. GenXers (born between 1965 and 1976) were 27 to 38 years old as they watched the first cruise missiles hit Baghdad in 2003, with a median age of about 32. For most of this cohort, the Vietnam War was something experienced as a child or adolescent at best, with the invasions of Panama or Grenada, the "collapse of communism," or the brief and overwhelmingly one-sided first Gulf War providing much more tangible touchstones to issues of foreign affairs. And DotNets (born after 1976) were in their teens and early twenties. For most of this cohort, the Iraq War was their introduction to international conflict in the post–Cold War era.

The unique experiences of these four cohorts — either by witnessing different collective events or living through broader technological, eco-

SELECTED EVENTS AND TRENDS
1966

Black Panther Party founded	Mao Zedong launches Cultural Revolution	Mass antidraft protests start in U.S.	*Star Trek* TV series premiere	2.9% inflation rate

AGE RANGE: Dutifuls = 21+   Boomers = 2–20   GenXers = 1

nomic, cultural, or political shifts—distinguish them from one another. They are also differentiated by the fact that experiences that are collectively shared are interpreted differently depending on one's age at the time they occur. While dramatic events such as the assassination of a president or a terrorist attack affect all members of society, the impact is unlikely to be the same for each cohort because it is experienced at different points in the life cycle. For example, while several age cohorts lived through the Vietnam War, it was experienced very differently by middle-aged men who had fought in previous wars, younger men who were eligible to be drafted, and elementary school boys whose only knowledge of the fighting may have been glimpses of the evening news. This matters because research suggests that the events and conditions experienced in youth and early adulthood play a critical role in the development of an individual's and a generation's subsequent worldview (Sears 1975; Jennings and Niemi 1981).

But who experiences certain events and trends and how they experience them are not the only factors that lead to the formation of a generation. A key element in this process is the larger information environment in which such events occur. Most Americans "experienced" World War II through newspapers, radio, and occasional newsreels, the Vietnam War through taped footage broadcast nightly by one of the three news networks, the Gulf War through live network and cable coverage, and the war with Iraq through all of these, plus the Internet.

Finally, *perceptions*—about the nature and impact of particular events, longer term trends, and even particular age cohorts or generations themselves—can affect generational characters as much as the events, trends, and cohorts themselves, especially in the mediated world within which we currently live. Our collective stereotypes of the "roaring twenties," the "Depression era," the "tumultuous sixties," the "conservative eighties," or the "post–9/11 era," while based at least in part in reality,

SELECTED EVENTS AND TRENDS
1967

Che Guevara killed	First heart transplant	First Super Bowl	Six-Day Middle East War	3 astronauts killed in flight simulation	3.1% inflation rate

AGE RANGE: Dutifuls = 22+   Boomers = 3–21   GenXers = 1–2

can be as important as the reality itself. Similarly, our stereotypes of the community-oriented and self-sacrificing "greatest generation," the radical, politically engaged "sixties generation," or the cynical, lost, and self-absorbed "slacker generation" can be as important, even self-fulfilling, as the reality upon which they are only partially and broadly based.

In our chapter 1, we described the four cohorts that form the American political landscape today, separating post–Boomers into two distinct groups. We defend this categorization in part through empirical means — and in subsequent chapters we use numerous measures of attitudes and behavior to document how Xers and DotNets are distinct from both each other and their elders. But our rationale for these differences is also grounded in the unique socialization of both Xers and DotNets — environments and experiences that we argue are different enough from those of their elders and each other that we would *expect* each cohort to possess distinct ways of acting in and responding to the political world.

In this chapter we provide a broad overview of the economic, cultural, political, and technological environments of the past 40 years. These developments provide a roadmap to the current nature of citizen engagement. And while the twists and turns along the way have shaped the habits and attitudes of all Americans, regardless of age, they have been experienced most intensely by the two generations that have come of age during this time. That is, the evolving values and the changing conditions that have had an impact on the opinions and behavior of all Americans are especially significant for DotNets and Xers because they experienced them during their "impressionable years." This explains in part why the current participation trends manifest themselves so strongly in today's youth. It also suggests that to fully understand citizen engagement today, we need an appreciation for the events and experiences that have shaped us over time.

SELECTED EVENTS AND TRENDS
1968

M. L. King assassinated	Robert F. Kennedy assassinated	Tet offensive	Prague spring protests occur	Cronkite "declares" stalemate in Vietman	LBJ announces will not seek reelection	Richard Nixon elected president	4.2% inflation rate

AGE RANGE: Dutifuls = 23+   Boomers = 4–22   GenXers = 1–3

GenXers and DotNets grew up in different worlds from those experienced by their predecessors. Throughout their childhoods and early adulthoods, the country witnessed the deterioration (and perhaps partial rejuvenation) of social institutions (such as public schools), a revolution in technology and communications, and a weakening of traditional political practices. They have experienced demographic busts and booms, unsurpassed economic prosperity followed by a recessionary bursting of the bubble, and a globalism that carries both everyday opportunities (international cuisine) and large-scale threats (terrorism). All of this has been accompanied by changes in the cultural environment that have reinforced the lessons of these phenomena and shaped the outlook of the young men and women who have come of age in the post-Boomer era.

While both cohorts shared many similar experiences, there are some key differences in the circumstances of their childhoods and the conditions of their early adulthoods. And as noted earlier, even shared experiences may be seen through very different lenses because of the different ages at which they were experienced by GenXers and DotNets. As we also noted earlier, the interpretations we develop of this period and of the generations emerging from it are as important as the actual conditions in which these cohorts came of age. For example, the socialization of GenXers is generally described in negative terms. Observers claim that as children, Xers bore the brunt of political and social changes in the larger society, and as young adults they disproportionately suffered from transformations in the economic realm. DotNets, in contrast, are often described as being coddled and cared for as children, and as entering adulthood during a period of widespread economic prosperity and possibility, only to have the rug pulled out from under them. While both descriptions may be as much perception as reality, they set the scene for how each age group is perceived, represented, and affected by larger

SELECTED EVENTS AND TRENDS

1969

Charles Manson and "family" arrested	Neil Armstrong walks on moon	*Sesame Street* airs	Chappa-quiddick incident	Woodstock Music Festival	Yassir Arafat becomes PLO Leader	First moratorium protests	5.5% inflation rate

AGE RANGE: Dutifuls = 24+   Boomers = 5–23   GenXers = 1–4

social and cultural forces and in so doing play a role in shaping each cohort's self-identity.

Understanding these social influences lends insight into the character of each individual generation — and our society more broadly. Indeed, just as differences between youth and their elders indicate changes in our society writ large, the experiences that have shaped these generations provide a window to view broad nationwide trends.

Growing Up after the Boom: Key Events and Trends

It is easy to forget (especially for those of us who can remember things like watching the Beatles perform on the *Ed Sullivan Show!*) how old we were during certain events, and, more important, how young GenXers or DotNets were at the time. As a way of putting important events or trends in a generational context, consider the events that are listed across the bottom of these pages. Included here are a host of political, cultural, economic, and technology-related events and conditions that have occurred since 1964, the generally accepted date at which the post–World War II "Baby Boom" came to an end. These events and statistics are presented by year, along with the age range that members of each of the four generations we focus on in this book would have been at the time. Before looking more closely at what these kinds of collective experiences might tell us about the formation of generational identities among GenXers and DotNets, a few general observations are in order. First, and most obviously, it is worth commenting on what is *not* included in the table because it happened before either of the two most recent generations were born. Crucial moments that arguably helped define Dutifuls and Boomers — the Great Depression and government's response to it through the New Deal; World War II and the Holocaust; the Korean

SELECTED EVENTS AND TRENDS

1970

U.S. troops accused of My Lai massacre	Beatles break up	First Earth Day Celebration	Kent State shootings	5.7% inflation rate

AGE RANGE: Dutifuls = 25+ Boomers = 6–24 GenXers = 1–5

War; the McCarthy era witch hunts; key moments in the civil rights movement such as *Brown v. Board of Education*, the state-federal confrontation in Little Rock, Freedom Summer, or the marches and protests in Birmingham and Selma, Alabama; the election and assassination of John F. Kennedy; the women's movement; and so forth — are little more than the subject of history textbooks for GenXers and DotNets.

Second, however, the list illustrates that many of the events we associate most closely with Boomers were also experienced — albeit at a much younger age — by many GenXers. The assassinations of Martin Luther King Jr. and Robert Kennedy, key moments of the Vietnam War and the domestic turmoil related to it, cultural events such as Woodstock, and the Watergate hearings and the subsequent resignation of Richard Nixon all occurred during the early lifetimes of GenXers. Third, the same events and others occurring prior to the late 1970s (for example the legalization of abortion or the Iran hostage crisis) are as foreign to DotNets as World War II or the civil rights movement are to GenXers. Fourth, many key events and experiences such as the Iran-Contra scandal, the *Challenger* shuttle disaster, the collapse of communism, and the Persian Gulf War were experienced by *both* GenXers and DotNets, though again at very different points in their respective, collective life cycles. Finally, while we talk in terms of distinct generations, this list exposes the fact that age differences between certain members of different cohorts (i.e., those at the beginning or end of a cohort) are often smaller than those within cohorts, complicating hard-and-fast definitions of when one generation begins and another ends. With these general observations and cautions in mind, let us now turn to an overview of the sometimes overlapping, sometimes distinct worlds in which GenXers and DotNets have grown up and the possible ways these conditions may have shaped their political attitudes and behaviors as adults.

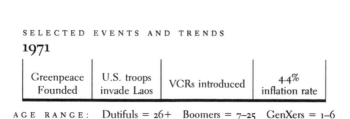

SELECTED EVENTS AND TRENDS
1971

Greenpeace Founded	U.S. troops invade Laos	VCRs introduced	4.4% inflation rate

AGE RANGE: Dutifuls = 26+   Boomers = 7–25   GenXers = 1–6

Xer Life at Home and in School: Turmoil and Risks

Each new generation is partially defined—by its members as well as by others—in comparison to the generation it succeeds. For Xers, this means a comparison with Boomers, an age cohort that experienced childhood under much more prosperous and stable conditions and entered adulthood in a highly politicized but economically prosperous era. Both situations set high and largely unmet expectations for the Xer world (and the Xer). Thus, it is little surprise that descriptions of Xers' early years are filled with examples of the failure of previously sound institutions and a general fraying of social threads—trends that began during the Boomer years but accelerated for and came to define Xers.

The hand-wringing begins with images of the breakup of the traditional two-parent family and the subsequent negative impact on Xers as children. Observers describe the late sixties and early seventies as representing the "disappearance of childhood," with stories of latchkey kids left to care for themselves and statistics documenting Xers' earlier experimentation with sex and alcohol (Lipsky and Abrams 1994). Much of this focus is on how changes in family situations left Xers with significantly less attention than that given to Boomer children. The number of divorces rose (Loeb 1994; Strauss and Howe 1993), average parent-child contact hours fell, and and television was seen as the new babysitter, filling in for an absent mom and dad (Holtz 1995: 52).[1]

Xer relationships outside their families were no rosier, as they were often conducted under the specter of AIDS. When it was first described as a "gay cancer" by the *New York Times* in 1981, the oldest Xers were adolescents (16 years old), the youngest just 5. In 1985, the year Ryan White was barred from attending school in Indiana and Rock Hudson died from the disease, Xers were between the ages of 9 and 20. By 1990, when the youngest Xers entered their teenage years and the oldest mem-

SELECTED EVENTS AND TRENDS

1972

M*A*S*H premieres	Pocket calculators introduced	Terrorist attack at Olympics	Watergate scandal begins	18- to 21-year-olds granted vote	Nixon reelected president	3.2% inflation rate

AGE RANGE: Dutifuls = 27+   Boomers = 8–26   GenXers = 1–7

bers of the generation marked their mid-twenties, the nation mourned as Ryan White, now a household name, died. In the same year, deaths from AIDS passed the 100,000 mark, almost twice the number who had died in the Vietnam War (AIDS Project Los Angeles 2003). If marriage and family appeared unstable or insecure while Xers were young, as they aged, romance and intimacy increasingly included the possibility of death.

Most popular accounts of Xers' schooling suggest little refuge from the failures associated with home, as it became commonplace to note the erosion of our public education system, once the pride of America. When the National Commission on Excellence in Education released their *Nation at Risk* report in 1983 (U.S. Department of Education 1983), in which they roundly condemned the system, most Xers were either in school or had recently graduated. In a direct reference to the implications of the system's failure for members of Generation X, the authors of the report stated: "For the first time in the history of our country, the educational skills of one generation will not surpass, will not equal, will not even approach, those of their parents" (Holtz 1995: 106). Some of this purported decline in the quality of education and the relative educational preparedness of GenXers may be more rhetorical than real, the result of an antisixties backlash and the beginnings of what would become the "culture wars." Regardless of the validity of the charges, however, the *public perception* that GenXers were the product of inferior education played an important role in the way the members of this age cohort were seen by others—and the way they came to see themselves.

One can easily imagine how each of these conditions could have lasting ramifications for Xers. Rising levels of divorce may have made Xers postpone marriage—and, indeed, the average age for marriage for men and women has continued to rise (United States Census 2003). Spending less time with parents may have made Xers especially vulner-

SELECTED EVENTS AND TRENDS

1973

Roe v. Wade decided	U.S. troops evacuate Vietnam	Vice President Agnew resigns	Draft ends	6.2% inflation rate

AGE RANGE: Dutifuls = 28+   Boomers = 9–27   GenXers = 1–8

able to messages from the broader culture and less likely to adhere to the traditional values held by members of older generations. Initiating and conducting relationships amid the fear of AIDS could be the cause for greater levels of distrust among individuals. And poor public education may have left this generation poorly equipped to deal with adult tasks—or at least to be regarded as unprepared and thus not given opportunities for such experiences.

All of these conditions, in turn, might explain why Xers are less politically active than older cohorts. Choosing to delay their entry into the adult world on a personal front might also account for their unwillingness to accept "adult" roles of citizenship, such as paying attention to the news or voting in elections. Another explanation might be that they lack the skills that are necessary for these roles (because of poor education) or they are considered immature and unprepared and thus are ignored by groups who mobilize and target citizens for action. Finally, their inactivity may be due to the fact that many are less likely to accept their parents' notions about the obligations of citizenship and more likely to reflect broader cultural attitudes that deride political participation as useless. Lacking trust in others, they may be unwilling to join organizations and work for common solutions and instead prefer to solve problems on an individualized basis. In sum, the early seeds of active citizenship—so important for later engagement—do not appear to have been sown for this generation.

Xers' Political Socialization: Government Ineptitude and Scandal

Xers' political experiences, which are replete with examples of governmental failure or suggestions of government ineptitude, did little to coun-

SELECTED EVENTS AND TRENDS
1974–1975

Patty Hearst kidnapped	Richard Nixon resigns	Arthur Ashe first black to win Wimbledon	Civil war breaks out in Lebanon	Pol Pot becomes Cambodian dictator	9.1%–11.01% inflation rate

AGE RANGE: Dutifuls = 29+   Boomers = 10–29   GenXers = 1–10

teract these early lessons. The oldest Xers (born in the late 1960s) may recall Nixon's resignation as their first political memory (Strauss and Howe 1993: 51); others would mention Carter's inability to resolve the Iran hostage crisis—complete with a botched rescue attempt—and long lines at gas stations, the events of their middle school years. By the time the youngest Xers reached elementary school, Reagan had come into the office denouncing government as "the problem, not the solution," an attitude toward the public sector that gained much popularity throughout the next decade. Indeed, Reagan's push for devolution and smaller government, which was continued by congressional Republicans, dominated much of public discourse as Xers traveled through middle school, high school, and college. When Xers began their own careers and started planning for the future, politicians warned that the future of Social Security—a governmental guarantee of assistance at life's end—was in jeopardy. Xers were learning not to have faith in government.

Indeed, the federal government appeared to be without fiscal responsibility. With each passing year, federal deficits ballooned, causing the debt to pass the one-trillion-dollar mark in 1981, and then tripling to $3.6 trillion in a decade, just as most Xers (now between the ages of 15 and 26) took their first independent financial footsteps. Five years later, when the youngest Xers reached their twenties and the oldest were in their early thirties, the Treasury Department reported a national debt of $5.2 trillion (Bureau of the Public Debt 2001).

A particularly striking example of governmental failure was the space program. Whereas Dutifuls and Boomers had witnessed man's first walk on the moon, this cohort—now between the ages of 10 and 21—sat in their classrooms and watched as the space shuttle *Challenger* exploded before their eyes. Around the same time, as the oldest Xers left high school and began to be more aware of political events, they faced a world replete with congressional hearings and investigations (from Iran-Contra

SELECTED EVENTS AND TRENDS

1976

Nadia Comaneci receives 7 perfect "10s"	Socialist Republic of Vietnam formed	Jimmy Carter elected president	5.8% inflation rate

AGE RANGE: Dutifuls = 31+   Boomers = 12–30   GenXers = 1–11

to the Savings and Loan bailout to the controversial confirmation of Justice Clarence Thomas), sending the message that politics and government meant back-room deals, investigations, and partisan attacks. Was it any wonder that government bureaucracy was incapable of launching a spaceship successfully?

In foreign policy, Xers experienced a world in which the truths averred so strongly by adults during their childhood appeared to be challenged and even abandoned as they grew older. American interaction in world affairs sent confusing messages to this generation. Having been raised to believe that the Soviet Union was a dangerous, powerful, and evil empire, they witnessed its almost overnight collapse. When the Berlin Wall fell in 1989, Xers, now in their teens and twenties, were left wondering what to make of the earlier characterization of the Soviet Union as a threat to democracy. Similarly, although Generation X was raised learning about the pitfalls of international combat (following Vietnam), throughout their youth and early adulthood they experienced American successes in three "wars" (the invasions of Grenada in 1983, Panama in 1989, and Iraq in 1991), the longest one lasting only six weeks—a far cry from the protracted engagement in Southeast Asia. Yet even these victories were ambiguous. For example, the Gulf War, which celebrated the triumph of American military prowess, resulted in a victory that did not include deposing the very man who had started the fiasco, a fact that would haunt the nation a decade later. Moreover, the notion that the motive for action appeared to be more economic (oil) than ideological (in the name of "democracy") was a lesson not lost on an already cynical youth, now between the ages of 15 and 26.

Certainly these conditions suggest that there are reasons for this age cohort to have withdrawn from public life. Researchers, commentators, and members of Generation X themselves have argued that while young people in the 1960s reacted (sometimes violently) to politics by wanting

SELECTED EVENTS AND TRENDS

1977

Elvis Presley dies	*Roots* miniseries airs	Stephen Biko killed in prison	*Star Wars* movie released	6.5% inflation rate

AGE RANGE: Dutifuls = 32+ Boomers = 13–31 GenXers = 1–12 DotNets = <1 to change government, youth of the 1980s and 1990s came of age at a time when government was disgraced. Xers were subjected to a political environment that bashed government and politics and a disjointed national agenda that failed to provide a focus for Xer concerns. The media reinforced this perspective, turning news coverage into largely negative accounts of political backbiting, deal cutting, and promise breaking (Patterson 1993). Nightly news shows aired regular features, such as the "Fleecing of America," where news anchors or reporters recounted how the government was wasting taxpayers' money. Politicians campaigned for office by running against a "corrupt" system. And parties, candidates, and interest groups spent inordinate amounts of time raising larger and larger sums of money from a very select group of corporations and wealthy individuals—and less and less time courting actual voters. All of these conditions could certainly lead to a tuning-out of politics by Xers, who would expect to see little good in government, a lot bad in the political system, and no reason to get involved (especially since they have no money to contribute).

Older generations were subject to the same messages, of course, but they faced them later in the life cycle, when they had already internalized habits of participation and engagement from earlier eras and were less vulnerable to these influences. Some of the younger Dutifuls for example, came of age in the 1950s, when government was not mistrusted, disgraced, or seen as irrelevant. Instead, Americans were oriented toward the use of government to solve problems. In their youth, Dutifuls witnessed the rebounding of Western Europe following the infusion of American funds, elected and then reelected a war hero as president, and, as they entered their late twenties, watched as the United States placed the first man on the moon. Indeed, these young men and women matured into a world where government was used to protect them from both internal and external threats to democracy from communism.

SELECTED EVENTS AND TRENDS
1978

First test-tube baby born	John Paul II elected pope	Jonestown suicides	7.6% inflation rate

AGE RANGE: Dutifuls = 33+   Boomers = 14–32   GenXers = 2–13   DotNets = 1

Similarly, although it would be an exaggeration to characterize the entire Boomer generation as actively involved in politics, the effect of Vietnam, the civil rights and women's movements, and the political violence of the period created an atmosphere in which "politics permeated the times in ways that made not thinking about and being affected by it next to impossible" (Delli Carpini 1986: 40). Boomers were socialized into the practice of grassroots politics, with an emphasis on the ability of individual citizens to affect government policy, and during which citizen action groups exercised significant leverage. Xers, on the other hand, did not have either the belief in government of the Dutifuls or the practice in political expression of the Boomers, which made them much more likely to absorb the negative messages of their times. In a poignant example, one Xer argued that the belief that "the system is broken" is, "outside of having divorced parents, the most common characteristic of my generation" (Meacham 1995: 22).

Finally, Xers also missed out on an alternative socializer to action — the impulse to get involved because of a particular issue. In the past, issues on the national agenda in the mid-1960s and early 1970s directly affected youth. Most obvious, of course, was the way the Vietnam War and the draft (which made serving an obligation, not a choice) connected top political issues of the day to the personal lives of youth. No issue of the late 1980s and early 1990s — at least none discussed by politicians, emphasized in the media, repeated by political pundits, or put forth by campaigns — had this impact. Even issues that arguably did matter to young people during this period were framed in terms that did not resonate with them. The future solvency of the Social Security program, for example, which one could argue might be most likely to affect younger cohorts as either recipients or payers, seemed too remote to have much import. Moreover, in an

SELECTED EVENTS AND TRENDS

1979

Shah of Iran toppled	Three Mile Island nuclear disaster	Sony introduces Walkman	Mother Teresa wins Nobel Prize	U.S. embassy workers taken hostage in Iran	Margaret Thatcher first woman PM of Great Britain	11.3% inflation rate

AGE RANGE: Dutifuls = 34+ Boomers = 15–33 GenXers = 3–14 DotNets = 1–2

age where government was viewed as ineffective at best and problem-
atic at worst, many issues that hit home for youth (such as AIDS)
were often seen as questions to be addressed by personal behavioral
changes rather than public, collective action. In short, Xers arguably
have been uninvolved in government and politics not because they
affirmatively shun it but because they fail to see its relevance. They
see little connection between their own lives and the decisions made
by government officials or the issues they address (Loeb 1994).[2] They
do not understand how government affects them — or how their own
involvement in politics might make a difference in their daily lives or
the lives of those they care about.

Economic Realities: No Safety Net

The broader economic environment, offering little stimulus to action,
did little to refute the messages from parents, schools, the media, and
politicians. Termed "America's most economically disadvantaged generation" (Lipsky and Abrams 1994; Strauss and Howe 1991: 32), Xers faced
a world of diminishing opportunities.[3] In the 1960s, the Department of
Labor classified 36 percent of jobs as professional or managerial; by the
1980s, 28 percent were categorized as such. For Xers, this meant that in
the 1960s, 1 in 10 college graduates were "underemployed"; in the 1980s,
3 in 10 were (Lipsky and Abrams 1994). There were similar drop-offs for
high-paying, nondegree work in the manufacturing and transportation
sectors. And when Xers did find jobs, they were seldom secure. Of the
1.45 million jobs that were lost nationally during the 1990–1992 recession,
16- to 24-year-olds, comprising 17 percent of the workforce, bore 65 percent of the loss (Holtz 1995).

SELECTED EVENTS AND TRENDS

1980

John Lennon killed	Mt. St. Helens erupts	Ted Turner founds CNN	Ronald Reagan elected president	Failed rescue attempt of U.S. hostages	13.5% inflation rate

AGE RANGE: Dutifuls = 35+   Boomers = 16–34   GenXers = 4–15   DotNets = 1–3

When the oldest Xers graduated from high school (in 1983) or college (in 1987) they faced continually rising housing costs. By 1993, the cost of renting an apartment had risen 50 percent since 1983 (Lipsky and Abrams 1994). This is not simply a reflection of inflation. While the cost of living rose 170 percent from 1972 to 1987, housing costs soared 294 percent during the same period (Holtz 1995). In 1967 the percentage of income required for a down payment on a first home was 22 percent; 20 years later, this number had risen to 32 percent (Chakravarty and Weisman 1988). Even the areas in which Xers seemed to succeed were marred by additional financial burdens. Although they attended college in record rates, early Xers graduated with an average of $10,000 of debt (Lipsky and Abrams 1994).[4]

Generation Xers' diminished economic opportunities and power may be a contributor to their alleged political apathy (Cohen 1993; Cutler 1980; Strauss and Howe 1991, 1993). For example, relative to older generations, Xers seem to have missed out on the American promise of home ownership—a symbol of the many ways in which the members of this generation have been disappointed by the larger economic conditions they inherited. Similarly, some argue that Xers have had to spend so much time trying to gain a foothold in the financial world that they have little time or energy left over for "postmaterialist" pursuits. When comparing the activism of college campuses in the 1960s to the relative quiet found in universities in the 1980s, these observers argue that most Boomers didn't have to worry so much about their economic futures, so they could concentrate on issues such as free speech. Xer students were forced to be more concerned with trying to make sure they were competitive in an increasingly shrinking labor market, leaving little leftover drive for political causes.

Alternatively, Xers may simply value material goods (over postmaterial

SELECTED EVENTS AND TRENDS
1981

AIDS identified	PC introduced by IBM	PACMAN introduced	Princess Diana and Prince Charles wed	First woman appointed to Supreme Court	Assassination attempt on Reagan	Assassination attempt on pope	10.3% inflation rate

AGE RANGE: Dutifuls = 36+   Boomers = 17–35   GenXers = 5–16   DotNets = 1–4

pursuits) because they have been socialized into a materialistic culture. In this way, Generation X is viewed as an extreme representation of a greater depreciation of public values across American society (Conger 1988; Crimmins, Easterlin, and Saito 1991: 32; Dunn 1992; Easterlin and Crimmins 1991; Loeb 1994; Meredith and Shewe 1994; Putnam 2000; Rahn 1998).

The New Media Environment: Non-News Options

The political, social, and economic realities of Xers' youth and adulthood occurred amid a revolution in media technologies. The advent of cable (and later satellite) television changed the face of American news consumption. Previously, the three major news networks—ABC, CBS, and NBC—had dominated the television marketplace, offering three different versions of news at the same time. Cable brought more options, many of them non-news, to the table. When the oldest Xers were infants, the three commercial network nightly news broadcasts had a combined rating of 50 percent—that is, half of all television sets in the United States were tuned into one of these three shows. By 1980, when the same Xers were just entering adolescence, their ratings had fallen to 37 percent. Ten years later, when the bulk of Generation X was either in high school or college, just 30 percent of evening television viewers were watching nightly network news (Project for Excellence in Journalism 2005). Thus, as Xers grew up, all Americans increasingly lost their evening news rituals. Some moved to cable news options, but many opted for entertainment television instead, ultimately consuming less news altogether, as evidenced in the general decline in newspaper readership over the same period. Xers, taking lessons from the larger culture, would learn

SELECTED EVENTS AND TRENDS
1982

E.T. the Extra-Terrestrial released	Michael Jackson releases *Thriller* album	6.2% inflation rate	"No Nukes" Rally in New York City

AGE RANGE: Dutifuls = 37+   Boomers = 18–36   GenXers 6–17   DotNets = 1–5 less about politics and government because they would have fewer opportunities to (even passively) learn about the key issues. More important, perhaps, are the larger cultural messages that the variety of options — and the general decline in news attentiveness overall — sent to this generation. News gathering and attention to public issues were no longer societal norms but simply one of many options offered by the marketplace.

After the Boom: The Xer Bust

A final element of Xers' socialization that has implications for their political behavior in adulthood is their demographic pedigree. They are significantly fewer in number than Boomers (40 million versus nearly 71 million, respectively). Indeed, the sheer number of Boomers created a force that marketers catered to and politicians listened to — conditions that were not in place for Generation X, which was termed the "Baby Bust" by some advertising magazines.[5] Generation X's relatively smaller size may be one reason that Xers have been less likely than prior generations to be *invited* to participate in politics. Of course, widespread changes in political practices have led to significantly less mobilization of all Americans, regardless of age (Rosenstone and Hansen 1993; Skocpol and Fiorina 1999b).[6] But in an era when fewer invitations are being extended in general, ignoring Xers — who never learned the habits of participation in the first place — results in a self-fulfilling cycle of mutual neglect in which politicians (and also the mainstream media) see Xers as inattentive and uninterested. When they do target individuals, they focus on older age groups who are more likely to listen to their messages. Young people, well aware that they are being ignored, become frustrated

SELECTED EVENTS AND TRENDS

1983

U.S. invades Grenada	U.S. embassy in Beirut bombed	Soviets shoot down Korean airliner	Sally Ride first U.S. woman in space	Reagan announces plans for SDI	Cabbage Patch Kids phenomenon	3.2% inflation rate

AGE RANGE: Dutifuls = 38+   Boomers = 19–37   GenXers = 7–18   DotNets = 1–6

with the process, see no incentive to pay attention, and thus tune out. This in turn creates little incentive for politicians to spend time and energy courting the youth vote or for the news media to tailor its coverage to this age group. The cycle repeats itself and perpetuates the problem (Freyman and McGoldrick 2000).

And, finally, Xers are also much more ethnically and racially diverse than previous cohorts. Coupled with their small numbers, Xers may feel more disparate and divided than earlier generations, leaving them with less of sense of themselves or their potential power.

A Generation of Slackers?

As our brief overview suggests, GenXers came of age in an inherited world that was economically, culturally, socially, and politically less optimistic than what had preceded it. These differences were real, but they were also exacerbated and at times exaggerated by the end of "the sixties" and the ensuing debate over the positive and negative consequences of that period. In many ways GenXers became caught in the resulting finger pointing, serving as poster children for both the Left and the Right's complaints about what was wrong with American society in the latter half of the twentieth century.

Perhaps the best example of the resulting image of GenXers is the one painted in popular culture. The 1991 film *Slacker* (released when Xers were between the ages of 15 and 26) solidified the image of the apathetic Xer in American life and introduced a new entry to the list of derogatory names applied to this generation. The overeducated and underemployed men and women in this film pass their days hanging out in coffee shops, discussing their personal philosophies on life, movies,

SELECTED EVENTS AND TRENDS
1984

Indira Gandhi assassinated	Ronald Reagan reelected	PG13 rating for movies introduced	First woman V.P. candidate for major party	Lethal gas leak in Bhopal, India	4.3% inflation rate

AGE RANGE: Dutifuls = 39+ Boomers = 20–38 GenXers = 8–19 DotNets = 1–7

and the mundane. Political discussions are limited to endless arguments about the feasibility of alternative conspiracies surrounding the Kennedy assassination. The formal trappings of adulthood — structured jobs, career tracks, and commitment — are all anathema to youth in the late 1980s and early 1990s. This is a decidedly unengaged generation. Indeed, as the label "Generation X" suggests, it was a generation without an identity or purpose — generation *not*.

How accurate is this portrayal? Although Xers have written about the film with an appreciation for its humor, they have consistently derided it for the inaccuracy of its image (Cohen and Krugman 1994; Russkoff 1994). Many claim that the apathetic and uninvolved picture of Generation X is a media creation, an attack on youth that occurs with every new generation. If Xers have committed the sin of political idleness, they argue, it is a result of their youth, not their generation. As they age, they will become more like the cohorts who preceded them — more engaged and more interested with each passing year. Regardless of whether the image is real or created, it has stuck — and it is this picture that the next generation, DotNets, are compared with.

Raising DotNets: Time, Attention, and Money

Although DotNets have begun only recently to draw attention, discussion, and speculation regarding this emerging generation generally pit them against their immediate predecessors, just as observers compared Xers to Boomers. This time, however, it is the younger of the two cohorts that is — rightly or wrongly — most often held up as the ideal. Popular accounts portray DotNets as the new "organization kids" (Brooks 2001) or optimistic team players who "believe in their own collective power"

SELECTED EVENTS AND TRENDS
1985

Titanic found	Hole in ozone discovered	Famine in Ethiopia	New Coke hits market	Gorbachev calls for glasnost and perestroika	3.6% inflation rate

AGE RANGE: Dutifuls = 40+   Boomers = 21–39   GenXers: = 9–20   DotNets = 1–8

(Howe and Strauss 2000) — a far cry from the slacker image that dominated descriptions of Xer youth. Comprising the "echo" of the Baby Boom, DotNets, much like their Boomer parents, have the advantage of size, outnumbering Xers (in 2002) by 10 million. Even more than Xers, DotNets are extremely diverse. One-fifth have parents who are immigrants, and 1 in 10 has at least one parent who isn't a citizen (Howe and Strauss 2000: 83). However, perhaps because DotNets first emerged during an era of economic prosperity, most observers paint this ethnic mosaic in much more positive terms than was ever the case for Xers. While it is an overstatement to conclude that the DotNet years represented a full-scale reversal of the social and economic problems that have been attributed to the era in which Xers were socialized, there are indications that many of the so-called negative trends and social practices begun in the 1960s and characterizing the socialization of GenXers were slowed or reversed during the years in which DotNets were raised. At a minimum, during the period in which most DotNets were children, society at large (and their own parents in particular) focused much more time and attention on both individual children and issues of childhood than was ever the case for Xers. As if paying amends for past sins, news media stories about "soccer moms" who spend hours in their minivans, shuttling young DotNets from after-school activities to sports leagues, are typical portraits of the care the generation has received. Sociologists point out that the 1990s represented "the first decade since the 1920s in which federal spending on kids rose faster than spending on working-age adults or elders" (Howe and Strauss 2000: 111).

Howe and Strauss (who label DotNets the "Millennial Generation") emphasize rising levels of education along with falling rates of homicide, abortion, and teen pregnancy (Howe and Strauss 2000). Specifically, in 1997, when the oldest Nets were 20 and a substantial number were in

SELECTED EVENTS AND TRENDS

1986

U.S. bombs Libya	Space Shuttle *Challenger* explodes	Chernobyl nuclear disaster	Marcos flees Philippines	Iran-Contra scandal begins	Mir space station launched	1.9% inflation rate

AGE RANGE: Dutifuls = 41+   Boomers = 22–40   GenXers = 10–21   DotNets = 1–9

their teens, two-thirds of high school graduates went on to either two- or four-year colleges. The abortion rate, which had peaked in 1990, had dropped 15 percent by 1995, when the oldest Nets were just entering adolescence (Infoplease 2001). In 1993, environmental pollution ebbed, and teen AIDS levels started falling (Howe and Strauss 2000).

A comparison of efforts aimed at public education characterizes some of the differences between the generations. For example, while A *Nation at Risk* warned adults that Xers were receiving substandard training, among the DotNet generation more students are taking calculus, the major sciences, and advanced placement exams (Howe and Strauss 2000). In public schools attended by DotNets across the country, local communities and national politicians began making efforts to reinvest in the system by raising teacher salaries, enforcing academic standards, or calling for school uniforms (Strauss and Howe 1993; Whitmie 1996). When the elder George Bush ran for president, he vied to be the "Education President," a different message from his Republican predecessor, who had vowed to dismantle the Department of Education during the Xers' childhood. Reagan's goal was not to undermine education, of course, but to extract the federal government from education policy. Eight years later, as Reagan's successor, Bush—perhaps responding to public opinion concerns about the quality of education—no longer had this goal. And when his son, George W. Bush, came to office in 2000, he pushed through federally-directed education reform.

While some say that these changes have had an effect, citing rising SAT scores, others argue that the school system for DotNets is no better than that of Xers.[7] Although the true state of public education is difficult to answer because generalizing across the thousands of school systems in rural, suburban, and urban America is difficult, what is clear is that the public attitudes toward the issue differed considerably over time. For Xers, discussions about education usually revolved around documenting

SELECTED EVENTS AND TRENDS
1987

DNA first used to convict criminal	New York stock market collapses	3.6% inflation rate	Supreme Court nominee R. Bork rejected

AGE RANGE: Dutifuls = 42+   Boomers = 23–41   GenXers = 11–22   DotNets = 1–10

the flaws in the system—and the students it produced. By the time Nets entered school, improving education had become a national, *bipartisan* priority.

Schools also began curriculum changes that carried new messages of activism and endorsed particular ideologies. Many school districts started teaching students about contributing to their communities by facilitating, or in some cases requiring, community service programs. Science classes were also altered to focus on the outside world, including lessons on how individuals can personally work to improve the environment and instituting in-house recycling efforts and school "cleanup" days.

Economically, the picture for DotNets also showed some signs of improvement, though this improvement was mixed at best. The earliest years of older Dot Nets, occurring during the 1980s, were characterized by a kind of economic prosperity, albeit a selective one that was fueled by growing personal and national debt and characterized by a "greed is good" mentality on Wall Street. As the first DotNets transitioned into the world of young adulthood in the 1990s, many of the personal financial trends evident among the Xer cohort continued unabated, although the larger economic context in which they occurred was noticeably improved. For example, like their predecessors, DotNets faced rising housing costs and increasing levels of college loan debt, but with lower interest rates relieving some of this burden. Moreover, at least the oldest members of the youngest cohort faced higher prices amid apparent economic prosperity and opportunity. Inflation and unemployment remained low throughout their teenage years, while these rates dropped for working teens (Howe and Strauss 2000: 279). Gross domestic product expansion continued almost unabated for nearly a decade. Poverty dropped by 20 percent between 1993 and 1999 (Caplow, Hicks, and Wattenberg 2000). In March 1999, just before the oldest DotNets were set to graduate from college, the Dow Jones broke the 10,000 mark. These

SELECTED EVENTS AND TRENDS
1988

Willie Horton ad airs	George Bush elected president	U.S. shoots down Iranian airliner	Pan Am flight 103 downed by terrorists	4.1% inflation rate

AGE RANGE: Dutifuls = 43+   Boomers = 24–42   GenXers = 12–23   DotNets = 1–11

young people had witnessed almost miraculous increases in the Dow throughout their late teens and early twenties: from 1995 to 2000, the Dow rose 15 percent a year. Throughout the late 1990s and into the beginning of 2000, the nightly news was rife with stories of Silicon Valley millionaires who were retiring at age 35 to pursue mountain climbing, world travel, or community volunteering. The first messages for these DotNets, with little memory of tighter financial times, was that the possibilities were endless.

Politics and Government: Mixed Messages

In the realm of government and politics, the picture is more clouded. Scandal (and resulting investigations) became an almost daily but perhaps less startling fact of life as DotNets aged. During the mid- to late 1980s, when DotNets were between the ages of 1 and 12, the Iran-Contra scandal drew attention, though as much for the way a defiant Oliver North captured the public's and media's imagination as for the outrage over a potential misuse of presidential power. The Clarence Thomas confirmation hearings, occurring while DotNets were between the ages of 3 and 14, raised fundamental issues regarding the state of racial and sexual relations in the United States. And the nearly eight-year saga of the Clinton scandals, beginning with persistent rumors of financial impropriety (Whitewater) and ending with the Monica Lewinsky affair and subsequent impeachment (along with the "collateral damage" of Newt Gingrich and Henry Hyde), occurred as many DotNets passed through adolescence into early adulthood. These hearings continued the pattern of scandal and partisan reactions to it as part and parcel of politics in contemporary America. Perhaps significantly, however, the bulk of these

SELECTED EVENTS AND TRENDS
1989–1990

Berlin Wall falls	Exxon Valdez Alaskan oil spill	Tiananmen Square massacre	Hubble Space Telescope launched	Lech Walesa becomes Poland's president	Nelson Mandela freed	4.8%–5.4% inflation rate

AGE RANGE: Dutifuls = 44+ Boomers = 25–44 GenXers = 13–25 DotNets = 2–13

scandals, especially those occurring when DotNets were more likely to be politically aware, were cases in which public servants were under scrutiny not for official acts of government betrayal but for personal transgressions that reflected poorly on their moral character. Governmental failure for Xers was institutional; for DotNets, government is full of flawed personalities, not necessarily flawed procedures. Neither image is necessarily a ringing endorsement for the world of politics.

Overall, the events of late 1980s through the end of the twentieth century sent mixed messages about politics and government. Clinton, who came into office as the oldest Nets were 15 and stayed in office as more and more of their cohort aged into political awareness, proclaimed that "the era of big government is over," while also restoring interest in government and politics as a pathway to social and economic change. For every failure directly or indirectly attributable to government—the Exxon Valdez oil spill, the Savings and Loan debacle, the Oklahoma City and first World Trade Center bombings, the botched attack on the Branch Davidian compound, the civil unrest following the Rodney King police brutality verdicts—one can point to notable successes such as the tearing down of the Berlin Wall, the end of apartheid in South Africa, improved relations between the United States and Russia, the easing of nuclear tensions, the successful use of diplomacy and force in Serbia and Haiti, the erasing of decades of a national deficit, and so on.

These developments occurred amid a fragmentation of the news media that was even greater than that experienced by Xers. By 2004, just 20 percent of television sets were tuned into the nightly news on the major TV networks, a trend that captures the continued overall decline in news attentiveness (Project for Excellence in Journalism 2005). By the time DotNets had reached maturity, most Americans (including their parents), had lost the habit of sitting down to either read a paper or watch the

SELECTED EVENTS AND TRENDS

1991

Collapse of Soviet Union	Operation Desert Storm/ Gulf War	Clarence Thomas/ Anita Hill hearings	South Africa repeals apartheid laws	4.2% inflation rate

AGE RANGE: Dutifuls = 46+   Boomers = 27–45   GenXers = 15–26   DotNets = 4–14

news. At the same time, as the twenty-first century unfolded, many alternative news outlets began combining news with entertainment or opinion. Thus, Nets came of age in an era that taught them that consuming the news is not a regular task that involves learning facts and staying current but an outlet for the expression of interests, political or otherwise (Pew Research Center for the People and the Press 2005c).

In general, then, the political world inherited by DotNets is a complex one that appears to be simultaneously both similar to and different from that of Xers. Like Xers, DotNets have been brought up to expect a world in which politicians bash politics, the campaign for dollars seems to overshadow the campaign for votes, and negative advertising, mudslinging, and scandal are the norm—all of which might explain why they, like Xers, appear to eschew involvement in public life. But there are some differences as well, particularly in international relations. Unlike Xers, who came of age with the United States and the Soviet Union battling for dominance in situations around the world, DotNets experienced life with the United States as the world's only superpower. Confident that there were no real threats to their security, for them battles over foreign policy, nationhood, and borders were for the history books. DotNets don't remember the "Miracle on Ice," when the U.S. hockey team defeated Russia in the 1980 Olympics—a national rallying point for older Xers. This may explain why some accounts suggest that DotNets shun such nationalism, reflecting their upbringing in a more international and interconnected world. Culturally, their increasing globalism means that DotNets live in an era when salsa replaces ketchup as the most used condiment, Japanese toys can take the American market by storm (Pokemon), and one can dine on Indian takeout in the midwestern heartland. Politically, it means that issues such as child labor in Pakistan and the exploitation of developing nations are at the forefront of college campus activism. Protests at World Trade Organization conferences in

SELECTED EVENTS AND TRENDS

1992

Rodney King beating trial	Bill Clinton appears on MTV and Arsenio Hall	Bill Clinton elected president	3.0% inflation rate

AGE RANGE: Dutifuls = 47+   Boomers = 28–46   GenXers = 16–27   DotNets = 5–15

Seattle—which included large numbers of youth—suggest that many DotNets feel a solidarity with other nations and an anger with perceptions of American imperialism.

Adding to this sense of globalism is the information and technological environment in which Nets have grown up. DotNets have come of age when personal computers and cell phones are natural everyday appendages, not a new tool to be mastered. They can have e-mail conversations with students in China, trade music with young people in Africa, send pictures to friends who are traveling the Andes. They have the ability to develop "communities" that cross geographic boundaries, connecting them to others who share their beliefs, habits, or outlooks. And, if they are so inclined, technological advances make it easier to coordinate activist campaigns that cut across traditional boundaries of time and space.

Even the mixed and modest improvements that DotNets experienced seemed to come to a crashing end with the advent of the twenty-first century, however. The first presidential election in which they could take part (in 2000), ended up in an ugly dispute that was decided by the Supreme Court and put into office a president who received fewer votes than his opponent. The decade-long economic bubble, spurred in large part by the dotcom revolution, burst, and with it the hope of almost assured financial security. And of course the terrorist attacks of September 11, 2001, and the subsequent invasions of Afghanistan and Iraq undermined the sense of comfort and security at home and suggested that globalism could have repercussions that were harmful not just to others but to ourselves.

Thus, in many ways the experiences of GenXers and DotNets are mirror images of each other. Xers entered a world reeling from the political tumult of the 1960s, and characterized by real and rhetorical reverberations of that era, including a withdrawal from politics, a conser-

SELECTED EVENTS AND TRENDS

1993–1994

Branch Davidian sect disaster	World Trade Center bombed	Internet use begins exponential growth	Conservative sweep in Congress	Nelson Mandela elected South African president	2.6%–3.0% inflation rate

AGE RANGE: Dutifuls = 48+ Boomers = 29–48 GenXers = 17–29 DotNets = 6–17

vative social backlash, a deterioration of basic institutions of politics and society, and an extended period of economic decline. By the late 1980s through the 1990s, however, when most Xers were in their late teens through late twenties, economic, social, and political conditions showed signs of improving. For DotNets (especially older members of this cohort) the circumstances of their lives were almost the reverse, with their early years characterized by signs of improvement and their teens and early twenties characterized by much more unsettled times.

Millennials Rising or Generation X Redux?

DotNets are still a generation in the making, which makes the story of their socialization as yet incomplete and certainly less clear than that of Xers. Yet, in this first systematic look at the DotNet generation, we illustrate their generational character as it presently stands. The picture is a nuanced one. At times they are similar to Xers, and at times they are different. Many of these comparisons can be traced to their socialization over the past two decades.

To begin, there are several reasons that might explain why DotNets are similar to Xers. The argument given earlier for Xers—that inactivity among youth is simply a result of life cycle effects and not real genera-

SELECTED EVENTS AND TRENDS

1995

Ebola virus spreads in Zaire	Gas attack in Tokyo subway	Yitzhak Rabin assassinated	Oklahoma City bombing	O. J. Simpson acquitted	2.8% inflation rate

AGE RANGE: Dutifuls = 50+   Boomers = 31–49   GenXers = 19–30   DotNets = 8–18

SELECTED EVENTS AND TRENDS

1996

Mad cow disease hits Britain	Diana and Charles divorce	Unabomber is arrested	Bill Clinton reelected	3.0% inflation rate

AGE RANGE: Dutifuls = 51+   Boomers = 32–50   GenXers = 20–31   DotNets = 9–19

tional differences—could work for DotNets as well: one should expect youth to be disengaged; young people have always been less involved then their elders. Give them time, let them "grow up," and they'll soon be active.

Alternatively, the lack of political engagement among DotNets could be attributed to the political and cultural environment in the twenty-first century, which may be as alienating for youth today as for Xers in the late 1980s and early 1990s. Politics is still considered corrupt, investigations have reached the level of presidential impeachment proceedings, and money still dominates elections. Recent economic strains and ballooning deficits have created a sense of insecurity that is reminiscent of the Reagan-Bush eras. And the September 11 attacks have revealed the country and the world to be a much more dangerous place than was previously conceived. In fact, the same argument could explain why, in some cases, DotNets have levels of engagement that fall *below* those of Xers. Raised in an era of prosperity and promise and then handed a world of economic and political anxiety could cause DotNets to be even less trustful of the political process and less willing to engage than Xers. Questions about the Bush administration's veracity concerning evidence for the Iraq war—a conflict that garnered strong support among youth at the onset—could exacerbate cynicism and reinforce their desire to abstain. Alternatively, they could be so satisfied, having experienced very

SELECTED EVENTS AND TRENDS
1997

Hong Kong returned to China	Princess Diana dies in car crash	First sheep is cloned	Tiger Woods wins Masters	2.3% inflation rate

AGE RANGE: Dutifuls = 52+   Boomers = 33–51   GenXers = 21–32   DotNets = 10–20

SELECTED EVENTS AND TRENDS
1998

India and Pakistan test nuclear weapons	Movie *Titanic* breaks box office records	Clinton impeached	Viagra introduced	1.6% inflation rate

AGE RANGE: Dutifuls = 53+   Boomers = 34–52   GenXers = 22–33   DotNets = 11–21

little personal struggle and not asked to sacrifice, that they feel no need to be involved. The volunteer forces fighting in Iraq and Afghanistan, for example, are starkly different from the drafted troops that sacrificed in Vietnam.

Others have argued that the early positive experiences of DotNets are more significant than recent negative events, and that the supportive, upbeat environments of their youth have made them *more* involved than their predecessors. Indeed, this is certainly the picture painted by Howe and Strauss, who predicted that this generation as would be highly civic, committed, and involved in the world around them. They directed readers to "check out Kids Voting USA, Children's Express, or the web world, and you'll see kids discussing issues, participating in polls, and organizing mock elections" (Howe and Strauss 2000: 231). In this scenario, globalism and the advances in technology that have transformed the world have made DotNets keenly aware of the issues of social justice throughout the globe — and given them tools to tackle them politically. Many early pictures of DotNets predicted that they would be better informed than previous cohorts, in large part because of the Internet, which provides them with instant information on a wide range of topics whenever they want it and makes activism an easy choice for this generation. While there is evidence to support some of this (e.g., there are certainly increased levels

SELECTED EVENTS AND TRENDS

1999

Euro introduced	Y2K bug scare	JFK, Jr., dies in plane crash	Columbine High School killings	NATO troops attack Serbia	Panama Canal returned to Panama	2.2% inflation rate

AGE RANGE: Dutifuls = 54+   Boomers = 35–53   GenXers = 23–34   DotNets = 12–22

SELECTED EVENTS AND TRENDS

2000–2001

Florida election debacle	George W. Bush elected president	9-11 terrorist attacks	2.8%–3.4% inflation rate	Enron scandal

AGE RANGE: Dutifuls = 55+   Boomers = 36–55   GenXers = 24–36   DotNets = 13–24

of tolerance among DotNets), our data also refute other predictions (e.g., increased levels of political knowledge).

Finally, some have argued that DotNets do not differ from older generations in terms of the *quantity* of their political engagement but are distinct in terms of the *nature* of this activity. DotNets came of age in an era when commerce—not government—dominated much of culture. Their demographic ballast means that they have been marketed to since their birth (Howe and Strauss 2000), a fact that is not lost on this market-savvy generation. In Bill Gates they have witnessed the power of a single industry. In his efforts to combat world disease, they see the power of a single captain of industry stepping in where governments have lagged. They have watched as Michael Jordan—an athlete—is credited with contributing 10 billion dollars to the economy (Johnson 1988). They have seen Nike respond to challenges to its labor practices and stood on the sidelines while one corporation after another donated hundreds of thousands of dollars to various presidential campaigns. Nations that have been adversaries of America have provided them with their everyday essentials: their clothes are made in China, their stereos are assembled in Vietnam. To DotNets, the center of power may not be government but the marketplace, and the object of their participatory efforts may be business and not the political system. Our data, which provide a unique

SELECTED EVENTS AND TRENDS
2002–2003

U.S. invasion of Afghanistan	War with Iraq	*Columbia* shuttle disaster	Second NYC blackout	Human Genome Project completed	1.6%–2.3% inflation rate

AGE RANGE: Dutifuls = 57+   Boomers = 38–57   GenXers = 26–38   DotNets = 15–26

SELECTED EVENTS AND TRENDS
2004–2005

Abu Ghraib prisoner abuse scandal	Indonesian earthquake and tsunami	Massachusetts legalizes gay marriage	Battle over Terri Schiavo's right to die	London terrorist bombings	Hurricane Katrina

AGE RANGE: Dutifuls = 58+   Boomers = 39–58   GenXers = 27–39   DotNets = 16–27

opportunity to investigate this arena, do show DotNets using their power as consumers to send political messages.

Youth Generations: Refraction and Reflection

Capturing the nature of youth engagement today is important both for what it tells us about where we are going and what it reveals about where we've been. The habits and preferences of today's young people give us a glimpse of what the future will be like, as DotNets and Xers grow older and began to take up the reins of leadership in our nation. Equally important, however, is how the character of these generations helps us to understand our political culture more broadly. The values and behaviors of the post-Boomer generations reflect the lessons that they learned along the way, from parents, peers, schools, the news media, politicians, and political activists—and from the events and trends that have framed these interactions. Whether perfect mirrors of the dominant culture or refracted images, they are us as we are now. We turn now to a detailed look at that reflection.

Engagement in Public Life

In the spring of 2001 we traveled to several locations around the country, inviting randomly selected people to participate in small group discussions to talk about their communities, how they spend their time, and their views on citizenship and politics. We found that most of the people we met were comfortable talking about their communities, their day-to-day activities, or their (mostly negative) opinions about politics and politicians. They also talked easily and openly about the sometimes episodic, sometimes regular volunteer work many of them engaged in. When we turned the discussion to more explicitly political forms of public engagement, however, it was a very different story. Few were able to describe their own political lives. Most had not thought much about it. Asked if citizenship carried any responsibilities, the few people who answered spoke mostly of good conduct, looking after one's family, and occasionally being a good neighbor. Surprisingly few mentioned voting, staying informed, or participating more generally in the political world.

While this pattern was evident in almost all the groups we spoke with, it seemed especially true for GenXers and DotNets. True, many of these young people had volunteered only haphazardly and sometimes at the prodding of teachers or even the criminal justice system. But many were regular and active contributors to their local communities. On the other hand, for most of these young people, awareness of the more traditional world of politics seemed almost nonexistent.

The pattern that emerged from these admittedly unrepresentative discussions was amply confirmed in our systematic surveys. While few Americans see themselves in explicitly political terms, young people are particularly uninvolved—both behaviorally and psychologically—in the world of candidates, campaigns, public policy debates, and the like. This is not to say they are disconnected from the wider world, or are apathetic about the problems facing society. But if they are engaged at all, it is apt to be through civic activity rather than through conventional political behavior.

To some degree, this pattern is nothing new. With only a few exceptions in our history, most young people have been slow to get involved in the rough-and-tumble of politics. Less explicitly political activities such as community service have always been a more accessible route for youth to become involved in the world beyond their own families and circle of friends.

But we believe we are seeing something beyond the usual patterns associated with one's place in the life cycle. Today's youngest citizens, along with their immediate predecessors, grew up in an extraordinarily complicated and change-filled era, as the brief history in chapter 2 makes clear. The image of the public and private sectors underwent significant change, new forms of communication arose, the diversity of the population increased, and social beliefs and practices were reevaluated. In response to these changes, we believe that a foundational, generational shift in the public life of citizens may be underway. This shift has been gradual, and its impact is most apparent on younger Americans. In its simplest form, it is marked by a growing gap in voter turnout between the youngest Americans and those in earlier cohorts, accompanied by increasing levels of volunteer and community service among youth. But it is more than this, and we begin to examine the change and its implications in this chapter.

The Multifaceted Nature of Public Engagement

Citizens can participate in public life in a myriad ways, from donating time at a local homeless shelter, to working for a candidate for elected office, to calling a local official to complain about street repairs in one's neighborhood. Given this wide range, empirical studies have attempted

to develop measures of participation that capture its various manifesta-
tions. In their classic study, Verba and Nie (1972) identified four dimensions: voting, election campaign activity, contacting public officials, and
cooperative activity (for example, working informally with others to solve
a community problem). Their research was particularly significant in its
recognition that civic behavior was a domain apart from more explicitly
political activities such as voting and campaign work.

Subsequent research built upon and expanded this work. In his comprehensive review, Brady (1999) distinguished between electoral (voting
and campaign activity) and nonelectoral activities, with nonelectoral
work sorted into categories of "conventional" (informal community work,
contacting elites, organizational memberships, attending meetings) and
"unconventional" (signing petitions or participating in demonstrations or
boycotts) behavior. More recently, Putnam distinguished between what
he called cooperative activity (defined in similar fashion to Verba and
Nie) and expressive forms of behavior (such as writing letters or discussing public affairs) (Brady 1999; Putnam 2000; Verba and Nie 1972). These
distinctions remain relevant and guided much of our work.

Political versus Civic Engagement

The forms of political engagement differ in many ways: in the goals, the
targets of activity, the institutions or places in which they take place, the
level of effort entailed. In the analyses that follow, we attempt to capture
the wide range of ways citizens can participate in public life. But we are
particularly interested in the divide between political and civic engagement. As described in chapter 1, political engagement is activity aimed
at influencing government policy or affecting the selection of public
officials. For most Americans most of the time, this means participating
in the electoral process, usually by voting. Civic engagement, on the
other hand, refers to participation aimed at achieving a public good, but
usually through direct hands-on work in cooperation with others. Civic
engagement normally occurs within nongovernmental organizations and
rarely touches upon electoral politics. The most obvious example of this
kind of participation is volunteer work in one's community.

The distinction between political and civic engagement is an important one with deep roots, pitting direct individual, community, and pri-

vate associational responses to public issues against the more formal and indirect mechanisms of representative government (Hanson 1985; Morone 1990; Putnam 2000; Skocpol 2003; Tocqueville 2001). Each form of public action is valuable, but neither alone is sufficient to address the myriad collective decisions that must be made in advanced democracies. At its best, the U.S. system combines elements of both civic and political participation. But the "proper" balance is a delicate and changeable one — and dependent on one's own values. As such, knowing if one type of public engagement is expanding and another is in decline — either in general or among new generations of Americans — is revealing not only of individual choices but more broadly of how our national conception of citizenship is evolving, and the impact of this evolving notion on the health of our democracy and on policy outcomes.

Yet despite the importance of the distinction, we also recognize that the boundaries between political and civic engagement are not clear ones. While civic engagement occurs largely outside the domains of elected officials and government action, it can have important consequences for matters with which the government is also concerned (for example, public safety, homelessness, education, even national security). And since civic engagement often pertains to *public* matters and not solely to private questions, government may not be directly involved but may serve as arbiter, facilitator, supporter, or enforcer of decisions and activities in the civic realm.

This observation is not a new one. But recent scholarship has underscored both the normative and the empirical linkages between civil society and democratic government. Robert Putnam's 1993 study of regional government in Italy argued that an effective democratic public sector depends upon the existence of a strong civic sector (Putnam 1993), a view he brought to an analysis of the American case in *Bowling Alone* (2000). And beyond the debate over how strong the civic sector must be is the fact that America has always been, in Arthur Schlesinger's words, "a nation of joiners." Skocpol's work has demonstrated the long symbiosis between America's decentralized government and its network of voluntary groups and associations. "Throughout most of American history, active democratic government and a vibrant civil society centered in federated associations went hand in hand" (Skocpol 1999: 33)

Devolution and the Growing Importance of the Civic Sector

The civic world is becoming more important politically for another reason. As a result of strong political forces in the United States over the past 25 years—largely but not solely as a result of growing power among conservatives—federal and state governments are increasingly devolving their functions and powers not only to lower levels of government but also to the private and nonprofit sectors. As noted in chapter 2, young people may be more sensitive to this power shift, with more DotNets than other cohorts telling us that business has more influence on their lives than government does. As this shift occurs, the line between public and private—and thus between political and civic engagement—is blurred even further. In such an environment, where the locus of power shifts from government and elected officials to the private sector and nongovernmental organizations, citizens may see the need to achieve public goals through cooperative work that engages or targets institutions other than the government. These interactions encompass a wide range of activity: donating money or labor to nonprofit service organizations, boycotting commercial products, protesting in front of corporate head-quarters, or just writing letters to company executives. Accordingly, the line between strictly *political* activity on the part of citizens and private actions becomes more porous.

Indeed, not only might much of what passes as civic involvement be considered politics by other means, but the very act of "deciding" whether an issue should be addressed in the civic or governmental realm is inherently political. As E. E. Schattschneider noted, the basic pattern of politics is that "the outcome of all conflict is determined by the scope of its contagion," and managing the scope of conflict is thus a key political task (Schattschneider 1960: 2). Power is exercised when a public problem is defined as appropriate or not appropriate for governmental resolution—that is, whether it is deemed to be in the political sector or not. Thus, the devolution of government and the growth in privatization underway today reflect the exercise of political power.

In the end, however, privatization and government devolution may have changed the locus of conflict but have not yet succeeded in removing the underlying issues themselves (for example, poverty or crime) from the public realm. Public efforts to deal with such problems continue, albeit increasingly in the civic rather than the governmental sector. As a result, civic involvement—even if it is occurring outside the formal mechanisms of elections and government policy—might still be seen as an inherently political activity. At a minimum it is certainly a public activity.

Public Voice and Cognitive Engagement

Beyond political and civic activities are two other kinds of public engagement. One is *public voice*, the ways citizens give expression to their views on public issues. Included here are activities such as signing petitions, engaging in e-mail campaigns, starting or contributing to political blogs, or writing letters to the editor. Contacting public officials—a quintessential political act in Verba and Nie's schema—is usually done for the purpose of affecting government's behavior and may be the most direct type of expression of public voice (Barnes and Kaase 1979; Verba and Nie 1972).[1] These activities tend to "go together" conceptually and empirically—that is, people who express their voices in one way (e.g., signing petitions) are likely to do so in other ways as well (e.g., contacting the media). Notably, the expression of public voice is characteristic of *both* political and civic activists.

The fourth type of activity is *cognitive engagement*, that is, paying attention to politics and public affairs. Cognitive engagement includes such activities as following the news in newspapers, talking about politics with friends and family, or simply being interested in public affairs. Cognitive engagement is necessary—though not sufficient—for effective citizenship. Moreover, participation stimulates cognitive engagement, and it, in turn, stirs people to further action, whether civic or political. For young people who have yet to develop habits of political participation, attention to politics and public affairs may be a valuable indicator of likely future participation.

Methods and Data

In this chapter and those that follow, we present evidence from a variety of research efforts, some by other scholars, but most by us, funded by a grant from the Pew Charitable Trusts in 2001. The first two stages of our research were qualitative. We felt it important to start tabula rasa, as the extant literature seemed, to us, very definitive on voting behavior but less so on other avenues of citizen engagement. Thus we chose a bottom-up approach. That is, rather than asking how young people participated in traditional political and civic activities, we asked what young people were doing, and then considered whether these activities were civic or political.

In March and April of 2001 we convened two panels of experts who worked with active youth. We used what we learned from these panels to guide the development of questions for use in 13 focus groups conducted in four widely separated locations (Chicago, New Jersey, North Carolina, and northern California). Most groups were homogenous racially and generationally, stratified by age into one of the four groups we have described, with most being DotNets and GenXers.[2]

To test new measures of engagement, we conducted preliminary surveys in Virginia and New Jersey during their gubernatorial elections in the fall of 2001, and a national survey of approximately 1,200 15- to 25-year-olds in January and February of 2002, focused on volunteering, other civic and political behaviors, attitudes toward politics, and high school and college experiences related to public engagement (referred to as the National Youth Survey [NYS] in the following pages).

We then launched our primary data collection activity: the National Civic Engagement Survey (NCES1), a 25-minute national telephone sample of 3,200 respondents conducted in April and May 2002. We drew disproportionately large samples of the youngest two cohorts: 1,000 DotNets (ages 15–25 at the time of the survey), 1,000 GenXers (26 to 37), and 600 each of Baby Boomers (38–56) and Dutifuls (57 and up). This was followed by NCES2, a second national telephone survey of 1,400 adults (18 and older) conducted shortly after the 2002 national elections with the goal of testing the stability and reliability of our measures, and exploring some unexpected findings from the NCES1 survey.

We also draw liberally upon the data collection activities of others: a survey of young people in August 2003 conducted by the National Conference of State Legislatures (NCSL); the surveys of college freshman conducted annually by the Higher Education Research Institute of the University of California, Los Angeles (UCLA); the national surveys conducted by the Pew Research Center (PRC) for the People and the Press over the past 18 years. The National Election Studies of the University of Michigan and the General Social Surveys conducted by the National Opinion Research Center (NORC) at the University of Chicago have also been very useful. (More detail about our methods and data can be found in the appendix.)

Our Measures

To provide a comprehensive assessment of the current state of public engagement, the relationship between different types of engagement, and generational and life cycle differences in patterns of engagement, we developed a set of survey questions, drawn where possible from prior scholarly research. The measures include 19 activities covering political and civic engagement and public voice. Each of these activities can be consequential, but each is also common enough to be captured in a survey of the general public (see figure 3.1).[3] Some forms of participation may be highly consequential but so uncommon that we would be unlikely to encounter more than a few cases in a typical survey of the public (e.g., running for elected office, forming a new advocacy organization). So there was a trade-off between the importance of the activity and how common it is. We also included nine measures to gauge cognitive engagement.

The notion of four interrelated but ultimately distinct dimensions of activity described earlier — political, civic, and expressive (public voice), plus cognitive engagement — makes intuitive and theoretical sense, and seemed consistent with the patterns we observed in our focus groups. But it also turned out to be a good description of patterns we observed in our systematic surveys of the public. After conducting our first national survey (NCES1) that included the 19 behavioral items, we evaluated how the items were related to one another, looking to see if certain combinations of activities were more commonly performed by some people, while different combinations were more commonly performed by others. Using factor analysis, we found that our 19 items fit reasonably comfortably into three distinct dimensions that corresponded to the theoretical distinctions discussed earlier in this chapter (see the appendix).[4]

Table 3.1 shows the items (with their exact wording) sorted into the four categories of engagement. Two points regarding these measures and their categorization are important to note. First, our measures of political

TABLE 3.1
The Core Indicators of Engagement

Civic indicators

- **Community problem solving:** Have you ever worked together informally with someone or some group to solve a problem in the community where you live? IF YES, Was this in the last 12 months or not?
- **Regular volunteering for a nonelectoral organization:** Have you ever spent time participating in any community service or volunteer activity, or haven't you had time to do this? By volunteer activity, I mean actually working in some way to help others for no pay. IF YES, Have you done this in the last 12 months? I'm going to read a list of different groups that people sometimes volunteer for. As I read each one, can you tell me if you have volunteered for this type of group or organization within the last 12 months? An environmental organization; a civic or community organization involved in health or social services—this could be an organization to help the poor, elderly, homeless, or a hospital; an organization involved with youth, children, or education, any other type of group. Thinking about the work for (type of group) over the last 12 months, is this something you do on a regular basis, or just once in a while?
- **Active membership in a group or association:** Do you belong to or donate money to any groups or associations, either locally or nationally? Are you an active member of this group/any of these groups, a member but not active, or have you given money only?
- **Participation in fund-raising run/walk/ride:** [Now I'm going to read you a quick list of things that some people have done to express their views. For each one I read, please just tell me whether you have ever done it or not. (FOR EACH YES, PROBE: And have you done this is the last 12 months, or not?)] Personally walked, ran, or bicycled for a charitable cause—this is separate from sponsoring or giving money to this type of event?
- **Other fund raising for charity:** And have you ever done anything else to help raise money for a charitable cause?

Political indicators

- **Regular voting:** We know that most people don't vote in all elections. Usually between one-quarter to one-half of those eligible actually come out to vote. Can you tell me how often you vote in local and national elections? Always, sometimes, rarely, or never?
- **Persuading others:** When there is an election taking place do you generally talk to any people and try to show them why they should vote for or against one of the parties or candidates, or not?
- **Displaying buttons, signs, stickers:** Do you wear a campaign button, put a sticker on your car, or place a sign in front of your house, or aren't these things you do?
- **Campaign contributions:** In the past 12 months, did you contribute money to a candidate, a political party, or any organization that supported candidates?
- **Volunteering for candidate or political organizations:** From volunteering sequence, respondent indicated having volunteered for "A political organization or candidates running for office"

Indicators of public voice

- **Contacting officials:** [Now I'm going to read you a quick list of things that some people have done to express their views. For each one I read, please just tell me whether you have ever done it or not. (FOR EACH YES, PROBE: And have you done this is the last 12 months, or not?)] Contacted or visited a public official—at any level of government—to ask for assistance or to express your opinion?
- **Contacting the print media:** Contacted a newspaper or magazine to express your opinion on an issue?

(continued)

TABLE 3.1 (*continued*)

- *Contacting the broadcast media:*. Called in to a radio or television talk show to express your opinion on a political issue, even if you did not get on the air?
- *Protesting:* Taken part in a protest, march, or demonstration?
- *E-mail petitions:* Signed an e-mail petition?
- *Written petitions:* And have you ever signed a written petition about a political or social issue?
- *Boycotting:* NOT bought something because of conditions under which the product is made, or because you dislike the conduct of the company that produces it?
- *Buycotting:* Bought a certain product or service because you like the social or political values of the company that produces or provides it
- *Canvassing:* Have you worked as a canvasser—having gone door-to-door for a political or social group or candidate?

Indicators of cognitive engagement

- *Following government and public affairs:* Some people seem to follow what's going on in government and public affairs most of the time, whether there's an election or not. Others aren't that interested. Do you follow what's going on in government and public affairs most of the time, some of the time, rarely, or never?
- *Talking with family and friends about politics:* How often do you talk about current events or things you have heard about in the news with your family and friends—very often, sometimes, rarely, or never?
- *Political knowledge (two questions):* Would you say that one of the parties is more conservative than the other on the national level? IF YES: Which party is more conservative? How much of a majority is required for the U.S. Senate and House to override a presidential veto?
- *Attention to the news media (five questions):*I'm going to read you some ways that people get news and information. Over the past seven days, please tell me on how many days you have done each of the following: A. Read a newspaper. B. Read magazines like *Newsweek, Time,* or *U.S. News and World Report.* C. Watch the national news on television D. Listen to the news on radio. E. Read news on the internet.

engagement are dominated (with the partial exception of volunteering for a candidate or political organization) by activities associated with campaigns and elections. This is largely intentional, since for most people, engagement with government (beyond things like paying taxes or receiving money or services) occurs through the electoral process. We acknowledge, however, that we may be missing certain aspects of political engagement not captured by these measures. Second, and related, our measure of contacting public officials could logically fit with political engagement rather than public voice, since it involves interactions with government officials. In our factor analyses, however, this variable showed a stronger connection to other expressive forms of participation than to electoral behavior. It also was as strongly related to civic behaviors as to political ones. We believe this is an indication that the lines between civic and political engagement, while meaningful, are porous, and that this interrelationship is captured in our "public voice" measures — a point we return to later in this chapter.

An Overview of Engagement in Public Life in the United States

We begin our portrait of public engagement with some bold strokes and then soften the picture with some shades of gray and a few details. While we will provide a detailed explanation of how we make this determination later in this chapter, the bottom line is as follows. About half of all Americans can be characterized as engaged in public life in some way. About one in five specialize in the explicitly political realm (by voting and working for a candidate or party, for example, but doing little or nothing in the civic realm); about one in six confine their efforts to the civic realm (working on problems in their community, raising money for charities, or volunteering). Those who are active in *both* the civic and political arenas (also about one in six overall) work to shape their communities through voluntary civic activity and also try to influence the policy direction of the government through the political and electoral process. Among those active in one or the other of the two major spheres, these "dual activists" are not especially different from others in terms of race, gender, or political persuasion, but they are much more vocal than other citizens, using a broader variety of means — petitions, letters to editors, direct contacts with officials, and so on — to let policy–makers and their fellow citizens know what they think. Dual activists are also much more attentive to politics and much more knowledgeable about it.

How Much Engagement?

Of all the indicators of public engagement, registration to vote is the one accomplished by the greatest number of individuals.[5] About four in five of those aged 18 older (79 percent in the spring of 2002) say they are registered.[6] Involvement in public life is less common as the level of commitment and effort needed increases. We know from actual turnout data over the past 30 years that approximately 50–60 percent of the public typically vote in presidential elections (an estimated 54 percent of the voting age population in 2004—and possibly as much as 64 percent of the eligible citizen population). A similar percentage (51 percent) in our survey reported "always voting" in elections.[7]

During presidential elections, many people take part in campaign activities, either formally as part of an organization or on their own, persuading others as to the wisdom of voting for a particular candidate. According to data from the National Election Studies in 2000, 42 percent of adults engaged in some type of campaign activity beyond voting: trying to persuade others how to vote, working for a candidate, donating money,

FIGURE 3.1
Activities in the past 12 months.

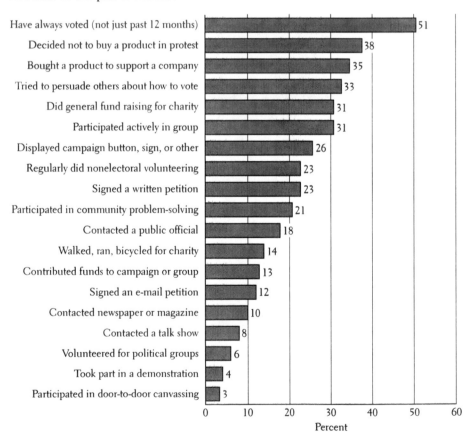

Source: NCES1 Survey.

attending a meeting or rally, or displaying a sign, button, or bumper sticker. Trying to persuade others is by far the most common activity, with about one-third (34 percent) saying they engaged in this in the election of 2000.

In the electoral realm, our 2002 surveys asked about activities that the respondent generally undertakes, since no national election fell within the past year (which was our time frame for most of the other activities we probed). One-third (33 percent) told us they generally talk to people and try to show them why they should vote for or against a candidate or party, about the same level as seen in the 2000 election. For other activities, our survey found higher levels of activity than the NES surveys that focus on a single election: one-quarter (26 percent) said they demonstrate their support through posting a house sign, wearing a campaign button or putting a sticker on their car. Half as many (13 percent) report having contributed money to a political party, organization or candidate. And referring to the past 12 months, 6 percent said they had volunteered for a candidate or political organization.

In the civic world, several activities capture the attention of significant minorities of the public. We define *civic activity* as organized voluntary activity focused on problem solving and helping others, a definition that obviously encompasses a vast range of settings, goals, and behaviors. Over half of the public — and according to some measures, well over half — belong to at least one kind of group or organization. Nearly one in three (31 percent) say they are an active member of at least one group, and 27 percent say they belong to a group involved in politics or public issues. Volunteer activity for organizations is also a fairly common activity. Nearly two-thirds of Americans say they have volunteered at some point in their lives, and — depending on how one measures the activity — somewhere between one-third and 40 percent say they have done it in the past year. As we will see, volunteering is a very slippery concept, one that is not amenable to easy measurement. But asking about *regular* volunteer work helps to clarify the issue: most people who do it regularly know that they do, and those who don't, know that they don't. About one-quarter (23 percent) report *regularly* volunteering time to a nonelectoral organization, such as a religious, environmental, youth or community organization.

Beyond the general world of volunteering and group activity, about one in five (21 percent) reports working with others to solve a problem in their community within the past year. Participation in fund raising for charities also represents a type of civic engagement, and 31 percent say they did some type of general fund raising activity for charity in the past year. Fourteen percent walked, ran, or biked for charity; 36 percent did one or both of these types of fund raising.

When people want their opinions heard by other citizens, the private sector, or the government, they turn to a variety of channels. Nearly one-quarter (23 percent) say they have signed a written petition on behalf of some interest or cause in the last year. Slightly fewer say they have contacted a public official (18 percent), signed an e-mail petition (12 percent), contacted a newspaper or magazine to register an opinion (10 percent), or tried to contact a television or radio talk show (8 percent). Finally, just a very few report having taken part in a protest or demonstration in the past year (4 percent) or gone canvassing door-to-door (3 percent).

The political use of consumer power attracts little scholarly attention, but our surveys suggest that it is quite widespread. Over one-third (38 percent in spring 2002) say they have *not* bought a particular product in the last 12 months because they dislike the conditions under which it was made or disapprove of the conduct of the company that produced it—a boycott, for all intents and purposes. Nearly as many (35 percent) say they have purchased a particular product or service because they like the political or social values of the company that produces it—sometimes called *buy*cotting. Participation in these two individualistic activities, although admittedly a low bar of involvement, is the most common of the nonelectoral activities in the survey and deserves more serious scholarly inquiry.

By almost any measure, many—perhaps most—Americans do not regularly follow the political world. According to the results of our survey, less than half (45 percent) acknowledge they follow politics and government most of the time. And while 60 percent say they talk about current events with family and friends very often, just one in three (32 percent) say they have discussions about politics. Accordingly, levels of political knowledge about many topics are low. For example, only about half of the public (49 percent) can name the Republicans as the more conservative of the two major parties.

A Simple Typology of Civic and Political Engagement

Despite the general hesitancy of most people to talk or even think about themselves in explicitly political terms, throughout our conversations with citizens in 2001 we did encounter people who were engaged in public life. Some of these people were active in campaigns, elections, and efforts to influence government policy but were relatively indifferent to the world of informal civic life. Others were active in the civic realm but not in the world of more traditional politics. We also found some citizens who were active both politically and civically. Our impression was that these three types of people—not to mention those who were completely unengaged—were very different from each other.

To pursue this more systematically, we decided to sort our survey respondents according to the pattern of their involvement in these two key arenas of public engagement. To undertake this sorting, we first needed criteria for judging someone as engaged or not. Since engagement—like age, weight, and height—is best thought of as a continuum, we recognize that any attempt to divide people into "engaged" and "unengaged" is likely to be arbitrary. But we sought a standard that would balance an academic ideal based on measurement theory and a common-sense standard that was reasonable on its face (so-called face validity). We settled on a metric that would judge someone as engaged in a domain if they took part in two of the five activities in that domain: two civic acts or two political acts. Different thresholds are certainly possible, and perhaps a single act—especially if it requires great effort or ongoing involvement—is arguably indicative of activism. But our two-act standard seems to work in practice.[8]

People in our national survey were considered to be *civically engaged* if they participated in two or more of the following civic activities.

- Regular volunteering for an organization other than a candidate or political party
- Working with others to solve a community problem in the past year
- Raising money for charity, through a run/walk or any other means in the past year
- Actively participating in a group or association

About one-third of those surveyed (32 percent) qualified as civically active using this standard. Similarly, people were considered *politically engaged* by the same standard: two or more activities from among the following:

- "Always" voting (or, for youth under 20 who have not yet had an opportunity to vote, intention to always vote)
- Volunteering for a political organization or a candidate
- Trying to persuade someone how to vote
- Displaying a button, bumper sticker, or sign on behalf of a candidate
- Contributing money to a party or candidate in the past 12 months

Just over one-third of those surveyed (36 percent) met this standard.

Significantly, a portion of the civically and politically engaged groups overlapped: according to our survey results, 16 percent, or about one of every six Americans, meet the standard in both arenas (figure 3.2). They are the *dual activists*. The same percentage—16 percent—are civically active but do not meet the standard for electoral activity. These are the *civic specialists*. A slightly larger group—20 percent—is politically but

FIGURE 3.2
Engagement among Americans age 15+.

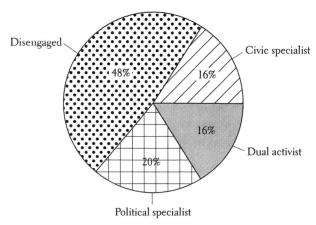

Source: NCES1 Survey.

not civically active. These are the *political specialists*. Finally, in these two arenas at least, nearly half of the public — 48 percent — meet neither standard. They are the *disengaged*.

The Relationship of Civic and Political Engagement with Voice and Cognitive Engagement

Sorting citizens into civic specialists, political specialists, and dual activists implies that these realms of public engagement are distinct. Yet we know that the measures of activity in one domain are also correlated with those in other domains, suggesting that the dividing lines are not impermeable. This implication is further supported when we consider the relationship of civic and political behavior to cognitive engagement and public voice. If at least some civic activity has a more political component to it, we might expect civic activists to use the same kinds of tools that mainstream political activists use to send messages and convey their views to policy makers, interest groups, and other citizens. And indeed we find that even those who concentrate their efforts in the civic arena, while eschewing involvement in traditional politics, nevertheless express their views to the same extent and through the same channels that those

TABLE 3.2
Relationship of Voice to Civic and Political
Dimensions

Activity	Civic Dimension	Political Dimension
Contact officials	.30	.34
Contact media	.27	.27
Talk show	.25	.21
Canvass	.19	.24
Protest	.18	.15
Paper petition	.17	.16
E-petition	.17	.15
Buycott	.16	.22
Boycott	.12	.15

Note: Entries are correlation coefficients showing relationship between the item and the factor score for the dimension.
Source: NCES1.

active in the traditional politics do. More generally, as table 3.2 shows, most activities in the realm of public voice are correlated with *both* civic and political activity.

Similarly, cognitive engagement is strongly associated with activities in the political dimension, but we also observe that civically active people are paying attention to the political world as well—even if not quite as closely as the politically active.

Public Engagement by Age:
A View across the Generations

A snapshot of the citizenry's engagement in public life reveals great variability across age groups in the population. The general picture is one of rising engagement with age, at least through middle age, but there

FIGURE 3.3
Engagement by age.

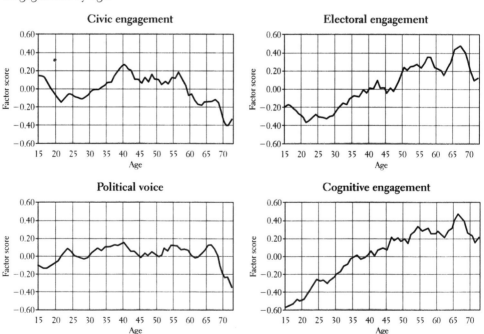

Source: NCES1 Survey.

are substantial differences in the patterns seen for political versus civic engagement, and no clear trend by age for the expression of public voice. Using the NCES1 survey, we plot indexes computed from items in each of the three dimensions of engagement (plus cognitive engagement) by age; data for people in five-year groups are aggregated to smooth out the trend lines (see figure 3.3).[9] Keep in mind that these trends are taken from a single point in time (spring 2002) and thus the patterns reflect a combination of life cycle differences (changes that happen as people move through the natural phases of life) and generational differences.

Political engagement increases as age increases, reaching a peak after age 65 and then falling sharply among individuals near and beyond 70 years of age. Attentiveness, or cognitive engagement, follows a nearly identical pattern, suggesting that the way this concept is measured is picking up conventional engagement in electoral politics more than in the civic world. By contrast, the patterns are different for civic engagement and public voice. In the civic realm, the youngest respondents exhibit higher levels of activity than do those slightly older, consistent with the notion that high schools and families provide important training, encouragement, and facilitation for this behavior. After a sharp fall from the teenage years, the rates of civic engagement rise among those in their late twenties, continuing through about age 40, after which the pattern is relatively flat.[10] Declines appear as early as the mid-fifties, with people in their sixties and beyond showing lower levels of civic activity than any other age group.

For voice, there is little trend by age, except for a sharp fall–off after age 65. Although this measure does not capture differences in intensity

TABLE 3.3
Civic and Political Engagement

	All %	DotNet %	GenX %	Boomer %	Dutiful %
2 or more civic activities	32	28	34	39	25
2 or more political activities	36	26	26	39	48
2 or more voice activities	24	21	25	27	21
Gets news from at least 1 source every day	75	52	66	81	92

Source: NCES1.

or the extent to which individuals are engaging in particular actions, it does indicate that younger people are undertaking at least as many different kinds of expressive activities as their elders.

Another way to describe these patterns is to compare the four age cohorts on the summary measures of civic and political activism used in the typology (table 3.3). By these standards, 28 percent of the DotNets qualify as civically active (having performed two or more civic activities), a percentage only slightly below the national average (32 percent) and comparable to the Dutifuls (25 percent). At 34 percent, GenXers match the national average, and Boomers (39 percent) are the most civically active of the four generations. In the more explicitly political sphere, however, both of the youngest generations (26 percent) are much further behind the national average (36 percent) with Boomers (39 percent) and Dutifuls (48 percent) leading the way.

Using the same two-activity standard for public voice, we see relatively small variations by age: Boomers score best (at 27 percent), followed by GenXers at 25 percent and DotNets and Dutifuls at 21 percent each. But there are vast cohort differences in attentiveness to the news: just half of DotNets (52 percent) say they get daily news from at least one of five sources, compared with 81 percent of Boomers and 92 percent of Dutifuls.

Political Activities

Differences across age cohorts in voter registration and regular voting are quite dramatic. Fewer Baby Boomers are registered or habitually vote than the generation that came before them, and there is an even larger fall-off from Boomers to the succeeding generations (table 3.4). Whereas almost three-fourths (72 percent) of Dutifuls say they always vote, just over half (53 percent) of Boomers and only about one-third (34 percent) of Xers say they do. Only one-quarter (24 percent) of DotNets who have been eligible to vote for at least a couple of years (aged 20 and older) say they always vote, even though "always voting" for most of them spans a very limited number of elections.[11] And, among DotNets who are old enough to vote, just 60 percent say they are registered. In addition, Dutifuls (34 percent) and Baby Boomers (28 percent) are considerably more likely than GenXers (18 percent) and DotNets (20 percent) to display a candidate or party preference by wearing buttons, putting up yard signs, or slapping bumper stickers on their cars.

There is also a significant age difference in contributing money to campaigns: 17 percent of Dutifuls and Boomers report giving money to a party or organization that supported candidates in the previous 12 months, compared to just 11 percent of Xers and 4 percent of DotNets. Finally, very few DotNets (3 percent) report volunteering for a party or candidate in the previous 12 months. The rate among GenXers is comparable (5 percent) and only somewhat higher for Boomers (8 percent); 6 percent of Dutifuls said they did this.

Some of these differences across age groups are significant, but are they larger than those seen in the past? As table 3.5 shows, prior to the 2004 election, the gap in voter turnout between younger and older people had grown larger in the 1980s and 1990s than it was in the 1970s. Surveys conducted by the U.S. Census Bureau show that 52 percent of youth aged 18–24 voted in the 1972 presidential election, while in 2000 only 36 percent voted. By comparison, among those 25 and older, voter turnout in 2000 was only 5 percentage points lower than in 1972 (63 percent versus 68 percent). In 2004, the gap had between older and younger voters dropped to 19 percentage points, compared to 27 points in 2000. The relatively stronger performance of the youngest cohort in 2004 is

TABLE 3.4
Political Activities

	All %	DotNet %	GenX %	Boomer %	Dutiful %
Registered to vote	79	60	70	83	89
Always votes	51	24*	34	53	72
Tries to persuade others	33	36	33	32	32
Displays campaign button/sticker/sign	26	20	18	28	34
Contributed money to political group in past 12 months	13	4	11	17	17
Volunteered for political group in past 12 months	6	3	5	8	6

*Among DotNets age 20+.
Source: NCES1.

intriguing, perhaps a response both to the greater efforts at mobilization, as well as qualities these young people brought to the election from their own socialization.

Beyond voting, young people do not fall as far behind older ones on some measures, and there is evidence that the big gaps seen in the 1980s and 1990s are diminishing. Figure 3.4 presents one way of gauging this. For each of five types of campaign activities, it compares the youngest cohort (those roughly the age of our DotNet cohort today) with adults in middle age (roughly corresponding to the ages of Baby Boomers today). Bars extending to the right indicate that the older group is more active than the younger group. Bars extending to the left indicate that the younger group is more active. The length of the bar shows the percentage difference between the two age groups. According to data from the National Election Studies, which have asked questions about campaign activities since the 1950s, youth have generally been less engaged in the electoral world than citizens in their forties and fifties. This pattern is most consistent exactly where we would expect it: donating money to candidates. Older individuals have been about seven to eight percentage points more likely to report doing this. Given the relatively low percentage of citizens donating money (approximately 8–16 percent over the period), this gap is substantial, if unsurprising. Similarly, older citizens have been more likely than younger ones to attend meetings or rallies

TABLE 3.5
Voter Turnout among Citizens 1972–2004

	Age 18–24 %	Age 25 + %	Gap %
2004	47	66	19
2000	36	63	27
1996	36	62	26
1992	49	71	22
1988	40	66	26
1984	44	69	25
1980	43	69	25
1976	44	65	21
1972	52	68	16

Source: Postelection surveys by U.S. Census. Tabulations by the Center for Research on Civic Learning and Engagement (2005b).

FIGURE 3.4
Percentage difference in campaign participation by younger and older citizens (% doing each activity among those age 38–56 minus % among those 18–25).

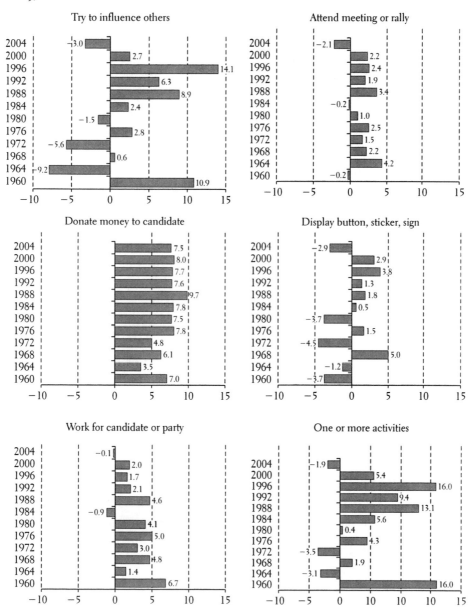

Source: National Election Studies.

for candidates throughout the period; after falling short of their elders for several elections, younger citizens slightly surpassed the older group in 2004. Older citizens have also been consistently more likely to volunteer to work for a party or candidate, though this gap appears to be slightly smaller in more recent elections and was nonexistent in 2004.

We do not wish to make too much of these often small and volatile differences. For example, while young people were actually more likely than older Americans to try to persuade others how to vote in three of the six presidential elections between 1960 and 1980, youth in 2000 and 2004 were much closer to their elders than they had been since 1984 (and indeed, scored well on this activity in our 2002 survey). For the first time since the 1980s, the youngest age group outpaced, by a modest amount, older voters in two other types of activities: displaying a sticker or sign and attending a meeting or rally. As a result of these activities, for the first time since 1972 the youngest group was slightly *more* likely than the older group to engage in at least one of the activities. Although it is certainly too soon to argue that a trend is developing, the relatively better performance of young people in 2000 (an election that did relatively little to stimulate voters) and 2004 marks the DotNet cohort as increasingly different from GenXers in electoral participation. There is the hint in these data that the sizeable generation gap in electoral participation, which had been growing since 1980, is now stabilizing.

Civic Activities

In contrast with the explicitly political world, the youngest cohort has been holding its own in the civic world of volunteering, organizational activity, fund raising, and the like. We will show that Generation DotNet is doing reasonably well in this arena, and then will take up the tougher question of how this performance compares to that of earlier generations. In looking at participation today, we consider five activities mentioned earlier: working with others in one's community to solve a problem; participating in a walk, run, or bicycle ride for charity; other activities to raise money for charitable causes; doing volunteer work for nonelectoral groups on a regular basis; and active participation in a group or organization.

Community involvement goes to the heart of civic engagement, and one of the most telling indicators may be having "worked together informally with someone or some group to solve a problem in the community where you live." On this question, despite younger people possibly having fewer reasons to be invested in their communities (being more mobile and less likely to own their own homes), GenXers and DotNets are very much like Baby Boomers in recent activity (table 3.6). This is an impressive hallmark and one that portends continuity in the tradition of civic involvement.

One-quarter of Boomers (25 percent) say they have worked in their communities in the last year, as have 22 percent of Xers and 21 percent of DotNets. Indeed, it is Dutifuls (15 percent) who have been the least active in this area in the last year, although another 27 percent of them report doing this at some point in their lives.

Volunteer work with organizations is also something that young people increasingly have taken up. Today's 15- to 25-year-olds actually post the highest rates of at least occasional volunteering. Fully 40 percent say they have given time to a group in the past year, compared to one-third

TABLE 3.6
Civic Activities

	All %	DotNet %	GenX %	Boomer %	Dutiful %
Community problem solving					
Last 12 months	21	21	22	25	15
Ever done	21	17	14	22	27
Volunteer work for nonelectoral organization					
Regular volunteering	23	22	25	26	19
Ever in past 12 months	8	18	7	6	3
Walked, ran, or bicycled for a charitable cause					
Last 12 months	14	16	16	15	8
Ever done	24	25	29	24	19
Other activity to raise money for charitable cause					
Last 12 months	31	28	29	37	26
Ever done	23	23	21	23	26
Member of group or organization					
Active member	31	22	29	40	27
Member but not active	30	19	30	31	36

Source: NCES1.

of Xers and Boomers (32 percent each) and just 22 percent of Dutifuls. Much of their advantage is due to the influence of high schools and colleges. Among high school students—many of whom are encouraged or required to do community service work—over half (54 percent) have volunteered for a nonelectoral group. Over 4 in 10 among college students (41 percent) have done so. By contrast, among youth who are not in high school or college, 25 percent say they have volunteered.

But DotNets do not have an advantage when *regular* volunteering for nonelectoral groups is considered: 22 percent of DotNets report doing this, compared with 25 percent for GenXers and 26 percent for Boomers. Nonetheless, it is a good omen that this young cohort is *starting* where GenXers and Baby Boomers are now, and is slightly ahead of Dutifuls (19 percent).

Members of the three younger generations are also equally likely to have participated in a walk, run, or bicycle event for charity—some 15–16 percent of each group in the last year, with roughly another quarter (25-29 percent) reporting having done so at some previous point in their lives. Moreover, DotNets match GenXers and the Dutifuls in other activities to raise money for charities (Baby Boomers are most likely to have done this in the past 12 months). About half of Dutifuls, Xers, and DotNets have done this at some point in their lives, and over a quarter in the last year. The figures for Boomers are 37 percent in the last year and a total of 60 percent at some point in their lives.

DotNets are much less likely than other cohorts to belong to a group or association (41 percent versus 60 percent for the sample as a whole), but the gap in *active* membership is smaller: 22 percent of DotNets are active members, compared with 29 percent of GenXers and 27 percent of Dutifuls. Boomers (at 40 percent) are the cohort most likely to report active group membership.

How do these patterns compare to the past? How did Generation X do when it was just coming of age? And for that matter, what about the Baby Boomers? Unfortunately, good measures of the broad range of civic activity over time are not as plentiful as those for electoral activity. Still, there are enough to allow us to believe that youth today may be future leaders of a revival in civic participation in at least some forms of activity.

The available evidence indicates that, at least since the late 1980s, the picture is either improving or remaining stable. One excellent source of trend data about youth is the series of surveys of incoming freshmen at four-year colleges and universities in the United States, conducted by the Higher Education Research Institute (HERI) at UCLA. According to these very large surveys, the percentage of freshmen reporting volunteer activity is now at its highest point since the question was first asked in 1984. Moreover, reported volunteer activity during the senior year in high school grew from 44 percent in 1987 to 70 percent in 2001, and the number of hours devoted weekly rose as well. At the same time, the percentage of students watching television — one of the villains in Putnam's story — has declined, as has the mean number of hours watched.[12]

Two other attitudinal indicators have remained stable, suggesting no further deterioration in relevant predispositions toward civic involvement. According to the HERI surveys, the number of students saying that it is essential or very important to become a community leader now stands at 31 percent (in 2004), about the same as it has been through much of the 1990s and considerably higher than it was in the early 1970s. The percentage of students placing a similar priority on participating in a community action program has been relatively stable (in the low to middle twenties) for the past two decades, though it is lower than levels seen in the 1970s (low thirties).

Public Voice

Political and civic activity is intended to solve problems directly in the civic world or to affect the selection and behavior of government officials. But both of these aims can be pursued indirectly through various tactics of communication and persuasion. Collectively, we call these efforts at persuasion "public voice." We focus on nine specific activities (table 3.7).

Little studied but surprisingly common is *politically motivated consumer activism*: in the last year, about one-third of the public reports not buying a product or service for political reasons, and a similar number say they have purchased a product from a particular company to reward it for some corporate values or behavior. Politically motivated consumer behavior appears to be as common among younger as older citizens. Because of the widespread nature of the activity and its potential as an expanded channel of activism, we discuss it in greater detail later in the chapter.

A significant number of citizens also join in the constitutionally sanctioned process of petitioning, in this case by literally signing their names (or e-mail signatures) to a document. Between one in five and one in four in each cohort report having signed a petition in the past year, with at least as many reporting they have done so at some point in their lives, except for the DotNets. Petitioning through the Internet is an avenue of participation more heavily traveled by the two younger generations.

TABLE 3.7
Expression of Public Voice

	All %	DotNet %	GenX %	Boomer %	Dutiful %
Contacted a public official					
Last 12 months	18	10	16	20	21
Ever done	17	9	15	21	19
Contacted newspaper or magazine to express opinion					
Last 12 months	10	10	8	12	12
Ever done	14	8	10	18	17
Called in to radio or TV talk show to express opinion					
Last 12 months	8	7	7	10	8
Ever done	5	4	4	5	6
Taken part in protest, march, or demonstration					
Last 12 months	4	7	5	3	3
Ever done	13	8	12	18	12
Signed an e-mail petition					
Last 12 months	12	14	15	11	9
Ever done	6	6	7	5	4
Signed a written petition					
Last 12 months	23	20	23	24	21
Ever done	24	12	24	31	24
Worked as a canvasser					
Last 12 months	3	2	2	3	4
Ever done	11	5	5	13	19
Boycotted					
Last 12 months	38	38	43	41	28
Ever done	18	13	17	20	19
Buycotted					
Last 12 months	35	35	42	37	25
Ever done	10	9	8	9	13

Source: NCES1.

About 15 percent of Xers and DotNets have signed an e-mail petition at some point in the last year.

Members of the youngest cohort are least likely to say they have contacted a public official in the past year—10 percent have done so, half as many as among Boomers (20 percent) or Dutifuls (21 percent). GenXers fall in between (16 percent). It is perhaps not surprising that this behavior is much less common among younger citizens. It requires a good bit of information (who is your representative, what is his or her address) and seems unlikely to yield much in the way of tangible benefits. Unfortunately, by comparison with letters, e-mail communication with elected officials is often ignored.

Yet younger people are not especially reluctant to voice their opinions, compared with older people. There are only small age differences in trying to contact the electronic media (a television or radio talk show) or in having actively taken part in a demonstration, protest, or march, and in door-to-door canvassing. More DotNets than other cohorts report having demonstrated (7 percent, versus 5 percent for GenXers and 3 percent each for the two older cohorts).

A Closer Look at Political Consumerism

A surprising finding of our study is that nearly half of Americans report having engaged in some form of consumer activism in the past year. That is, 49 percent say that political and social concerns have influenced retail decisions in the last year. More Americans report engaging in consumer activism than any other single type of political behavior, with the exception of registration and voting. Over half (56 percent) of Americans report boycotting a company or product at some point in their lives, with 38 percent saying they have done this in the past 12 months. And *buy*cotting is only slightly less prevalent. Under half (45 percent) report having done so at some point in their life, while 35 percent have used the consumer carrot in the past 12 months. Both forms of consumer activism are about as prevalent among the youngest cohort as among GenXers and Boomers. Only the Dutifuls lag behind in the rate of consumer activism.[13]

The high reported rates of political activism by consumers led us to a closer examination of this phenomenon and its potential. What we found is that while genuine political motivation underlies many purchasing decisions, boycotting and buycotting is sporadic and largely unorganized, and many people who say they engage in these practices have trouble remembering specific instances of it.

In two different surveys, we asked people to describe what they boycotted or buycotted. In both a Virginia survey, which used a question that offered a few examples of boycotting, and in our fall 2002 national survey, half or fewer of those who said they had done something in the past year were able to give an appropriate example of a something we considered politically relevant consumer behavior. Clearly, some people misunderstood what we were asking for: one young person told us he boycotted Busch beer, " 'cause it doesn't do anything for me." Others described poor service or bad product quality as their motivation. Many people simply said they could not remember.

But many answers resonated very clearly. Lots of people say they "Buy American" if they can. Environment-friendly products and companies were frequently mentioned. Numerous mentions of sweatshop and child labor were heard. Significant numbers of people — both conservative and liberal — talked about the attitudes of companies toward gay rights, abortion, and other highly charged social issues.

We took two lessons from this effort at validation. First, although politically motivated consumerism may be broadly practiced, for many people it is not something that is constantly on their minds while shopping. Second, while fewer than half of those who said they boycotted or buycotted could volunteer a clear example of the activity, we suspect that it may be more prevalent than this would indicate. We cannot conclude that people who gave inappropriate responses do *not* engage in political consumerism; it is also possible that they misunderstood our question or could not think of what they done. Perhaps a different question would have elicited a different answer. Indeed, the transcripts of the responses show that some people would come up with one or two inappropriate examples before telling us about something that readily fit our conception of the activity. As with many phenomena in survey research, we feel confident that we could generate higher incidences if we took respondents through a list of products, services, and causes, asking whether they had considered social or political values in purchasing decisions for each. Our approach was a fairly conservative one and put much of the burden on the respondent.

Given the fact that many people can't give concrete examples of politically motivated consumer activism, it came as no surprise that relatively small numbers of people say it's something they do regularly. Among those who report buycotting or boycotting during the past year, only about one-fifth (23 percent for boycotting, 19 percent for buycotting — about 11 percent of public overall) say that this is something they do every week (table 3.8). Comparable numbers say they do it about once a month (18 percent for boycotting, 25 percent for buycotting). Over half say they are boycotting and buycotting only a few different types of goods or services.

People engaged in consumer activism overwhelmingly see it as an individual activity rather than as part of an organized campaign. Among those who've boycotted or buycotted in the past year, only 7 percent each (and 9 percent overall) tied the most recent occurrence to an organized campaign; the rest said it was something they just decided to do on their own. This may be a function of how people conceive of their personal choices, rather than an indication that such activity is completely isolated from campaigns undertaken by activists and organizations. In response to a question about where people got the information that helped them make a decision to boycott or buycott, a plurality (35 percent for boycotting, 33 percent for buycotting) mentioned the news media. Fewer (16 percent and 23 percent, respectively) mentioned friends or family members, and only around 1 in 10 (9 percent and 11 percent) mentioned groups or organizations. The Internet was also mentioned, but by only 7 percent for boycotting and 6 percent for buycotting.

Citizen consumer activists do not have a great deal of hope that this activity will be successful in changing the behavior of businesses. Only 14 percent say they think it can change businesses a great deal, and 26 percent say "a fair amount." The vast majority of people who boycott or buycott — 79 percent — say they do it for altruistic or self-expressive reasons . . . because it's a good thing to do.

People who are more plugged into the political and civic life of their communities are also more likely to be consumer activists. A much greater share of those who have done volunteer work in the past 12 months, taken part in group activity, or contacted a public official have engaged in consumerism than their less active counterparts (see table 3.8).

In addition, people who incorporate politics and public affairs into their daily life are more likely to be consumer activists. Boycotting and

TABLE 3.8

Consumer Activism

Frequency	Boycott* %		Buycott* %
Every week	23		19
About once a month	18		25
Less often	58		55
Don't know	2		1
Total	100		100
Organized campaign?			
Yes	7		7
No	90		90
Don't know	3		3
Total	100		100
Information from . . .			
Friend or family	16		23
News media	35		33
Internet	7		6
Group or organization	9		11
Somewhere else	26		22
Don't know	7		5
Total	100		100

	Boycotted or Buycotted† %	Neither† %	Total %
Activities in past 12 months			
Volunteered	63	37	100
Did not volunteer	38	62	100
Contacted official	75	25	100
Did not contact official	39	61	100
Group activity			
Active in group	61	39	100
Not active in group	37	63	100

Note: Based on people who said they had engaged in boycott or buycott in past 12 months.
Source: NCES2.
†*Source:* NCES1.

buycotting happen more frequently among those who are attentive to politics, report Internet usage, and use a variety of media sources for news and information. Still, consumer activity can best be described as a sleeping giant. It is largely inchoate, disorganized. Many are inclined to do it, but there is no systematic source of information about it, no regular spur. Most of the media messages citizens receive are provided *by* corporations on behalf of their products, through media organizations that depend on advertising for the bulk of their revenues. It is perhaps not surprising that this channel for political activity remains more potential than potent.

Cognitive Engagement

Adding further evidence to the generation gap in political engagement, age differences in basic attention to politics — a precursor to participation in this realm of public life — are striking. Whereas 60 percent of Dutifuls and 50 percent of Baby Boomers claim to follow politics and government "most of the time," just 37 percent of GenXers do so, falling to an even lower 25 percent of DotNets (see table 3.9).

Echoing these cohort differences, DotNets are less likely than older cohorts to say they often talk about current events with friends and family, and especially unlikely to say these conversations focus on politics. While 38 percent of Boomers and 35 percent of Dutifuls say their discussions with friends and family include items about politics or government "very often," just 28 percent of Xers and 22 percent of DotNets say the same.

The age differences in political interest manifest themselves in big differences in exposure to news via the mass media. In data that will come as no surprise to media organizations, there is a big cohort gap in newspaper reading and watching television news and, to a lesser but still significant extent, listening to radio news. Defining "regularly" as having been exposed five of the last seven days — having a news habit — newspaper readership drops from two-thirds (66 percent) of Dutifuls to half (48 percent) of Boomers, and then to 32 percent of Xers and 30 percent of DotNets. Regular television news viewing declines from a committed 85 percent of Dutifuls to a healthy 63 percent of Baby Boomers. However, just 47 percent of Xers and 38 percent of DotNets have this level of exposure. The differences for radio news are smaller, but still dramatic.

By contrast, the news about news magazines is somewhat better. Nearly 4 in 10 DotNets (37 percent) read a news magazine at least once a week, compared with 28 percent among GenXers, 34 percent among Boomers, and 37 percent among Dutifuls.

Some suggest the Internet could be a great leveler, allowing young people to get as much news as their elders, just from a different source. There was tantalizing evidence in support of this idea in the 2002 survey,

TABLE 3.9
Cognitive Engagement

	All %	DotNet %	GenX %	Boomer %	Dutiful %
Follow government and public affairs "most of the time"	45	25	37	50	60
News media consumption					
Newspapers (at least 5 days/week)	46	30	32	48	66
National television news (at least 5 days/week)	60	38	47	63	85
Radio news (at least 5 days/week)	52	33	52	61	55
News on the internet (3 or more times/week)	24	28	32	24	14
News magazines (at least once a week)	34	37	28	34	37
Political knowledge					
Margin to override veto (April 2002)	32	30	29	35	32
GOP more conservative (April 2002)	49	40	51	56	47
GOP has majority in Senate (June 2003)*	63	51	63	64	70
Name Trent Lott as senator who resigned his leadership post (January 2003)*	45	21	40	53	53
North Korea developing nuclear weapons (January 2003)*	64	46	62	69	69
Name current vice president (May 2002)*	61	48	69	64	57
Name secretary of state (May 2002)*	48	28	42	57	54
Name of European currency (May 2002)**	44	35	40	50	45

Source: All data from NCES1 except as noted.
Source: Pew Research Center.

and more recent surveys show significant growth in young people's use of the Internet for news. A June 2005 Pew survey found 23 percent of young people (aged 18–29) saying they get news every day online, and over half (55 percent) read newspapers either in print form or online — both figures that are comparable to those of older Americans (Pew Research Center for the People and the Press, 2005b).

Given these patterns in news consumption, political discussion, and interest in government, it is hardly surprising that similar generation gaps exist in political knowledge. DotNets fall behind their elders, including GenX, on factual knowledge that requires regular surveillance of the political landscape, such as naming public officials or knowing that Republicans have a majority in the Senate or are more conservative than the Democrats. They do about as well as other cohorts on a measure of civics knowledge — that a two-thirds majority is needed for congress to override a presidential veto.

There is no question that young people today are less attentive to traditional politics than their elders. But are they more cognitively disengaged than young people 10, 20, or 30 years ago? One of the clearest indicators that they *are* more disconnected comes from the HERI annual survey of college freshmen — though there is at least a suggestion that the decline in attention has reached a plateau. The percentage of students saying they consider it essential or very important to keep up to date with political affairs declined from 60 percent in 1966 to as low as 28 percent in 2000, before rebounding a bit to 34 percent in 2003 and 2004 (figure 3.5). By this measure, the early wave of college-bound DotNets displayed less interest in politics than did much of Generation X at a similar age. The slight upturn in interest of late is also mirrored in the HERI item on political discussion: in 2004, 26 percent said they discuss politics on a regular basis, the highest number since 1993.

On a different question related to politics, the pattern has been relatively stable over the years. Only about one-fifth of freshmen (20 percent in 2004) say it's essential or very important to influence the political structure, but this is virtually the same as it's been since the question was first asked in 1969.

National surveys of the general public indicate that the percentage of people who are completely inattentive to politics has been rising over the past 16 years, even as the percentage who are *very* attentive has remained about the same. Youth are not immune to these trends. The

PRC has conducted regular assessments of political values since 1987, including attention to politics. On an index that combines responses to four different questions, DotNets in 2002–2003 score disproportionately at the bottom, especially compared with GenXers surveyed at about the same ages in 1987–1988 (see table 3.10). In the current surveys, 24 percent of DotNets score zero on the index, compared with 21 percent of GenXers in the same surveys. But in 1987–1988, only 12 percent of GenXers scored at the bottom. And Boomers and Dutifuls have also slid back over this period. This pattern reflects an overall shift in which a greater proportion of the entire public now scores at the bottom of the scale — 17 percent, compared with 7 percent in the earlier surveys. Thus DotNets' poor showing reflects both the usual lack of interest among youth *and* the nature of the times. At the other end of the scale, only 14 percent of DotNets achieve the highest score, and this is comparable to GenXers' score in 1987–1988. The overall percentage scoring at the top is unchanged.

One concrete indicator of engagement clearly shows a generational decline: newspaper reading. While declines in daily reading of a newspaper could be offset by growth in the use of other media such as the Internet, it is abundantly clear from the General Social Survey that, compared with the cohorts that preceded it, smaller percentages of each new

FIGURE 3.5
Freshmen consider it essential or very important to . . .

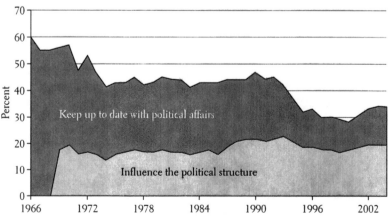

Source: Freshmen surveys by UCLA Higher Education Research Institute.

cohort over the past 30 years report reading a newspaper every day (figure 3.6). As with data on political interest from the HERI survey, however, there is an indication in the most recent surveys (2000 and 2002) that a floor may have been reached, though it is a low floor. In daily newspaper reading, DotNets enter adulthood only 6 percentage points below where Generation X did at a comparable age in 1991–1993. (By comparison, Generation X had entered about 20 points below the Boomers.)

Summarizing Age-Related Patterns in Public Engagement

While Americans have always had numerous ways to participate in public life, our analyses, like many that have come before, find that a significant minority is not meaningfully engaged in any of them. Of those who do participate, they are fairly equally split among those who choose the traditional political routes available in our republican system, those who opt for civic activities, and those who engage in both the civic and the overtly political world. Underneath this broad conclusion is a more tell-

TABLE 3.10
Attentiveness to Politics

	COMPLETELY INATTENTIVE TO POLITICS		
Generation	1987–1988	2002–2003	Change
Born pre-1918	7%	–	–
WWII (1918–1945)	5%	11%	+6
Boomer (1946–1964)	8%	16%	+8
Gen X (1965–1976)	12%	21%	+9
DotNet (1977–)	–	24%	–
Total	7%	17%	+10
	HIGHLY ATTENTIVE TO POLITICS		
Generation	1987–1988	2002–2003	Change
Born pre-1918	23%	–	–
WWII (1918–1945)	27%	25%	–2
Boomer (1946–1964)	20%	23%	+3
Gen X (1965–1976)	13%	19%	+6
DotNet (1977–)	–	14%	–
Total	22%	21%	–1

Source: Pew Research Center Surveys.

ing one, however, that may provide a glimpse into the future contours of democratic citizenship in the United States. Younger Americans — especially members of the DotNet generation — show a pattern of engagement that, while similar to that of the population as a whole, is distinctive in intriguing and mixed ways. On the one hand, they are less engaged in traditional political activities — especially voting — than older Americans. On the other, they are about as engaged in civic life as their parents and older siblings.

The import of these findings for the future shape of citizenship in the United States depends in part on whether younger Americans are different because they are still young or because their generations are different from those who were socialized in earlier eras. While the data we have mustered in this chapter could only partly and imperfectly address this issue, the evidence suggests that both life cycle and generational processes are at play, and thus that at least some of the patterns we uncovered are likely to last and perhaps even grow as DotNets and GenXers age. If this interpretation is correct, then it is possible that absent larger structural changes or unforeseen events, we may be witnessing a subtle but important shift in citizenship, away from a focus on govern-

FIGURE 3.6
Daily newspaper readership by cohort.

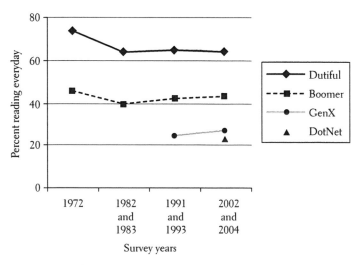

Source: General Social Survey.

ment and elections as the mechanisms for determining the public good and toward alternative avenues such as the private sector and the non-governmental public sector.

We believe the implications of this shift in emphasis from traditional political activities to civic engagement for the future of our democracy are ominous, though the extent of our concern depends in part on whether or not it represents a rejection (conscious or not) of the goals of political action (that is, collective, codified efforts to determine and implement the public good) or instead is an at least partial substitution of alternative means for achieving the same political ends. If the former, then young Americans may be little more than "canaries in the mine," serving as especially sensitive indicators of broader trends in our culture that are pushing the public away from the political world. If the latter, then while there is still reason for concern, the ultimate impact will depend on whether or not this new form of "civic politics" can be effective in translating the public will into the public good.

4

Through the Looking Glass:
Attitudes toward Public Engagement
through a Prism of Cohorts

Our examination of citizen behaviors across a wide variety of engagement argues not so much for a mixed generational pie of participation as it does for the existence of two separate pies. The pie of civic engagement looks to be well formed and sweet enough: each slice is roughly the generational size it ought to be, and the fruit is nicely distributed among the four sections. However, the pie of electoral participation is cut into slices of unequal size and clearly has a greater proportion of ripe fruit, giving it a different flavor.

What accounts for these differences? Why do the four age cohorts seem to behave quite similarly in the civic arena but so differently in the political one? To further explore these questions, in this chapter we examine the *attitudes* that underpin behaviors—the ingredients in the recipes for the pies. Even though there seems to be a clear line of electoral cleavage between the oldest and youngest two generations, we will show some important differences between DotNets and GenXers on the one hand and between Baby Boomers and Dutifuls on the other. We begin by presenting new data on reasons people give for why they do not participate in electoral politics. We then look *inward* to citizens' sense of themselves as actors in the political drama: How (if at all) does having a sense of being a part of a unique generation relate to participating in politics? What are the "norms" of citizenship held by each of the different generations, and how do these norms relate (if at all) to participation? We then turn the lens *outward*: To what extent do people trust others to be fair with them? What are their expectations of the political system? What should be the role and scope of government? What are their views of politicians and the political process? Finally, to what extent do they believe they can impact the political system through their actions? Whenever possible, we try to examine the relationship between these various civic and political attitudes to the behaviors presented in chapter 3.

Why Young People Do Not Participate in the Electoral Arena

The evidence shows there is now a two-generation–wide schism in the realm of electoral participation. A national survey conducted for the Council for Excellence in Government in early 2002 found just 20 percent of those between 18 and 25 stated that voting was "extremely important" to them, followed by another 32 percent who said it was "very important."[1] Correlatively, about half of those between 18 and 25 described voting as just "somewhat" important or less. Just one-third of those in this age range described voting as "a responsibility" or "a duty." Another third described voting in purely elective terms as a "choice," while the remaining third described voting simply as "a right" — neither fish nor fowl in terms of citizen obligation. What is behind this? Is it that younger people have been turned off from politics and have consciously rejected participation in the political system? Or, have younger people simply never tuned in and thought about participation? Is there a generational difference in the perceived relevance of politics and government? Or is it that younger people feel more empowered by acts of civic versus political involvement?

We were able to look closely at the reasons people gave for not voting on two national surveys. The second National Civic Engagement Study (NCES2) was conducted immediately after the 2002 congressional elections and asked people if they were registered and had voted in that election. Those able to vote but who chose not to (*eligible but not registered* and *registered but not voting*) were read a closed-ended list of reasons and asked to indicate which best characterized their situation. The study conducted by the NCSL in the summer of 2003 also delved into reasons for not participating in the electoral process. Those saying they did not vote "all the time" were presented with a similar list of reasons for not voting, and asked to indicate which best fit their particular situation. Both inquiries covered the same conceptual reasons for non-involvement—lack of interest, alienation, efficacy, self-perceptions of the adequacy of one's political knowledge, relevance, perceived partisan differences, and the convenience of voting—while they differed in mode of administration, the gatekeeper question to identify nonparticipants, and some of the motivations asked about.[2]

The data on reasons for nonvoting in the 2002 national elections are presented in table 4.1. At the outset, it is important to keep in mind two points. First, these data are based on all those eligible to vote (registered or not) who could have voted in 2002 but chose not to do so. Second, the data apply to very different proportions of the four age cohorts. While applicable to 38 percent of all Americans, nonparticipants encompassed 55 percent of DotNets, half (49 percent) of GenXers, a third (34 percent) of Baby Boomers and just a quarter (23 percent) of Dutifuls.

The results are more interesting than enlightening. *None* of the reasons offered to DotNets struck much in the way of a responsive chord, a telling finding in itself. Just 16 percent said they did not vote or were not registered because they were not interested; only 12 percent said their vote wouldn't make a difference. In fact, the data make a fairly compelling case that DotNets could not articulate a clear reason for their lack of participation. Our reading of these data leads us to four main conclusions, as follows. First, no single reason stands out why those DotNets who were eligible to vote in the elections of 2002 chose not to do so. As a corollary observation, we can suggest no magic bullet to stimulate involvement. The most frequent response, given by less than a quarter, was that they had recently moved and were not registered at their current address. We believe this to be less a barrier to voting than a matter of inconvenience, and one that is easily overcome with a bit of engagement. In their look at voting among young citizens, the Council for Excellence in Government found only 3 percent saying it was "very difficult" to register to vote.

Second, we note that for almost *half* of eligible DotNet voters, there was *no* major reason given why they did not vote in the election. We are reminded once again of the difficulty in asking survey questions to learn about things people have *not* done. People are much better equipped to tell interviewers calling unexpectedly why they have done the things they have done, rather than why they haven't. But the lack of coherent top-of-mind responses points to the absence of a compelling reason or reasons for nonparticipation. It is not a survey artifact. We believe that if there was a reason there, we would have found it.

Third, there are a number of differences between DotNets and their older counterparts, although most of the differences are between the

TABLE 4.1
Reasons for Not Voting in the 2002 Elections among Those Eligible

	DotNet	GenX	Boomer	Dutiful	All
Major reasons given for not voting in 2002*					
I recently moved and haven't registered at my current address	23%	23%	13%	15%	19%
I'm not interested in politics	16%	20%	23%	25%	21%
It's too hard to get information about who to vote for	13%	29%	20%	14%	20%
My vote wouldn't make any difference in what happens in my life	12%	13%	18%	21%	16%
I really dislike politics and government	8%	14%	22%	17%	16%
There's no difference between the two parties	7%	10%	15%	20%	13%
Voting is too much trouble	6%	7%	7%	7%	7%
Number of reasons described as major by respondents					
0 reasons	48%	34%	39%	44%	40%
1 reason	33%	36%	30%	25%	32%
2 reasons	12%	15%	15%	11%	14%
3 or more reasons	7%	15%	16%	20%	15%
Total	100%	100%	100%	100%	101%
Mean number of reasons	0.9	1.2	1.2	1.2	1.1
Percent of cohort not participating in election	**55**	**49**	**34**	**23**	**38**
Number of cases	83	151	152	80	466

*Multiple responses accepted; entries are expressed as percentages.
Source: NCES2.

DotNets and GenXers on the one hand and the Boomers and Dutifuls on the other. We note that it is a larger number of GenXers (29 percent) than others who seem perplexed by the system, not knowing where to turn or whom to trust for relevant, accurate information. But we also note that among nonparticipants, the older two generations are better able to give *any* reason at all, to give a greater number of reasons, and to give specific reasons for why they have opted out of the system. More of those Boomers and Dutifuls who do not participate seem to have reasons why. That is, they have consciously decided not to participate. In contrast, the data presented in table 4.1 argue that *young people have not so much dropped out as they have never tuned in*. Just 12 percent believe their vote would not make any difference in an election outcome, only 8 percent say they dislike politics and government, and 7 percent feel there is no difference between the two parties. These beliefs may grow in time, but for right now *it appears that the members of the youngest cohort have not rejected the political system so much as they are indifferent to it*.

Taken on their own, the data in the NCES2 survey are suggestive rather than conclusive, due to the small sample sizes in the four age groupings. For this reason we replicated the analysis on the NCSL data, not without its own limitations, where we were only able to compare DotNets versus all other nonparticipants.[3] Our analysis of these data led us to three central observations. First, DotNets were again less able to articulate any reason for not voting in all elections. Second, fewer non-participating DotNets acknowledged purposive (closed-ended) reasons for not voting, such as being alienated, being turned off by the negative character of politics, and not seeing a difference between candidates they are asked to choose between. They were much more likely than older respondents to feel they didn't have enough information to cast an informed vote, and somewhat more likely to say they did not vote for reasons of convenience. Finally, and we believe this to be important in the civic education debate, very few DotNets (or others for that matter) said they did not vote because they think they can make more of a difference by volunteering in their communities. That is, it does not seem that civic participation drives out, or replaces, electoral involvement. The totality of our evidence suggests that DotNets' (and perhaps GenXers') lack of involvement *seems to be more due to a lack of relevancy than rejection*. This is an important distinction for those looking for a ray of hope with regard to young people's future participation in the system, as it may be much harder to entice those who had consciously turned off, rather than simply never tuned in.

Looking Inward: How People See Themselves as Citizens

We are concerned with the attitudes people hold about themselves, and their role and responsibilities in a democratic society. We look first at the notion of "generational identity"—whether there is any group consciousness around being part of a specific age cohort—and then move on to examine views on the obligations of citizenship, again through a generational prism.

Generational Identity

What we heard from DotNets:

I think it is really easier now for us to let people know about things. We have the Internet compared with what they had [like] back in the days when guys ran horses and giving letters. Really, in that way [the] Internet is a great tool to spread your opinion. Look how many forwards you get at work. I mean you open a forward and you forward. . . . Something you share with them could effect them in their community. Right there if they send something back, you know what really influenced me into doing this? I made a difference.

Moderator: Do you think Generation X, if that's the generation that came before you, wasn't as accepting and tolerant?
Response: They were the first ones, they had to try it. We're the ones that are just continuing it. And we got it going—you know what I'm saying? They were pushing and . . . we're the ones that it's just the way it is. . . . I was trained to, like, hate certain people, because that was their generation, that's what they were like. "Oh my god, homos," you know. Now my generation is more accepting.

What we heard from Xers:

I don't think I'm part of a generation. I don't like to put myself
in groups. I like to be myself.

By the time I'm 30 I want to own my home, I want a BMW.

I'm not part of that generation. I'm my own self. Myself.

Moderator: Do you feel like you're part of a generation?"
Response: Yeah, sure. Everybody is. But I wouldn't put a label
    on it. . . .
Moderator: What about if you can't name it, or you don't like
    the name other people put on our generation? What are the
    best things about being in our generation?
Response: There are a lot of prisons.

In chapter 3 we suggested there may be something unique about the
DotNets, given the many ways their socialization has differed from that

FIGURE 4.1
Generational identification by cohort.

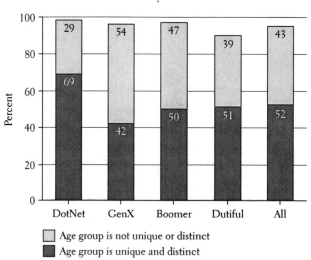

Age group is not unique or distinct
Age group is unique and distinct

Source: NCES1 Survey. "Don't know" responses have been omitted.

of GenXers. But do *they* think they are different? Data from the NCES1 suggests that they are at opposite ends of the spectrum in terms of believing there is something special about their particular age cohort. In fact, the idea of a generational identity strikes a resonant chord with a far greater number of DotNets than those in the other three generations. As shown in figure 4.1, fully two-thirds of DotNets agree with the statement "my age group is unique and distinct from other generations," while just 29 percent agree "there is nothing particularly unique or distinct about my age group." Further, these responses are quite different from all the other generational groups. And the contrast to those who came before, GenXers, could not be sharper: whereas 69 percent of DotNets believe their generation is unique, 54 percent of GenXers believe theirs is *not*.

What we cannot answer, of course, is the question of whether it is *normal* for each age group to think of itself as unique when at a young age. This is an inherent limitation to a cross-sectional survey at a single point in time. But should the idea of generational uniqueness be due solely to one's position in the life cycle, we would expect this perception

FIGURE 4.2
Percent believing age group is unique.

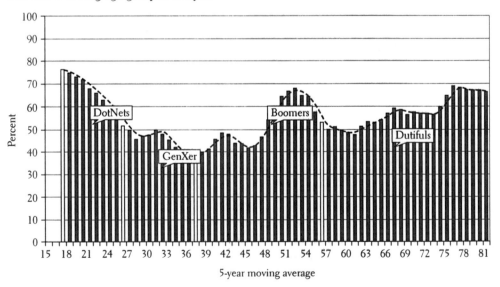

5-year moving average

Source: NCES1.

to recede with age and observe a linear decrease in the percentage in each age group giving this response. That is, the scores of DotNets would be highest, followed by GenXers, Boomers, and then Dutifuls. Obviously this is not the pattern in our data. Figure 4.2, which is based on a moving average across age, shows several interesting patterns. First, the youngest DotNets have the strongest identity. Second, Generation X has the weakest identity. But there are two other peaks on the graph as well. One is those in their early to mid-fifties, the heart of the Baby Boom generation who were socialized to politics in the 1960s and early 1970s. Later Boomers are much less likely to have a strong generational identification. The final peak is among the very oldest respondents, those in their late seventies and eighties, who represent the remnants of the "Greatest Generation."

Group consciousness does not always lead to greater political or civic participation. While there is some indication that increased racial consciousness leads to greater participation among blacks (Barker, Jones, and Tate 1994; Gurin, Hatchett, and Jackson 1989; Tate 1993), there is little evidence that feminist or gender consciousness does so for women (Jenkins 2003; Miller, Gurin, and Malanchuk 1981; Tolleson-Rinehart 1992). For younger people in particular, a sense of generational identity may be both a cause and effect of paying attention to the wider world. Our own evidence on the question is mixed. In the sample as a whole, generational identification is modestly related to engagement in all its forms. The correlation between generational identification and political and civic activity, as well as with public voice, is positive and statistically significant but small.

Obligations of Citizenship

What we heard from Dutifuls:

I have my father's notes when he went to night school to learn the Bill of Rights and all this and he became a citizen. And from that time on, since I was a little girl, I can remember him going to vote because he earned that right, and as a citizen he had to put his vote for whoever he believed in. . . . Every time there was an election he would go, make it a point, first thing before he went to work, he would go and vote. So he studied that and he felt that that was his right that he had earned by coming here and becoming a citizen.

I think we have an obligation to educate ourselves on civic matters, make a choice, and vote. I think that is an obligation. It's what we give back. If we don't we're giving nothing.

What we heard from Xers:

I don't lie, steal. So basically you don't break any laws—yeah just be a generally good person, help out people if you see they need help. Around a year ago I went in a grocery store and this kid's sitting on a railing and he fell back and I grabbed him. But that's more reaction than anything else.

I don't vote. Honestly there's a lot of stuff I don't understand. And if I don't understand it, I shouldn't go in a vote on it. And I guess that's my fault that I've never taken the time to understand.

What we heard from Boomers:

We are very, very blessed with a wonderful country, and [although] some of the people [who are] elected might not be my choice, it still beats the heck out of a lot of other countries. And I want to make sure that our freedoms are passed down to the best of my ability as one person can do.

What we heard from DotNets (responding to the question *What makes you a good citizen?*):

Uphold the law. Anybody can be a citizen, go take a test and bam, you're a citizen, it's no big thing. I was born here so I had no choice.

Response: I'm just an average [citizen], I uphold the law. I don't go out and do any drug heists or anything. I don't bad-mouth anybody big. I just chill, I mind my business.

Moderator: So you purposely don't get involved?

Response: Yeah. I don't find any interest in politics at all.

Moderator: What about staying informed? Do you think that's a responsibility? To stay informed, know what's going on in your community, current events, nationally?

Response: It's a personal choice. It takes a lot of time to stay informed, read the newspaper, watch the news. People are doing other stuff. I'm doing homework all the time, running, hanging out with my friends, I don't have time to do all that stuff.

In our expert panels, we were impressed with the conviction of those working with youth that there was a strong sense of generational identification and that young people were committed to being involved and "making a difference." We took this hopeful expectation into our focus groups of young people, and were somewhat disappointed. When asked for the qualities that make one a good citizen, most of our participants seemed slightly puzzled by the question, as if it was not one to which many had given prior thought. Common responses were that a "good citizen" obeys the laws or is not a burden to society or other people.

As these excerpts indicate, we found little in the way of expressions of active or *positive obligations* of citizenship among the younger two cohorts, that is, that a good citizen would be expected to make a contribution to the collective good in some way. Another theme in these discussion groups was that *while being involved was fine, it was also fine that some people* chose *to do so* and others did not. The focus groups led us to believe that DotNets were not much different from GenXers in the sense of having an obligation to make the world around them better.

Empirically, we found little consensus on whether citizen involvement is viewed as a duty or an option in the country today. Responses split down the middle—overall 47 percent feel it is their "responsibility" to get involved, and 48 percent characterize it a "choice" to do so, with few cohort differences. And, as shown in figure 4.3, it is just the barest of majorities (53 percent overall) who believe that being a good citizen entails having some obligations. However, a far greater number in the younger two generations embraced the more passive view of citizenship: 58 percent of DotNets and 48 percent of Xers chose the option that "simply being a good person" is enough to qualify for good citizenship, compared to just one-third of Boomers (35 percent) and Dutifuls (32 percent). It is worth noting that DotNets are coming into the electorate at a lower level than even GenXers, who have been widely scorned for their nonparticipation. Moreover, we do not believe this is simply a difference in response "style," with younger people more likely to say they do *anything* out of a norm of obligation.[4]

The national survey by the National Conference of State Legislatures focused on the issue of civic duty in its various forms, and its results echo and elaborate upon the findings in the NCES1.[5] The survey asked if each of six activities *was* or *was not* necessary for someone to do in order "to be considered a good citizen." Items encompassed obeying laws, voting, being attentive, contacting officials, donating money, and volunteering time.

There is quite a range in the number of Americans subscribing to each of these values. There is near universality in the belief that a good citizen must obey the laws—92 percent of all and 97 percent expressing an opinion believe this to be so, including every single one of the Dutifuls interviewed in the course of conducting the study.[6] Three-quarters

FIGURE 4.3
Obligations of citizenship by cohort.

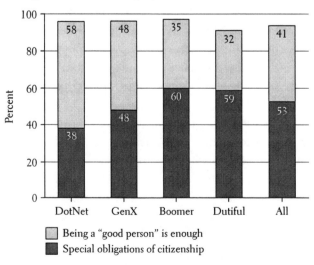

Source: NCES1 Survey. "Don't know" responses have been omitted.

(75 percent) at least pay lip service to the value that a good citizen votes in elections, and two-thirds (66 percent) say it is a citizen's duty to pay attention to government and politics, even if far fewer engage in these activities in practice. There is little consensus that the norm of good citizenship requires people to contribute their own resources of time (54 percent) or money (41 percent) in the country as a whole (see table 4.2).

While there may not be a simple generational pattern in the responses presented in table 4.2, there is a clear and quite interesting one. First, there are no cohort differences in the belief that a good citizen must obey the laws of the land, a view held by all of those in the two older generations and 9 in 10 of those in the younger two. In a sense, this is the gold standard of what generational transmission could be. This basic value is obviously fully held by all groups and certainly serves as societal glue against cynicism and doubts about the legitimacy of government. The rules of the game are in fact *rules*. No matter if Al Gore won the popular vote for president in 2000; George W. Bush won the electoral vote as interpreted by the legitimate arbiter of the Supreme Court, and is the rightful president. Transitions in other countries may not be this smooth, lacking the consensual value that "those are the laws and all must obey them." The universal nature of this value among the U.S. public also suggests that the public assumes that the process by which the laws are made is, on the whole, a fair one.

Second, there is a canyon of difference between the younger and older two generations *across those obligations focusing on the necessity of citizen involvement and attention.* A significantly larger portion of the two older generations buy in to these responsibilities than do those in the two younger ones. Differences of 20 to 30 percentage points separate Boomers and Dutifuls on the one hand and DotNets and Xers on the other in terms of believing it is the responsibility of a good citizen to: (1) vote, (2) pay attention to government decisions and political happenings, and (3) contact legislative officials about issues of importance to them.

This means that we have two successive generations where half of each cohort *needs to be persuaded* to follow government and politics and to participate in elections. For the others, it is—or has become—a default value of the political culture. We also want to note that Dutifuls give a bit more support to each of these ideals than do Boomers, and that there is no appreciable difference between DotNets and GenXers.

TABLE 4.2.
Obligations of Citizenship by Cohort

	DotNet %	GenX %	Boomer %	Dutiful %	All %
Vote in elections					
Yes	66	69	84	94	75
No	20	13	8	3	13
Don't know/Blank	14	18	7	3	12
Yes/Yes + No	77	84	92	97	85
Obey the laws					
Yes	87	89	97	100	92
No	4	6	1	—	3
Don't know/Blank	9	6	2	—	5
Yes/Yes + No	96	94	99	100	97
Volunteer their time					
Yes	49	48	54	78	54
No	26	24	17	9	21
Don't know/Blank	26	28	30	14	25
Yes/Yes + No	64	67	77	90	72
Donate money					
Yes	34	35	44	64	41
No	38	36	27	18	31
Don't know/Blank	23	29	29	19	28
Yes/Yes + No	48	49	62	78	56
Pay attention to government and politics					
Yes	54	59	84	90	66
No	23	14	8	2	15
Don't know/Blank	24	27	8	8	19
Yes/Yes + No	70	81	91	98	81
Contact your legislators					
Yes	48	50	72	76	59
No	20	19	9	7	15
Don't know/Blank	32	31	19	17	25
Yes/Yes + No	71	72	89	92	80

Note: Yes/Yes + No figures are the percentage of *Yes* responses after excluding *Don't know/ Blank* responses from the base.
Source: NCSL.

Thus if this is a life cycle phenomenon, DotNets are entering the electorate at the same place that Xers are at after 10 to 15 years of citizenship, which may be encouraging.

Finally, the data in table 4.2 indicate that on the more selfless acts of affirmative participation—volunteering time and donating money—the primary difference is between Dutifuls and *all three of the generations that have followed them*. While Boomers are slightly higher than Xers and DotNets in believing these are obligations of citizenship, there remains an interesting schism between the oldest generation and all others on these items. The difference between Boomers and Dutifuls may be a function of time or money, which Dutifuls may have more of, but it may also reflect a central value difference in the culture.

What do we then conclude about DotNets? In many ways they look virtually identical to Generation X as a *cohort* at this point in time, with *both* groups lagging in engagement and attentiveness, although DotNets look somewhat better than Xers when viewed through the lens of the life cycle. If indeed this is an area where attitudes become more favorable to participation with age, there is reason for optimism about this youngest generation, in that 10 or 15 years from now we would expect them to be significantly advanced from where GenXers are currently. So the glass may be half full or half empty. The half-empty interpretation starts by noting that DotNets now look more like GenXers than any other cohort, which is cause for concern if we are witnessing a generational effect. The half-full interpretation starts with the same observation, but is a reason for optimism if we are witnessing a life cycle effect. The evidence reviewed in this section suggests that DotNets are something of a mixed bag in how they view themselves and their role as citizens. While they are starting out with a stronger sense of generational identification than did Generation X, we find DotNets to be less well developed than any other cohort in recognizing affirmative obligations of citizenship. We are not sure whether this is a worldview that people grow out of as they age. But, as is depicted in table 4.2, the degree to which these younger two cohorts so clearly lag behind in feelings of obligation to pay attention and to vote is an ominous sign for those hoping to see growth in their participation in electoral politics.

Looking Outward: How People
See Their Fellow Citizens,
Politics, and Government
Human Nature: Interpersonal Trust

What we heard from DotNets:

> *Response:* No, I don't really trust people I don't know. I trust
> family and friends, but not strangers, people I just meet.
> *Moderator:* So you feel like you couldn't . . . like if you needed
> help, if your car broke down?
> *Response:* If my car broke down on the side of the freeway and
> some guy stopped, I'd probably be running and hiding. I
> wouldn't be that trusting.

What we heard from Xers:

> *Moderator:* Do you think that's uncommon? Do you assume
> people can't trust another person until they prove otherwise?
> *Response:* Not any more. Definitely no.
> *Moderator:* Do you think it used to be different?
> *Response:* Yea. My parents trusted people. You could go out of
> the house without being a nervous wreck. Before I was mar-
> ried I trusted everybody. I was maybe a little too the other
> way. Ever since I met him and the stuff that he sees, that
> stuff that goes on, I'm just very cautious now. But I don't
> like to be that way. I like to give people the benefit of the
> doubt. But like I said, knowing the other side, what goes, it's
> hard to trust people.
> *Moderator:* What are you afraid of? What are you afraid will
> happen?
> *Response:* I guess mostly, more so, it's my kids, I'm over-
> protective of my kids. I'm afraid for their safety, for the ben-
> efit. You just never know. Believe me, being married to a
> police officer, I've seen the things crazy, crazy that people
> do and it amazes me every day what people do, steal from
> you. And I wasn't brought up that way. It's amazing to me.

What we heard from Boomers:

> when I was growing up when I was a child in, over on the west side on Western and Colton . . . you know, my mother worked nights so she slept until 11:00, till later in the evening then woke up and took care of business, made sure I got tucked in. And went off to work and dad worked in the day. When I was out with the rest of the neighborhood kids, I had a mother here, had one over here, had a mother over there. And if I got yelled at over here, believe the rest of the neighborhood knew about it. All the parents watched out for all the kids.

One of the most striking social trends during the 1970s and 1980s was the rise in interpersonal problems: crime, unwanted pregnancy, and divorce in particular—all amply documented on the news if not felt personally by much of the public. The framers of the U.S. Constitution differed in their personal assessments of the nature of humanity, but all agreed that one of the most important functions of government was to protect its citizens from the worst tendencies of their fellow citizens. But it is unclear how a darkening view of human nature would affect specific views of government and its responsibilities.

As a nation, we are far more suspicious of our fellow citizens than we used to be. One of the more striking trends in public opinion since the advent of modern polling has been the decline in the percentage of Americans expressing generalized trust in other people. And this trend is largely a generational phenomenon: older cohorts exhibit a higher level of trust and have tended to maintain it as they have aged, while newer cohorts have come into the system with lower levels of trust (much as we might expect, given the negative societal cues) (Brady 1999; Dahl 1989; Hanson 1985; Morone 1990; Pateman 1970). Our survey finds no exception to the pattern. We employed two commonly used indicators of interpersonal trust on the NCES1.[7]

The data presented visually in figures 4.4 and 4.5 are quite clear: the youngest cohort shows the continuation of a downward spiral of interpersonal trust. By a wide margin of 70 to 27 percent, DotNets are more likely to say that people just look out for themselves rather than trying to be helpful. The next most cynical group is Xers, but the margin here is a narrower 59 to 35 percent. Roughly equal numbers of Baby Boomers hold positive and negative views of human nature, while Dutifuls give the benefit of the doubt to others. The same pattern holds with the second indicator of interpersonal trust: 56 percent of DotNets feel that others would take advantage of them if given the chance, compared to just 41 percent of Xers, 36 percent of Boomers, and 29 percent of Dutifuls. Like GenXers who preceded them, DotNets are clearly coming into young adulthood with very little in the presumption of goodwill toward their fellow citizens.

While any assessment of the psychological profile of the outlook of the younger generation(s) would be incomplete without noting how they differ from their elders, we do not wish to make too much out of this trend at the present time. For we are unsure how important this difference in outlook among cohorts may turn out to be—striking though it is—with respect to political and civic engagement. Others have looked closely at the linkage, with mixed results (Rahn and Transue 1998; Uslaner 2000). It is clear that there is not a strong relationship between interpersonal trust and political participation, and we find the relationship with civic engagement to be similarly weak.

FIGURE 4.4
Views of other people as helpful or selfish by cohort.

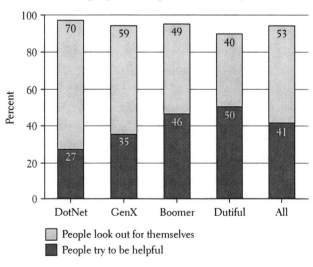

Source: NCES1 Survey. "Don't know" responses have been omitted.

FIGURE 4.5

Views of other people as fair or self-serving by cohort.

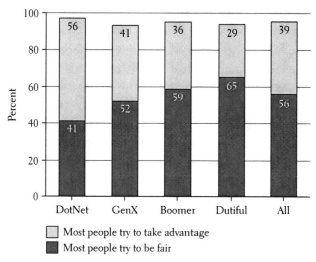

Source: NCES1 Survey. "Don't know" responses have been omitted.

Moreover, an experiment we conducted suggests that these standard questions may not really mean what they appear to mean. Our results are presented in table 4.3. In the NYS of 1,166 DotNets, half of the sample was asked if people would try to take advantage of "others" if given the chance, while the other half was asked if people would try to take ad-

TABLE 4.3

Question Wording Experiment on Interpersonal Trust

%	Belief
55	Most people try to take advantage of others if given the chance
21	Most people try to be fair in their dealings with others
23	Can't choose
1	Refused
100	Total (N = 586)
31	Most people try to take advantage of me if given the chance OR
46	Most people try to be fair in their dealings with me
22	Can't choose
1	Refused
100	Total (N = 580)

Source: NYS.

vantage "of me" if given the chance. When asked if people would try to take advantage of others, our young respondents answered much as they did in the NCES and other national surveys (55 percent distrustful, 21 percent trusting). But when the focus is moved from the more amorphous descriptor of "others" to the respondent's direct experiences ("of me") we note a far greater amount of trust. Just 31 percent believe that most people would try to take advantage of *them* if given the opportunity. Perhaps the DotNets are unusual in making this distinction, but we suspect that these questions—while they may be a good measure of sensitivity to the "mean world syndrome" described by George Gerbner and Larry Gross (1976) in the 1970s—are not necessarily predictive of future civic and political activity by young people.

Views of the Political System:
Of Politics, Government, and Efficacy

In 1981, Ronald Reagan said: "Government is not the solution to our problems. Government *is* the problem." This view has been echoed and elaborated upon by many politicians and other observers in the years since. Even Bill Clinton proclaimed in 1996 that "the era of big government is over." And throughout this period, public officials and politicians were vilified, especially by the press, for their ethical behavior, enslavement to special interests, and willingness to do anything to win election. Even consummate Washington insiders, such as Al Gore in 2000 and John Kerry in 2004, ran as outsiders "against the system."

Throughout much of the time that Generation X was socialized to politics, and while many of the DotNets were forming their first impressions, antigovernment rhetoric has flourished. Both DotNets and Xers are steeped in scandal, captured by cynicism and the unrelenting negativity of the news cycle. So there is much that would also argue for a similar worldview of disillusionment with politics and government. Can we see an impact of this acidic bath on the views of young people about government, politics, and politicians?

To answer this, it is important to make distinctions. There is government, and then there is politics. These are not the same thing. The evidence is that views of politics, for many young people, are distinctly negative. But government is viewed more analytically. President Reagan's criticism of government was more ideological than cultural, and ideology is inherently more contestable than culture. Those who grew up during Reagan's administration are somewhat more conservative and more critical of government than those who grew up during Bill Clinton's time in office (see chapter 6). But all who passed through this period may bear the evidence of the antipolitical culture of the times. Here we compare and contrast citizens' views of the political system, the scope, functioning, and perceived responsiveness of government. We offer more evidence in this section about the views of newest cohort in American politics—the DotNets. But of course we cannot tell if any of the views they hold are distinct without comparing them with the views of older cohorts.

Views of Politics

The modern rise in distrust of government did not begin with the Reagan era. In many respects, Reagan was the product of growing dissatisfaction with government rather than the catalyst of it. In fact, the past 40 years in the United States have witnessed sharp swings in view of government, with trust plummeting during the 1960s and 1970s, recovering in the mid-1980s, dropping again in the early 1990s, and rising through the rest of the decade to a peak in the aftermath of 9/11 (Pew Research Center for the People and the Press 1998; Council for Excellence in Government 2004).

TABLE 4.4
Motivations of Public Officials by Cohort

	DotNet %	GenX %	Boomer %	Dutiful %	All %
Most people elected to public office work to serve the public interest	24	36	36	48	31
Most people elected to public office work to serve their own personal interest	36	39	47	38	39
Not choosing	40	26	18	14	30
Serve own personal interest (as % of those with an opinion)	60	52	57	44	56

Source: NCSL.

The vast majority of Americans find the playing field of politics to be tilted: 56 percent agree that politics is a means for the already powerful to maintain advantage; just one-third believe that politics is a way for the powerless to acquire equal footing. Interestingly, in the NCES1 survey we found more (relative) affirmation about politics among DotNets than any other group. About 6 in 20 GenXers and Boomers alike viewed politics as a way for powerful people to keep power for themselves, compared to half of DotNets and Dutifuls. But the youngest cohort was no more sanguine about the motivations of politicians than other age groups — though a significantly larger percentage of them had no opinion, perhaps a positive sign that they are not yet reflexively suspicious. (Interestingly, the Dutifuls expressed the highest level of positive sentiment about public officials. See table 4.4.)

The question of how young people viewed politics was foremost in our minds as we undertook this project. Accordingly, we made it an important part of early exploration of opinion in the focus groups we

FIGURE 4.6
Associations with the word "politics" among DotNets only.

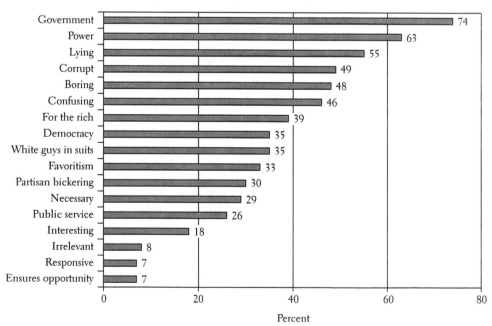

Source: NYS.

conducted across the country. While the questions we asked in these focus groups evolved over time and were occasionally tailored to the age group we were examining, a staple of each group was to pass out pencils and paper and ask participants to write down the first word that came into their minds when the moderator mentioned "politics" and "government." We then called on each in turn for their answers, listing responses on an easel to begin our discussion segment on views of the political system. The focus groups suggested a wide range of words — some positive, some negative, and some neutral in meaning. We carried this practice over to the NYS conducted in February 2002.[8] On basis of the focus group results, we chose 17 descriptive words or phrases that we had often heard in focus groups and asked respondents to "check off all the words below that come to mind when (you) hear the word POLITICS." The percentage picking each word or phrase is shown in figure 4.6.

At the top of the list of responses are fairly neutral descriptors: "government" and "power," acknowledged by 74 percent and 63 percent, respectively. Beyond this, however, the negativity in the general American political culture is readily apparent: 55 percent check off "lying," and half mark "corrupt," as words they associate with politics. Next are two words that are less overtly negative but nonetheless indicate young people's distance from the political system: "boring" (48 percent) and "confusing" (46 percent). These in turn are followed by a significant number who, similarly, find politics to be outside their purview, or *for others*: 39 percent say politics is "for the rich," and a similar number (35 percent) say politics brings to mind images of "white guys in suits" — the same number who thought of the word "democracy." At the bottom of the list are words such as "responsive" (7 percent), "ensures opportunity" (7 percent), "interesting" (just 18 percent), "public service" (26 percent) and "necessary" (29 percent). While we lack comparative data to know if the worldview based on these adjectives is distinct to the newest generation, all in all it is quite a negative and cynical picture of the political world held by our youngest citizens.

But of what consequence? Do the views of the political system held by young people matter at this point in their lives — that is, do they translate into more or less participation? We first factor analyzed the 17 statements, finding that they reduce to four underlying dimensions.[9] (See table 4.5.) Factor 1 is clearly defined by its negativity. The negative adjectives *corrupt, lying,* and *favoritism* most strongly identify this factor.

Factor 2 seems to be mainly descriptive observations without much in the way of emotional content: *government, democracy,* and *power* are the words that best define this factor. We think Factor 3 is best described as noting some distance or alienation from the respondents' life experiences to the political world. That is, politics is *for others.* It is *boring, confusing, for white guys in suits,* and, to a lesser extent, *for the rich.* The highest loadings on Factor 4 are positive associations with politics: *ensures opportunity* and *responsive,* followed by *interesting* and *public service.*

Because the adjectives were carried on only one of our surveys with a narrow scope, our ability to link these dimensions to concrete acts of participation is somewhat limited. This particular survey carried few of the dependent variables of participatory behavior that made up the core of the subsequent NCES. However, the survey did ask if our age-eligible respondents were registered to vote, if they had voted in the 2000 presidential election, if they followed news about government and politics, and the extent of their participation in voluntary organizations, giving us some purchase on how these views of the political world related to actual behaviors.

TABLE 4.5
Factor Analysis of Adjectives Applied to Politics by DotNets

| | COMPONENT | | | |
	Negative	Descriptive	For others	Positive
Corrupt	.80	.01	.05	−.03
Lying	.72	−.03	.22	.01
Favoritism	.69	.07	.11	.03
For rich	.59	.04	.37	−.04
Party bicker	.59	.16	−.01	.09
Government	.18	.73	.13	−.06
Democracy	.02	.63	.00	.24
Power	.41	.63	.06	.00
Public service	−.05	.54	−.08	.43
Necessary	−.06	.51	−.05	.32
Boring	.14	−.09	.72	−.00
Confusing	.06	.18	.72	−.03
White guys in suits	.30	.01	.55	.05
Ensures opportunity	.06	.11	−.03	.67
Responsive	−.12	.27	.09	.59
Interesting	.13	.30	−.37	.52
Irrelevant	.29	−.31	.29	.49

Source: NYS.

The pattern of results shown in table 4.6 is quite striking, and perhaps somewhat counterintuitive. Young people who have neutral responses to the word *politics* — who think descriptively in terms of government, democracy, power — are more likely to engage in conventional political activity. But so, too, are those who have negative views of politics — who see politics involving corruption, lying, favoritism. The emotional energy of these negative views does not drain away the willingness to engage.

But views of politics as distant — inscrutable, boring, the province of others — are associated with lower levels of engagement. Overall, the negative correlation between political engagement and views of politics as "for others" is nearly as strong as the positive correlation with views of politics that are clinical and descriptive. Although we will later present evidence that at least some civic engagement is politically motivated and has political consequences, views of politics among young people — at least in this context — are only weakly related to membership in voluntary organizations. And *positive* views of politics bear little relation to the level of engagement in either political or civic activity, suggesting that impressions of politics are far from fully formed and are yet to be strongly related to potential behaviors.

TABLE 4.6
Correlates of Views of Politics with Political and Civic Activity

Factor	Registered[1]	Voted[2]	Political activity[3]	Political and cognitive activity[4]	Voluntary activities[5]
Negative	.11**	.10**	.15**	.15**	.06
Descriptive	.14**	.15**	.18**	.24**	.08**
For others	−.05	−.12	−.11	−.20**	−.09**
Positive	−.02	−.01	.03	.11**	.09**

[1]Registered to vote — applicable only to those 18+.
[2]Voted in 2000 election — applicable only to those 18+.
[3]Political activity scale with 5 components: (1) registered; (2) voted in 2000; (3) signed an e-mail petition; (4) signed a written petition; (5) wrote a letter to a public official.
[4]Political and cognitive activity scale: includes 5 components of political activity scale, adding recently talked about the news, follows government and politics, follows political happenings.
[5]Scale from 1 to 9 on the number of voluntary organizations the respondent reported belonging to.
**Correlation is significant at .01 level.
Source: NYS.

The Role and Functioning of Government

What we heard from Nets and Xers after 9/11:

> I think instead of sitting here fighting against ourselves, the Republicans against the Democrats, always trying to find some dirty laundry, like on Bush, or this or that, this is how we should have been, how we are now, always not fighting against each other and trying to ruin each other. Focus, like on the terrorists. Why couldn't we have done this five years ago, try to track him down and end it five years ago? Because we're too busy fighting each other.

> *Moderator:* So you trusted them that in response to the terrorist attacks . . . take the right response . . .
> *Response:* Sometimes the politics inside a country . . . people get elected . . . people say anything to get into power. . . . If we're going to get attacked, the right thing to do, which they've done, is bomb them back.

> I trust them to take care of it. They will get to the bottom of it, they will find him, they will give justice. I trust them to do that. As far as truth and information and stuff like that, no, not always.

While many trends in the political and cultural *Zeitgeist* are arguable, one is not. The U.S. political system shifted to the right during the 1980s and into the 1990s. Republicans gained the U.S. Senate and White House in 1980, and although they lost the Senate in 1986 they won both houses in 1994, as well as a majority of governorships and state houses as well. Youth socialized during the 1980s were told that liberalism was a discredited ideology and offered a strong and charismatic conservative president in Ronald Reagan. The 1990s were more complicated, with intense antigovernment activity coupled with a charismatic and youthful Democratic president, Bill Clinton, ending in his personal scandal. The current decade has already proven highly eventful, with two razor-thin presidential election victory margins, a terrorist attack, and a war in Iraq, but of course its imprint on the political thinking of the citizenry is still being formed.

We will explore the ideological, partisan, and value profiles of our cohorts in greater detail in chapter 6. Here we simply observe that DotNets stand out for their generally positive view of government — both its core responsibilities and how well it has discharged them. Moreover, DotNets may be distinctive for another view: on where the locus of power in modern society resides. Our early evidence is that the youngest cohort sees business as more powerful than government today, while most people in older cohorts still see government as most influential.

DotNets certainly seem to be starting out with less suspicion and hostility toward government than the cohort they will be replacing. At the time the NCES1 survey was taken, the American public overall was evenly divided about the role of government vis à vis the private sector: 47 percent felt that government should do more to solve problems, and 45 percent said that government should leave things to business and individuals (figure 4.7). However, by a two-to-one margin, DotNets favored an expanded role of government (64 to 31 percent), as did a slight majority of GenXers (51 to 41 percent). Views of the proper scope of government were reversed among the older two cohorts. Majorities of Boomers and Dutifuls opted for a greater role for business and individ-

FIGURE 4.7
Government activity by cohort.

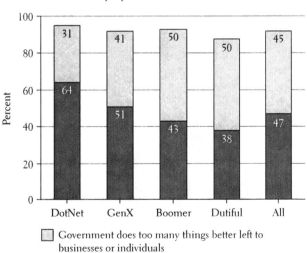

Government does too many things better left to businesses or individuals
Government should do more to solve problems

Source: NCES1 Survey. "Don't know" responses have been omitted.

uals, while about 4 in 10 favored a stronger government presence. These are some of the strongest cohort differences in all the attitudinal survey work we conducted or reviewed in the course of this project.

We observe a very similar pattern of responses on the issue of government regulation of business (see figure 4.8). Respondents were asked whether government regulation did more harm than good, or was necessary to protect the public interest. By margins of two to one, both DotNets and Xers take the proregulation side. Boomers and Dutifuls are less supportive of regulation; about half of each say regulation is necessary, but one-third of each are antiregulation. This survey question, and to some extent the previous one, juxtapose "government" against "business" in some fashion, so it is possible that younger people are not so much progovernment as they are antibusiness. However, we believe this not to be the case. The NCSL survey fielded in the summer of 2003 asked respondents how much power they believed a number of groups in society had. While 51 percent of DotNets felt that "business and corporations" had "too much power," the number of GenXers (62 percent), Boomers (65 percent), and Dutifuls (69 percent) were even higher. These relationships between age and opinion about government were as strong

FIGURE 4.8
View of government regulation by cohort.

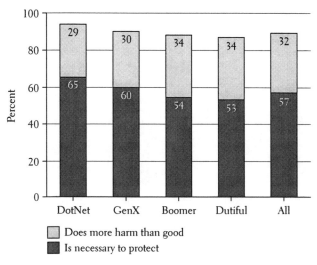

Source: NCES1 Survey. "Don't know" responses have been omitted.

as those between party and ideology on the one hand and opinions about government on the other.

Apart from views about what government should do with respect to problems in the society—largely, problems related to the functioning of the market, as well as peoples' successes and failures in it—is the question of how people perceive the market vis à vis the government. Surveys have long shown that the public distrusts big business just as it does big government, and is suspicious of the motives of corporate executives in much the same way that it casts a wary eye on public officials. Much has been said about the growth of antigovernment sentiment in the past few decades, but this has also been a time of concomitant growth in the power and influence of business. What is the public's perception of this phenomenon? In particular, how do young people see the balance shifting between the public and the private sectors?

Inspired by the suggestion of political scientist W. Lance Bennett, we tried to address this issue with a question on a statewide sample conducted in New Jersey in the spring of 2003.[10] Respondents were asked: "Who do you think has the most influence over how you live your life these days: the government, or business and corporations?" (table 4.7). Significantly more DotNets (over 18 in this survey) said business is more powerful than government, by a margin of 61 to 35 percent. The responses of GenXers also tilted fairly heavily toward business, while Boomers were evenly divided. And Dutifuls were a mirror image of DotNets, with the majority believing that the public sector exerts more control over them than does the private sector. Recognizing that this is a single question on a survey in a single state, the results are nevertheless intriguing.

TABLE 4.7
Relative Impact on Life—Government or Business

More Influence on Your Life	DotNets %	GenXers %	Boomers %	Dutifuls %	All %
Government	35	37	44	47	46
Business and corporations	61	54	42	36	39
Neither/both/don't know	4	10	15	16	16
Total	100%	100%	101%	100%	101%
Total (n)	69	186	439	281	1002

Chi square value p ≤ .001.
Source: Star-Ledger/Eagleton-Rutgers Poll No. 143, April 24–May 4, 2003.

Political Efficacy and Empowerment

What we heard from Boomers:

> Well, where I was from we had a neighborhood watch group, and practically all of our neighbors had the sign in their window that showed they were part of the watch group. And what they did was we looked out for each other, and if there was anything going on they called the police and the police would be there right away. Just preventing problems in the neighborhood.

> *Response:* So they [his town] want to put this cell tower there, and a lot of people are fighting that. And also, they just put a Starbucks in town, and that was a big uproar because there was a little café next to it that they were afraid big bad Starbucks would come in and put them out of business.
> *Moderator:* But it didn't stop it?
> *Response:* The cell tower is still going on. The Starbucks is there.

The public is almost evenly divided on the question of its ability to influence the political system. We find this to be true whether the referent is having a say "about what government does" or "making a difference in your (one's) own community." In both cases, there are no significant differences across age cohorts. If the "Millennials" are rising, they haven't yet fully felt their power (Howe and Strauss 2000). In both the civic arena and in conventional politics, most DotNets (and most citizens generally) don't see themselves as able to make a lot of difference in what happens.[11] Only about 1 in 10 DotNets believe they can make a great deal of difference in their communities; another 4 in 10 say they can make at least "some" difference. These answers place them near GenXers and Boomers, and a little ahead of Dutifuls, although all cohort differences are minor. And there is even less difference on the measure of political efficacy.

But this is an unsurprising result—at least on the political side—inasmuch as political scientists have never found significant age-related differences in political efficacy. We examined cohort trends in the National Election Study, which has asked a basic battery of efficacy questions since 1952; these show no consistent cohort differences (except that the oldest cohort, which is less educated, tends to feel that government is too complicated).

Summary and Conclusions

In this chapter we explored cohort differences across a range of political and social orientations, in light of expectations raised in our review of the world in which the DotNets and GenXers grew up. In some dimensions—trust in or cynicism about government, feelings of personal political efficacy—we found little difference across the age cohorts. But in many other areas, there are significant differences. Four in particular are worth restating:

1. DotNets and GenXers could not be more different on the existence of "generational identification." DotNets are far above the mean in believing that their age group is unique; GenXers are far below the mean, with Boomers and Dutifuls in the middle.

2. DotNets and Xers both badly trail Boomers and Dutifuls in the view that citizenship entails obligations. This is most apparent in the responsibility of citizens to be attentive, become informed, and vote. There is little difference between DotNets and Xers on this dimension.

3. DotNets and GenXers are the two most progovernment cohorts, giving it credit for its functioning and worrying less about an expansive scope. Generation X is more conservative than the DotNets, but on most measures both are more accepting of government than their elders.

4. DotNets are reaching maturity with less interpersonal trust than Xers, who themselves are far less trusting of their fellow humans than Boomers or Dutifuls. But this orientation seems to bear little relation to political and civic engagement. Moreover, we have significant questions about what it really signifies.

At this point, we are hesitant to draw too many bold conclusions about the newest cohort. While DotNets' first tastes of politics are indeed poisoned by the common well of negativity in the political culture, they are — for the most part — no more cynical than older Americans, and in some instances appear less so. Moreover, views of politics for them are not yet strongly related to civic and electoral behaviors. In fact, those with negative views are somewhat more likely to participate than those with positive ones. Those giving neutral descriptors such as one might acquire in high school civics courses (government, democracy, power) are among the most participative; those who feel the political system is something "for others" are the least. Thus at this early juncture, there is evidence that DotNets' initial negative introduction to the system does not necessarily pose serious negative consequences for future participation, although the lack of inculcation of civic norms among DotNets (and GenXers) certainly does. Finally, we also wish to note the tentative evidence that youth are more apt than their elders to perceive the private sector as more influential in their lives than government, and we hope this earns a place on future research agendas.

Generational Pathways to Participation

What we heard from a DotNet:

> I'm going to vote for myself. Every president, I think, is a liar.
> That's just my opinion because they're all trying to get one job
> and they're going to say anything to get your vote. And then
> when they get it they're not going to do what you say anyway
> . . . For young people, for old people . . . [when you] get down
> to it they don't do nothing for you.

What we heard from a Dutiful:

> It seems to me that politics is necessary and in a democracy it
> is going to be a problem. Because we can go get a king and we
> can throw away all these problems and let him take care of it
> for us . . . well if we don't want that then we've got to make it
> work. And the way we make it work is through politics. So it
> goes both ways.

These remarks are just a few of the many we heard in our focus groups
that highlight our cohorts' differences in their approaches to politics.
Many Nets see the political world as largely irrelevant and concentrate

their efforts in more private activities; most Dutifuls see their own participation as key to the process. As previous chapters have illustrated in detail, the differences represent the ways young adults have remixed the participation soundtrack, sampling some of the habits of older adults (civic work and the expression of political voice), while eschewing more overtly political acts.

There are three possible reasons for these differences. First, young people may lack key resources that traditionally steer individuals into political life. Some of these shortcomings may simply be a reflection of the cohort's relative youth and inexperience and will disappear as they grow older, settle down, find jobs, and get married. Thus, in this formulation, the relatively low levels of political engagement among DotNets today are due largely to their place in the life cycle, not their generational pedigree. For example, one of the most important predictors of engagement is advanced education; people who are more educated are more involved. As this point, many Nets are just starting college. As time passes and the cohort ages, more and more Nets will have attended college and gained the critical skills and orientations that will lead them into public life, and they may eventually become as politically engaged and involved as older folks.

The second explanation also argues that Nets' lack of political involvement can be traced to their weak showing on many of the important precursors to engagement. The critical difference here is the focus on Nets' unique generational character. In this explanation, young people may have fewer of the key resources commonly associated with an engaged life, but unlike the life cycle explanation, there is no age–related explanation for their shortfall. If youth today are less likely to hear parents talking about politics, less likely to possess strong attachments to the political parties, or less likely to attend religious services with much regularity, then we would expect them to be less involved in politics, since all of these conditions are negatively related to engagement. What makes this a generational and not a life cycle phenomenon is the fact that these conditions are not a function of age but of how they have been socialized. DotNets are not likely to outgrow them.

Third, in another generational explanation, DotNets may have all the key resources that led their elders toward engagement, but the younger cohort may be less politically involved because the connection between these traditional elements and participation is weaker now than in the past. They're not getting the same boost toward engagement that these influences provided earlier cohorts. This might mean, for example, that DotNets are just as efficacious as older adults, but that efficacy matters more for older cohorts. Older folks who feel more effective are more engaged; among younger people, efficacy doesn't matter.

In a rigorous examination of the pathways to participation for all four cohorts, we found support for the first two explanations and not the third. In other words, it is the fact that DotNets lack key resources and attitudes — not that they are taking a different path to participation — that explains why they are less politically active than older cohorts. A few of the characteristics they lack (such as high levels of education) are a function of their location in the life cycle and will improve with the passage of time. But they are also falling short on key characteristics (such as civic duty) that have little to do with the fact that they're young — a generational explanation.[1] Thus some of the low levels of political engagement among youth are typical of young people in any era. But some of it is unique to this generation.

There is little support in our data for the notion that the *process* of engagement is unique for DotNets. The same motivators work for DotNets that have worked for generations ahead of them. For example, individuals who grew up in homes with political discussions are more engaged adults than are their counterparts who were raised in homes with no such talk — regardless of the era in which they came of age. Thus, Nets' lack of political engagement is not due to the impact of influences having changed.

This chapter provides a detailed look at this process, beginning with an overview of the ways a host of resources are linked to participation.[2] Next, we build a model of citizen engagement that allows us to illustrate how a plethora of conditions, attitudes, and orientations come together to influence participation. Finally, we take a closer look at what young people are currently doing in their own environments (in and out of school), the ways their engagement is being spurred, and how these positive influences might account for the divide between the civic and political participation of this cohort.

The cross-sectional nature of our data sets prevents us from sorting out the relative impact of life cycle and generational effects on Nets' political disengagement. However, the cohort analyses from earlier chapters do shed some light on when and where generational or age-related factors might make an impact. Throughout this chapter, we turn back to these earlier analyses to help make sense of the puzzle of political participation among youth.

What Helps People Participate?
Modeling Citizen Engagement

The decision to participate seems pretty straightforward. You either do it or you don't — the "it" being any number of things that comprise the array of politically consequential behaviors. However, the process that leads to that decision is not so simple. There are a multitude of characteristics, traits, and experiences that inspire someone to be engaged in public life.[3]

In their work on citizen engagement, Verba, Schlozman, and Brady (1995) develop a model that situates the roots of political participation in a set of chronological stages. Some resources or influences develop early in life; some occur immediately before an individual takes action. We follow their lead, using our own data set (the NCES1), which contains a unique set of measures, to illustrate the process of engagement as a movement through time, where one may or may not acquire various precursors that spur activism.

We have developed a model containing eight steps that we think lead to involvement in public life. They are: initial characteristics, early socialization, education, television avoidance, generational identification, social capital, political capital, positive attitudes toward politics and government, and mobilization. Basically, our argument is that individuals have the potential to be exposed to important socializing experiences early in life that, in turn, put them in a better position to acquire skills, attitudes, and fortuitous contacts that add to the likelihood that they'll be engaged citizens. The model is built on the assumption that the acquisition of these precursors happens in stages and that each experience, characteristic, or attitude affects not only participation but the likelihood of acquiring other precursors as well. As it turns out, not all of the things we include in the model (such as gender or minority status) contribute very much to our understanding of why people are engaged. Others (such as early socializing experiences, political capital, and mobilization in particular) turn up time and again as especially potent. Importantly, when we compare the cohorts, we find that young people aren't that different from older citizens when it comes to the extent to which they have experienced various early socialization processes. But the members of the youth cohort possess significantly lower levels of political capital and are much less likely to have been mobilized. The youth deficit on these key precursors need not be the norm. More can be done to mobilize youth and inspire norms of civic duty. But that's a story for later. First, we need to spend some time describing and explaining the pathway to participation that is illustrated by this model. Table 5.1 shows the distribution of each cohort on a variety of potential influences on engagement.

Initial characteristics, or traits that one is simply born with, include gender, mother's education, minority status, and age.[4] Maternal education and age are believed to promote engagement, while being female or a person of color may have less sanguine effects on participation. Preliminary bivariate analyses supported this relationship. For example, individuals whose mothers attended college are more active than those whose mothers did not do so across most of the 19 indicators of engagement. But this characteristic cannot explain lower levels of political participation among DotNets. Fifty-one percent of Nets' mothers have some college experience, compared to just 32 percent of GenXers, 21 percent of Boomers, and 12 percent of Dutifuls. If anything, these higher levels of college education among Nets' mothers should have facilitated increased levels of activity among their children.

As for minority status, it's apparent that race and ethnicity remain important for sorting out who participates and who does not.[5] Across numerous measures, whites outpace nonwhites in their levels of participation, but minority status seems to have little overall impact when a host of other factors are taken into account. However, it's important to note the differences among whites and nonwhites across various activities. The reality is that minority participation (and minority voices) is disproportionately absent from the public realm.

DotNets are the most diverse generation — both in terms of immigration and race and ethnicity — to come of age in America. However, while this *might* account for lower levels of political participation among Nets, it does not explain why young people are holding their own in the civic

TABLE 5.1.
Precursors to Engagement by Cohort

	All	DotNets	GenX	Boomer	Dutiful
Step 1: Initial characteristics					
Average age	38	20	32	47	69
Gender (percent female)	52	50	51	51	56
Mother's education (percent some college)	32	51	32	21	12
Nonwhite (race black, Asian, other, or Hispanic ethnicity) (percent)	26	34	31	24	17
Not native-born (percent)	8	7	11	6	6
Step 2: Early socialization					
Someone in household volunteered (percent)	40	43	40	40	36
Frequent political discussions in household (percent)	19	16	17	19	24
Step 3: Education					
Education (percent with some college)	44	34	55	52	36
Step 4: Formative attitudes and behaviors					
Television avoidance (percent who watch 1 hour or less per day)	22	27	25	22	9
Generational self-identification (percent)	54	69	42	50	51
Step 5: Social capital					
Size of social network (percent 4 or more friends)	37	34	35	34	50
Attendance at religious services (percent weekly or more often)	40	37	37	42	49
Interpersonal trust (percent who endorsed two items measuring interpersonal trust)	28	17	26	35	41
Length of community residence (average number of years at current residence)	19	11	13	23	36
Step 6: Political capital					
Attention to politics (percent who follow politics and government "most of the time")	40	25	37	50	60
Percent with political knowledge (2 or 3 correct answers)	26	23	25	30	29
Efficacy (percent who believe individuals can make at least some difference)	49	48	53	54	40
Partisanship (percent strong partisan)	26	19	23	30	39
Sense of civic duty (percent who believe more rather than less is required of citizens)	28	21	30	33	31
Step 7: Attitudes about government and politics					
Positive attitudes toward government (percent)	23	31	22	19	14
Positive attitudes toward politics (percent)	9	11	9	6	10
Step 8: Mobilization					
Contacted by a political party or candidate (percent)	23	12	23	32	34

Source: NCES1.

and voice realms, especially since the relationship between minority status and participation remains — albeit weakened in the youngest cohort — regardless of the type of engagement under consideration.

Next in the model is early socialization, a composite measure that includes growing up with a parent or guardian who volunteered and hearing frequent political discussions with family members. Both of these contribute to more engagement through the benefits young people gain by having good role models in their lives. Our data repeatedly reinforce the importance of political socialization to engagement. Individuals who had frequent household political discussions while young and who grew up in homes where someone volunteered are more likely to be involved in a host of activities than are those who grew up without these experiences. While we find little difference in the rate at which the different cohorts had volunteer role models, DotNets (and GenXers) are somewhat less likely than Boomers, and especially Dutifuls, to report a home that had political talk (16 percent and 17 percent, versus 19 percent and 24 percent, respectively). Thus, we find that on a key precursor — political talk in the home — there are some generational differences between the age groups, which might account for the lower levels of political activism among youth.

Next comes education, something we've already shown to be related to more citizen engagement. Education is a tried-and-true motivator that works both directly and indirectly on engagement. In other words, education doesn't just affect levels of citizen engagement. It also affects many of the other precursors, which in turn go on to influence engagement.[6] Young people, of course, are at an inherent *life cycle* disadvantage at this step in the process, though DotNets are on track to have an advantage over older cohorts in the percentage who will ultimately finish college and even undertake graduate study.

The next stages in our model are two formative attitudes and behaviors: generational identification and television watching. If generational identity is formed as one is coming of age (when society and the media begin to react to the new "generation"), individuals with a strong sense of generational identity might think of themselves as part of a larger group, which is usually an empowering situation. That is, if one thinks of taking action, knowing that one belongs to a generation of like-minded individuals might promote engagement. Our evidence, even if tentative, seems to bear this out. For example, 37 percent of those with a generational identity report trying to persuade others to vote — or how to vote — when an election is taking place, compared to just 29 percent of those who do not think they belong to a unique generation. Youth seem to have the edge on this one, since, as we've shown earlier, Nets are the most likely to say their generation is unique and distinct from others.

Putnam and others have warned of television's baneful effects on an engaged citizenry. Simply put, television watching and engagement is viewed as a zero-sum relationship. The more you do of one, the less time you have to spend on doing the other.[7] There's some evidence for this relationship in our data. For example, 34 percent of those who report watching an hour of television or less on an average day say they regularly volunteer for a nonpolitical organization, compared to just 10 percent who watch more than six hours per day. Although Nets and GenXers are the two age cohorts who have popular reputations as couch potatoes, both cohorts spend about as many hours in front of the television as do older adults, and may even clock fewer hours there than do Dutifuls.

Next comes social capital. The term "social capital" is often used as a shorthand to describe the benefits that arise from extended social networks. By getting to know people through groups or organizations, attending religious services regularly, joining civic clubs, enrolling in school, or any other mechanism for meeting others, people increase their trust in others and develop habits of reciprocity. In short, a society abundant with social capital is one where its citizens are not motivated solely by selfish concerns but are aware of and concerned about the needs of others.[8] The indicators that we use to form a composite measure of social capital are the size of someone's social network, how often he or she attends religious services, his or her levels of interpersonal trust, and length of residence in a community. All are associated with more citizen engagement. For example, 59 percent of those who attend religious services more than once a week regularly vote, compared with just 47 percent of those who never attend religious services.

But while our analysis indicates that those with more social capital are, generally speaking, more engaged, we also don't find much evidence that levels of social capital vary among the cohorts. For example, Nets are about on par with older citizens in having large social networks — 34 percent of the youngest cohort report having six or more close friends, compared to 39 percent of Xers, Boomers, and Dutifuls.

Political capital follows social capital in the model and is best understood as the political resources that arise in citizens who are attentive, knowledgeable, efficacious, strongly identified with a political party, and infused with a strong sense of civic duty. What all of these traits have in common is an implicit recognition that the world of politics is important and relevant. Possessing these characteristics reduces the "costs" associated with participating by making the system familiar and providing the confidence to get involved, identifying the key issues on the agenda, and providing a psychological connection to the political process (either through a desire to see one's party succeed or a more general orientation to the process). We find strong confirmation for the relationship between all of these measures of "political capital" and engagement in its various dimensions (table 5.2). Of course, political capital is, in many respects, a desired outcome of positive socialization and is interwoven with participation—a "dependent variable" as much as an independent variable. It is as interesting as an "effect" of other forces as it is a "cause" for participation.

As for the relationship between these indicators and age, Nets and Xers are about equally as likely to believe in their own efficacy as older adults. About half of each cohort say they can make a great deal or some

TABLE 5.2
The Importance of Political Capital

	Percent who reported always voting in local and national elections
Correctly answered . . .	
3 political knowledge questions	71
1 political knowledge question	49
	Percent who reported working with others to solve a community poblem
Expressed . . .	
Strong sense of civic duty	30
No sense of civic duty	16
	Percent who reported signing a written petition
Score on index of Cognitive engagement	
Highest score	45
Lowest score	32

Source: NCES1.

degree of difference in effecting change. Civic duty, however, is a different story. As we discussed in chapter 4, fewer DotNets have a sense of civic duty. Fifty-six percent of Xers, Boomers, and Dutifuls believe that being a good citizen comes with special obligations, compared with only 38 percent of DotNets.[9]

Youth are also much less partisan than their elders, which puts them at a disadvantage since individuals who have developed ties to a political party are more engaged, especially in electoral politics. Nineteen percent of Nets report being strong partisans, compared to 29 percent of older citizens. As for Xers, they're only slightly less independent and slightly more partisan. Patterns observed over the past 40 years seem to show that this is more of a life cycle than a generational phenomenon and thus is likely to be self-correcting.

Cognitive engagement and political knowledge — two related and important elements of political capital — show significant differences across the age continuum. As we outlined in chapter 3, Nets lag behind everyone in their level of attention to politics and their news consumption; they are also significantly less likely to talk about politics with their family and friends. On questions that measure political knowledge, Nets are the least likely to give correct answers.[10] However, GenXers aren't showing remarkable improvement over Nets on attentiveness and knowledge.

The penultimate motivator for engagement is a composite measure of attitudes related to government and the political process. They come at this point in the model because they are less general orientations (like civic duty) and more assessments of the current political or government situation. Initially we expected that positive attitudes toward government or the political process would promote engagement. However, the evidence suggests that this isn't always the case. It's true that having a positive attitude toward the political process, or believing that, for instance, the political system works to ensure equal opportunity for everyone, is related to more activism across a variety of activities. Individuals who endorsed three statements attesting to the fairness of the political system are significantly more likely to regularly vote than those who endorsed none of the three statements (61 versus 47 percent, respectively). However, when it comes to endorsing positive statements about the *government* (e.g., government's role in regulating business and solving society's problems, as well as acknowledging the good that it does), the opposite is true. People who express more discontent with government are more engaged. About 4 in 10 (43 percent) of those who had good things to say about government's current functioning regularly vote, compared to 60 percent of those who said otherwise. Yet, as discussed in chapter 4, young people are no more disgusted about politics than are their elders, and they have somewhat more positive attitudes toward the role of government. Neither of these factors, then, looks like a reason for their lack of political participation.

Mobilization is the last stop on the way to engagement. The effects of being personally asked to participate in the political process, whether in the form of a request from a candidate to work on a campaign or an invitation from a friend to volunteer at a hospital, are powerful and operate above and beyond the boost provided by traditional political capital (table 5.3). Essentially, the effects of mobilization are unique enough to merit their own placement in a model of engagement.[11]

The importance of being asked to participate resonates not only for electoral activities but for civic and voice activities as well. Across all of the 19 core indicators of engagement, those who have been invited to participate were significantly more likely to have done the activity than were those who didn't receive an invitation. Yet young people, and in particular DotNets, are not the target that older people are. Just 12 percent of DotNets have been personally contacted by a campaign, party, or group to work for or contribute to a candidate. Almost twice as many (23 percent) GenXers have received such requests, and fully 32 percent of Boomers and 34 percent of the oldest cohort have.

It's important to note that the decision by groups or individuals to ask someone to participate is not a random act, and is often related to

TABLE 5.3
The Importance of Being Asked to Participate

	Received an Invitation	Did Not Receive an Invitation
Percent who reported trying to persuade others when an election is taking place	47	28
Percent who reported regularly volunteering for a non-political group	37	18
Percent who reported participating in a consumer boycott	47	34

Source: NCES1.

judgments about the likelihood that the request will yield a positive response. It may also be related to judgments about the effectiveness of the participation likely to be undertaken by the person asked—for example, that they are educated, affluent, knowledgeable about the system. In other words, people who are already more likely to participate are also more likely to be contacted and asked to do so. To the extent that these assumptions are true, the act of being asked is not independent of other characteristics that also predict (or are correlated with) civic and political engagement. There is no easy way to identify the truly independent impact of mobilization, short of experiments that randomly assign people to be mobilized or not. Such studies have demonstrated the efficacy of efforts to mobilize the vote among young people, but cannot show the overall importance of mobilization vis à vis other influences (Green 2004).

Each of the steps in the model of participation—from initial characteristics through the effects of early socialization, advanced education, television avoidance, generational identification, and on through social and political capital, followed by attitudes toward government and politics, and the final boost of mobilization—follows the same path, regardless of generation. Any individual moves through this process, acquiring (or missing out on) various precursors throughout his or her life.

The process is the same for all age groups, yet Nets (and to a lesser extent, GenXers) trail their elders in their levels of political participation. The review of the evidence suggests that some factors are mainly life cycle differences between the cohorts, which will erode over time. As Nets age, they will gain in terms of education, which should help boost their involvement. Yet Nets and GenXers are less likely than their elders to have heard political discussions at home, clearly a generational difference. And the younger cohorts—especially the Nets—have a much weaker sense of civic duty, which could still develop over time but might be generational. And then there are a number of precursors in which lower levels among Nets and GenXers are probably the result of both life cycle and generational differences. For example, we know that young people are traditionally less partisan, attentive, and knowledgeable about politics. Yet the rates at which Nets trail older cohorts across these measures are greater than the traditional gaps, which suggests that there is more to the story than simply age. On the positive side, Nets have grown up with better role models in terms of volunteering than was the case with older cohorts.

The Path to Participation: Putting the Pieces Together

In building this model of participation, we have discussed only the bi-variate relationships between our precursors and engagement, or which factors are associated with higher levels of activism, without any regard as to what happens when all of these precursors come together. Yet, in reality, the process is much more complex. An individual is not simply attentive, or mobilized. Each individual—each cohort—is an amalga-mation of various characteristics. Thus, in order to fully understand how these characteristics operate, we need to take the various precursors into account at the same time. Doing so takes our understanding of citizen engagement to a different level. First, we'll be able to tell how much of an impact each precursor has on citizen engagement while holding con-stant the effects of everything else. For example, it's clear that people with more education are more involved than less educated individuals, and the same can be said for those who were raised in homes with frequent political discussions. Education and growing up in a politicized family tends to encourage more activism in public life. If households with political discussions are also disproportionately better educated, it could look like both of these are at work, when really only one influences matters. If both matter, if neither does, or only one makes a difference, taking both into account at the same time will help us sort this out.

Second, in conducting a path analysis, we'll be able to gauge the extent of a precursor's direct and mediated effect on citizen engagement. For example, we will gain from this analysis an understanding of how much education affects engagement, both directly and indirectly through its relationship to other precursors. For example, education not only boosts citizen engagement directly but also spurs activism through its effect on the development of partisanship (educated individuals are more partisan). Ultimately, this analysis allows one to assess education's direct, indirect, and total (i.e., the cumulative effect of education on citizen engagement by itself and through other precursors) effect on the various types of citizen engagement.

Tables 5.4 through 5.7 show the standardized coefficients for the di-rect, indirect, and total effects on citizen engagement for all of the pre-cursors in our model.[12] The models are broken down by types of partic-ipation—electoral, civic, and voice—as well as a summary measure of engagement that is an index of all of the 19 indicators. Only the variables that are significant are included in the table. So, to use the example of table 5.4, which details the pathways to a summary index of participation, gender (i.e., female) and minority status contributed nothing significant to the model. As such, they were excluded from this particular analysis but were included in subsequent analyses when they did make a contribution. Each model appears to do a good job in accounting for engagement. The normed fit index for each model approaches 1.0.

When it comes to overall participation (a measure combining 19 items in all three domains of participation), the single most important

TABLE 5.4.
Pathways to a Summary Index of Participation

	Direct effect	Indirect effect	Total effect
Age	−.08	.22	.14
Mother's education	.04	.20	.24
Early socialization	.10	.14	.24
Education	.07	.15	.22
Generational identity	.07	.04	.11
Television avoidance	.05	.01	.06
Social capital	.10	.01	.11
Political capital	.37	.05	.42
Positive attitudes toward the system	−.07	−.02	−.09
Mobilization	.25	n/a	.25

Note: Goodness of fit index = .98.
Source: NCES1.

TABLE 5.5
Pathways to Electoral Participation

	Direct effect	Indirect effect	Total effect
Age	.08	.14	.22
Early socialization	.07	.14	.21
Education	−.06	.16	.10
Generational identity	.04	.04	.08
Social capital	.07	.01	.08
Political capital	.37	.05	.42
Mobilization	.25	n/a	.25

Note: Goodness of fit index = .99.
Source: NCES1.

precursor is political capital. All other indicators pale in comparison to the importance derived from being attentive and knowledgeable about politics, having a strong sense of efficacy, identification with a political party, and endorsing an active approach to citizen responsibilities. The next tier of important precursors includes maternal and early socialization—both of which gain much of their strength through their indirect effects on later precursors—as well as education and mobilization. Consistent with earlier research, education is important in and of itself, but

TABLE 5.6
Pathways to Civic Participation

	Direct effect	Indirect effect	Total effect
Female	.03	−.01	.02
Age	−.10	.16	.06
Mother's education	.03	.13	.16
Early socialization	.10	.11	.21
Education	.12	.10	.22
Television avoidance	.09	.01	.10
Social capital	.13	.01	.14
Political capital	.22	.03	.25
Mobilization	.15	n/a	.15

Note: Goodness of fit index = .99.
Source: NCES1.

TABLE 5.7
Pathways to the Expression of Public Voice

	Direct effect	Indirect effect	Total effect
Age	−.14	.16	.02
Mother's education	.04	.16	.20
Minority status	−.04	−.02	−.06
Early socialization	.07	.09	.16
Education	.10	.11	.21
Generational Identity	.07	.03	.10
Political capital	.28	.04	.32
Positive attitudes toward the system	−.09	−.01	−.10
Mobilization	.18	n/a	.18

Note: Goodness of fit index = .96.
Source: NCES1.

also gains influence through its effect on things like political capital and mobilization. Age, generational identity, television avoidance, social capital, and *negative*, as opposed to *positive*, attitudes toward the political system make only minor contributions to overall engagement.

Electoral participation is spurred by many of the same influences that were important for overall participation, as is illustrated in table 5.5. Political capital, mobilization, and early socialization boost participation, although for some their importance is derived through their direct effect on electoral engagement (i.e., political capital), while for others strength is gained through their effects on later precursors (i.e., early socialization). Being older plays a larger role when electoral participation is considered by itself than when considering a summary index of participation (or behavior in the civic and voice realms).

While a few characteristics were especially important in predicting activism overall, and the same was true for behavior in the electoral realm, civic engagement is influenced by a broader array of predictors (see table 5.6). Education, maternal education, and early socialization, as well as political and social capital, are more strongly associated with civic activism. Mobilization is important, though less so than in the case of political activity, and television viewing (the avoidance of it) also correlates with civic engagement.

Finally, expressions of public voice seem to be encouraged the most by political capital and, to a lesser extent, education, maternal socialization, and mobilization. Similar to what was found in the summary index of participation, a negative outlook on the political system encourages expressions of public voice, suggesting that discontent drives engagement. But this is also the domain in which generational identity has a significant, if small, impact on engagement. Finally, this arena is the only one in which we find significant negative effects for non-native birth and being a member of a racial or ethnic minority.

Overall, we see that the path to participation is a varied one. From birth throughout the life cycle, individuals of all ages gain resources, develop attitudes, and receive invitations that encourage them to participate in public life. Some patterns are worth special note. First, the long-term effects of early socialization are important for all three kinds of participation. For years after individuals leave home, venture out on their own, and begin independent lives, they bear the marks of their early years. Those who had positive volunteer role models or who grew up in homes where politics was discussed are among those most actively involved in all realms of public life, even taking into account additional influences that one gains over the life cycle. Second, political capital pays off. Individuals who pay attention to the news, who are knowledgeable about politics and government, who have confidence in their ability to make a difference, who have strong ties to political parties, and who have a strong sense of civic duty are more involved, *ceteris paribus*, than those who don't possess these additional resources. Finally, mobilization matters. Even individuals who learn the early lessons of socialization or gain important political capital along the way are more likely to be brought into the process when someone asks them to take part.

When we compare cohorts across these key predictors, we again find evidence of both life cycle and generational explanations for why the mix of participation is changing in America. Young people are trailing older adults in ways that are due to both their age and their generation. Nets are less likely than older cohorts to have heard political discussions while growing up. This is clearly a generational phenomenon. Nets also score lower on the key ingredients in our political capital measure. Some of this (partisanship, knowledge) can be attributed to Nets' stage in the life cycle, but other factors (civic duty) have the look of generational effects, and still others (attentiveness) may be a combination of both. The same is true of mobilization. Nets are targeted less often than their elders. This may be because they are young, and therefore both harder to reach and less likely to respond, but it may also be because—as a generation—this age group has gained a reputation that has caused them to be written off.

But this is a story as much about remixing as falling behind. And, while these analyses provide insight into the key factors that promote engagement, and earlier analyses provided guidance as to when Nets' differences on these crucial elements were due to generational as opposed to life cycle influences, it is much harder to discern why Nets have created a unique mix.

To understand this better, we turn now to the particular ways young people are participating in public life (their unique approach). The rest of this chapter provides an in-depth look at youth involvement—in civic life, the political world, and the breeding grounds of high school and college. Along the way, we highlight the ways individuals, institutions and organizations are currently shaping the activism of this youngest cohort, and point to how these various influences may be favoring civic, as opposed to political, engagement.

A Closer Look at Youth

Much has been written about the long-term effects of participatory habits developed in high school and college. Previous studies have demonstrated that young people who volunteer in high school and college are more likely than their nonvolunteering counterparts to engage in volunteering and community activities as adults. Involvement in after-school activities also plays a role in socializing students into the world of civic and political life. Individuals who were involved in school organizations (except athletics) as teenagers are disproportionately more involved as adults, even when the impact of later influences such as marriage, children, and advanced education are taken into account.[13]

Yet, while this link between youth activism and adult engagement has been established, much less attention has been given to the question of what makes adolescents involved in the first place.[14] Our data offer us a unique opportunity to address this question. To do so, we will first describe what youth are currently doing. Next, building on the evidence that there are both short- and long-term consequences to early activism, we take up the more difficult question of why some young adults get involved in the first place. Why do some spend time on service activities while others stand on the sidelines? What leads some to start being active in issues and activities that extend beyond their campuses? How might we encourage more activity among young people? If, as our analysis in the first part of this chapter indicates, there are long-term effects of "early socialization," what exactly is going on during these formative years?

While we can answer these questions, the story is a complicated one. Youth engagement won't be boosted in a single stroke. There is no simple solution to apply, no magic tonic to administer, no engagement gene to alter. The pathways to participation are too wide and too varied, and they are influenced by too many factors — families, schools, clubs, groups, churches, even friends. But if this means youth civic involvement is unlikely to be spurred by a lone strike, it also suggests that there are multiple prods to encourage participation.

Before describing the influences, let us turn first to the question of what it is DotNets—especially high school and college students—are doing. We draw from both the NCES and the NYS, since each brings a unique set of measures to the task, and we focus on students because of the additional opportunities for involvement offered by high schools and colleges and the importance of these programs as training grounds for later engagement. Both surveys include questions about specific activities in and out of school—such as student government or other organizational work—and both ask about influences that are specific to being in high school or college.[15]

School-Based Opportunities for Engagement

The high school and college experiences provide many opportunities for civic and political engagement. Most of the avenues available to adults are also available to youth (voting is an obvious exception for most high school students); in addition, school-based organizations provide ready-made vehicles to serve a wide variety of interests and tastes. Schools increasingly facilitate—and in some cases, require—community service or volunteer work. In addition, the curriculum typically includes explicit civics and government content, as well as opportunities and incentives to pay attention to public affairs even in nongovernment courses.

Most current high school students are involved in at least one high school-based organization or group (table 5.8). The most popular draw is organized sports, with almost half of students participating in some way. About one-quarter (23 percent) are involved in band. A large minority of students is active in groups that range from foreign language clubs (15 percent) to student council (12 percent) to cheerleading (10 percent). Dance, newspaper, yearbook, and debate pull in about equal numbers of students. Only 22 percent of respondents say that are not involved in *any* organized groups.

Group activities outside of high school are also common. Not surprisingly, sports organizations are popular—44 percent say they are involved with athletic groups outside of school. Religious groups (with a participation rate of 37 percent) are a close second. Scouts (14 percent) and the YMCA (8 percent) are a distant third and fourth. Only small numbers report involvement in Boys and Girls clubs (5 percent), 4-H (3 percent), and FFA/FHA (2 percent). Just 1 percent are involved in explicitly political groups or Model United Nations programs.

A small percentage of high school students are involved in the governance of their schools. Just 8 percent report having been involved in elections or administration—either by running for office, working on a campaign of a student government candidate, or serving as a student representative. Student councils operate off the radar of most students, however; only 23 percent say that they pay at least "some" attention to the activities of their school student government; over one-third pay little to no attention.

Student involvement in college associations is less common than it is in high school, and more diffuse when it does occur. Fully 60 percent of college students are not involved with *any* campus groups, and no organization attracts even a large plurality of college students. The largest draws are sports and Greek organizations (13 percent and 11 percent, respectively), although almost as many report being involved with subject-oriented groups (9 percent) and honor societies (8 percent). Ethnic or religious groups pull in another 6 percent. Student governments garner 6 percent, while political organizations attract only 3 percent.

Similarly, even the scant attention afforded student government at the high school level outstrips the interest garnered by college student

TABLE 5.8

Participation in High School Organizations among Current High Schools Students

Activity	%
Organized sports	49
Band	23
Foreign language club	15
Other	15
Student council/student government	12
Drama club	12
Cheerleading, drill, flags, or spirit organization	10
Yearbook committee	9
Service club	9
Newspaper	8
Debate	7
Dance club	7

Source: NYS.

government. Just 11 percent of current college students in the NYS report paying at least some attention to their student government organization; 56 percent pay no attention. A minority are involved in other activities on campus. One in five college students has attended a speech, informal seminar, or teach-in about politics or national issues.

Pathways to Participation among Youth

In chapter 3 we demonstrated that while the members of the youngest age cohort are not as active as older Americans in the political realm, they are as active or more active in the civic arena and in expressing their political voices. And, while we have shown that many are taking advantage of opportunities for involvement in school as well, not all DotNets are equally engaged. For example, within the past year, 40 percent have volunteered for a nonpolitical group, 38 percent have participated in a boycott, and 20 percent have worn a campaign button, displayed a yard sign, or posted a bumper sticker on their car. What distinguishes these engaged youths (in one or multiple activities) from their less active counterparts? Good role models at home, skills training in schools, and the simple invitation from an outside group.

Charity Begins at Home

Many of the important lessons for engagement are learned at home. Young adults who grow up amid regular political discussions are much more involved in a host of activities. For example, more than one-third (35 percent) of those who often heard political talk while growing up are regular volunteers, compared to just 13 percent of those raised in homes where political talk never occurred—a finding that also suggests an interesting spillover from the political world to the civic. Similarly, among young people who are eligible to vote, 38 percent of those from homes with frequent political discussions say they always vote, compared to 20 percent of those without such dialogue. By talking about politics, families teach their children that it is important to pay attention to the world around them—and to take the next step of doing something.

Parents and guardians, even siblings, provide critical role models for civic behavior as well. Young people who were raised in homes where someone volunteered (43 percent of all youth) are highly involved themselves — joining groups and associations, volunteering, wearing buttons, or displaying bumper stickers at rates higher than those who did not grow up with such examples. Youth with engaged role models are also more attentive to news of politics and government and more likely to participate in boycotts or buycotts. Both of these influences continue to be significant when a host of other factors are taken into account — a finding to which we will return.

Lessons from the Schools: Practice, Practice, Practice

Family influences (which our earlier analysis demonstrated to have lifelong effects) are augmented by lessons learned in high schools and colleges. Schools can provide training grounds for civic involvement, offer opportunities for open discussions, and create avenues for service work — all of which lead to higher levels of youth involvement. Students who attend schools that provide civic training in the classroom or reward service opportunities are more involved than students whose schools do not.

Civic instruction is commonplace at the high school level, though it varies from current events requirements in classes to mandated service work in the community. Nearly three-quarters (70 percent) of current high school students took a course that required them to pay attention to government, politics, or national issues in one of the two previous school years. A slight plurality (48 percent) report that their "interest in things like politics and national issues" increased as a result of their taking such courses. About 4 in 10 (41 percent) say that the courses had no impact. Only 8 percent said that their interest decreased. Among college students, fewer have taken such courses (40 percent), although almost as many (47 percent) said that their interest increased as a result.

However, simply requiring attention to politics and government is not enough to foster greater involvement among high school students. Instead, it is when students report that teachers encourage open discussions about these matters that their scores on scales of civic behavior climb. This finding holds up even when other important influences are taken into account, which suggests that when teachers promote lively classroom participation, they are also encouraging involvement outside the classroom as well.

Open discussions are a regular part of the classroom experience for about half of today's high school students. Fully 49 percent report that teachers often encourage the class to discuss political and social issues in which people have different opinions; another 27 percent say that teachers sometimes do so. Slightly over half (54 percent) say that teachers encourage them to make up their own minds about issues; 31 percent say they sometimes do. Very few students say that open discussions and independent thinking are never encouraged (4 percent and 1 percent, respectively). Among college students, about half (47 percent) say that teachers often promote open exchanges, and fully 70 percent say they are encouraged to make up their own minds about issues.

Teachers can have a greater impact on engagement when they require students to develop specific civic skills, but not all students are being taught such skills. Eight in ten high school students have given a speech or oral report, but only half (51 percent) have taken part in a

FIGURE 5.1
Civic skills in high school pay off.

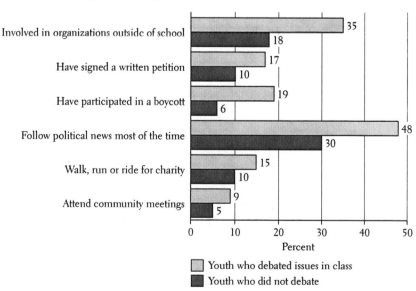

Source: NYS.

debate or discussion in which they had to persuade someone about something, and just 38 percent have written a letter to someone they do not know.

Students who have been taught these skills, especially letter writing and debating, are much more likely than those lacking such experience to be involved in a range of participatory acts inside and outside the school environment, even when other conditions are taken into account (figure 5.1). Again, the impact of these skills on participation is much stronger than that of the more generic course requirement to follow politics and national affairs.

Schools and Volunteering: The Impact of Carrots and Sticks

Many of today's students are active volunteers in part because high schools and colleges have facilitated such efforts and provided reinforcing classroom support. Three-quarters (75 percent) of high school students say that their school arranges or offers service activities or volunteer work for students; 65 percent of college students say so. A much smaller number of students say that volunteer work is required for graduation — 21 percent of high school students and 7 percent of college students say so.

Student involvement rises when schools facilitate volunteer work, and

TABLE 5.9
Encouraging and Requiring Service

	Percent who volunteer
High school arranges work	
Yes	45
No	33
High school requires work	
Yes	59
No	37
College arranges work	
Yes	38
No	13

Source: NYS.

participation steps up again when schools mandate it. Some 45 percent of students at high schools that arrange service work volunteered, compared to 33 percent of students who attended schools that don't provide such assistance (table 5.9). Fully 59 percent of students whose high schools required volunteer work actually volunteered last year, compared to 37 percent of students without such requirements.[16] Among college students, 38 percent whose schools arrange work volunteer, compared to 13 percent whose schools do not do so. (Too few colleges require such work to allow for an analysis of this effect.)

Again, classroom discussion can play a critical role in youth involvement. Student volunteers who are encouraged to talk about their volunteer work in class are much more likely to stick with it. Fully 63 percent of high school students and 58 percent of college students who volunteered within the last year had an opportunity to talk about their service work in the classroom. The members of this group are twice as likely to volunteer regularly as those who don't get the chance to talk about their experiences (64 percent versus 30 percent, respectively). They are also much more likely than those without such discussions to work on a community problem (47 percent versus 32 percent), to participate in a run, walk, or bike ride for charity (27 percent versus 15 percent), or to influence someone's vote (50 percent versus 34 percent). These findings remain valid even when a host of other factors are taken into consideration.

School Organizational Affiliations:
Political Training Grounds

Civic lessons are not limited to classroom settings. Many high school students are gaining significant training through their participation in extracurricular activities, especially when they are involved with political groups. As mentioned earlier, research has shown that students who participate in political groups in high school continue to be disproportionately civically and politically active after graduation.

The content of student groups matters. Our analysis indicates that simply being involved in high school organizations does not lead to greater involvement after graduation, but involvement in *political* groups does. Among high school graduates age 25 and under, those who participated in political organizations vote more frequently (38 percent versus 21 percent), are more attentive to news (36 percent versus 24 percent), and volunteer regularly at twice the rate of those without experience in these organizations (33 percent versus 15 percent). They are also more likely to give voice to their concerns through boycotting, signing petitions, or contacting public officials or the news media.

Other Intermediaries: Creating Connections

Young adults are not affected solely by the push and pull of families and schools. Outside groups and institutions also play key roles in boosting their engagement. A simple but direct invitation to participate can make a critical difference for those aged 15 to 25.

As noted earlier, current volunteers were asked how they first began working with their volunteer groups, that is, if they made the first contact, if the group contacted them, or if someone else put them together. Most of those in the DotNet cohort were active through outside initiatives — saying that "someone else put us together" (20 percent) or that they were recruited by the group itself (39 percent).

The tendency of youth to need a facilitator suggests that an obvious mechanism for increasing involvement among this age cohort would be to ask them more often. Especially in the political world, youth today receive fewer invitations to participate than their elders.

Across a range of activities, DotNets who were targeted by outside mobilizers were much more active than those who did not receive such attention. The exception is fund raising, which some use to argue that young people are targeted less often than their elders because they are less likely to respond positively. Indeed, just 13 percent of DotNets actually gave money in response to a request — compared to 22 percent of Xers, and 39 percent of Boomers and 42 percent of the oldest generation. But, this may simply be an indication that, as young adults, they have less money than older cohorts.

Among those aged 15 to 25 who were contacted by a political group in the past year, almost one-third (31 percent) volunteer regularly for a nonpolitical group, 42 percent have worked to raise money for charity, and 36 percent have worked to solve a community problem. For DotNets who were not contacted, the figures are 21 percent, 26 percent, and 19 percent, respectively. Indeed, mobilized DotNets outstrip those who haven't been contacted across almost every participatory measure—and these differences persist even when other factors (such as income, education, or family influences) are taken into consideration.

Other research has shown that churches and synagogues provide hospitable environments for the development of social capital and opportunities for effective training for civic engagement.[17] This survey reinforces that finding for young adults. DotNets who attend religious services regularly are much more active in both the civic and political realm than are those who do not take part in any religious activities. Presumably, by attending religious services, youth are coming into contact with individuals who provide volunteer opportunities, encourage them to get involved in their communities, or offer them political buttons and bumper stickers to display.

Predicting Engagement among High School Students: The Big Picture

We began this chapter with a discussion of the various influences (such as education, religious attendance, and income, among others) that predict engagement among all adults. While many of these influences are at work among DotNets as well, in our discussion of this youngest cohort we have highlighted the important role that families, schools, and outside organizations play—and we have argued that these influences continue to be significant even when we "take into account a host of other effects." What exactly do we mean by this? Young people are subject to a variety of influences, and they enter the public realm with a range of demographic characteristics and political attitudes, all of which have the potential to affect their level of engagement. When we use statistical models that allow us to take these factors into consideration, however, the storyline remains the same: parents, schools, and mobilizers are key to creating engaged youth. We turn now to a short discussion of this final point.

As mentioned earlier, with the exception of voting, high school students have the same opportunities to be engaged as older Americans. They can write letters to their members of Congress, sign petitions, participate in protests, canvass for political candidates, or volunteer at the local shelter for the homeless. In addition, a plethora of organizations in and out of high school offer opportunities for engagement. Thus, to measure students' overall level of involvement, we used the NCES1 to create a scale of engagement that incorporates 18 of our 19 indicators (save voting), along with a variable for participation in high school organizations and a summary indicator of a respondent's self-reported attention to news about government and politics.[18] We have consciously included this last measure (attention to the news) as part of students' overall level of engagement, not as a *precursor* to activity, because we believe that with voting—the most obvious form of participation—unavailable, paying attention to the political world is an alternative marker

TABLE 5.10

Predictors of a Summary Index of Engagement among High School Students

	Beta
Weekly Internet use	.21
Someone in the household volunteers	.17
Female	.17
Political knowledge	.14
Discussed politics while growing up	.12
Civic duty	.11
Number of friends	.11
Mobilized	.10
Income	.10
White	−.09
Mother's education	.09
Daily television watching	−.09
Discuss political and social issues in class	.08
Religious service attendance	.07
Strength of partisanship	.05
Efficacy	.05
Generational identity	−.05
Class requirement to follow politics	.04
Government regulation of business	−.04
Positive view of politics	−.03
Encouraged to make up mind about issues?	.03
Interpersonal trust	−.02
Age	.01
Length of residency	−.01
Non-native born	.00

Note: Coefficients in boldface are statistically significant.
Source: NCES1.

of student engagement.[19] The scale ranges from 0 to 25, with a mean of 5.8, a mode of 5, and a reliability of 0.68.

We conducted a parallel analysis with the NYS, which has an even richer set of measures of high school specific avenues for involvement—such as participation in student government and explicitly political organizations—and possible influences to action, along with a subset of the general activities available to all adults.[20] The scale ranges from 0 to 24, with a mean of 7, a mode of 6, and a reliability of 0.65.

Table 5.10 presents the standardized regression coefficients for an expanded set of predictors regressed on the NCES1 summary scale of engagement, based on a sample of current high school students. Table 5.11 presents the similar results for the NYS. The variables are sorted on the basis of the betas; all significant values are highlighted. Both models fit the data fairly well; we are able to explain about 40 percent of the variance in our summary measures (based on adjusted r-squares of 0.38 for the NCES and 0.40 for the NYS).

TABLE 5.11
Predicting Engagement among High School Students

	Beta
Learned to write a letter to someone you don't know	.21
Enjoys high school	.19
High school arranges volunteer work	.18
Discussed politics at home while growing up	.16
Learned to debate	.15
Female	.11
Household income	.11
Learned to give a speech	.08
Efficacy	.08
Perceived impact of government on daily life	.07
Issue mobilization	.07
Political knowledge	.05
Requirement to volunteer	.03
Taken a course on politics or government	.03
Hispanic	−.02
Interpersonal trust	.02
Age	.02
White	.01
Perceived ability to influence high school government	.00
Mobilization	.00

Note: Coefficients in boldface are statistically significant.
Source: NYS.

The analyses not only support the notion that the influence of families and schools continues even when taking into account various socioeconomic factors—such as race, income, or how long one has lived in the community—but also provide insight into the influence of other factors, such as various political attitudes. Specifically, both analyses reveal that students who reported more frequent political discussions were more active than those from homes with less frequent (or no) political talk, regardless of their income, race, perception of government relevance, or efficacy. Similarly, someone in the household volunteering (a measure available only in the NCES1 survey) was the second most powerful predictor of engagement, all things being equal.

The importance of proper support in high school holds up under this stringent set of controls as well. These institutions—and the teachers in them—play key roles by teaching students skills (especially debating and letter writing), as well as providing them with opportunities to be involved by arranging volunteer work. Notably, the *requirement* for volunteering was not significantly related to engagement. This last point deserves clarification. As the bivariate analyses earlier in this chapter illustrated, students who are required to volunteer were more active volunteers than those students who did not have the same requirements. However, if we look beyond volunteering to a broader measure of engagement and control for various influences, there are no statistically significant differences in the levels of engagement between students who attend schools with mandatory volunteering and students without such requirements. Providing opportunities for engagement (rather than mandating it) appears to have greater spillover effects for involvement in other arenas of public life.

The models diverge in their support for the power of mobilization— an effect that is significant for the NCES1 but fails to meet the threshold in the NYS. This difference is most likely due to slightly different questions; the NYS, which asked about a more narrowly tailored request, may have missed some outreach. The NCES1 also suggests that students who report a wider number of friends are more engaged—perhaps because the greater one's social network, the greater the likelihood that one will be invited to get involved.

Of the many attitudes included in these analyses, the only one that met the standard of statistical significance was a respondent's sense of civic duty. Students who felt a greater responsibility were more active.

This attitude trumps all others—including the belief that one can make a difference (efficacy), a sense of generational identity, and interpersonal trust, none of which was significantly related to participation.

In both models, greater levels of engagement are associated with two demographic variables—income and gender. Wealthier students may be more engaged because they can afford to spend time in political or civic activities instead of working to earn money—or family wealth is a marker for other resources relevant to participation, such as books in the home, travel to foreign countries, and the like. The finding that female students are more involved than male students is in keeping with other studies of young women's civic engagement.[21]

There are a few lessons from models (not shown) that examine the influence of these factors across the different political, civic, and voice domains described in detail in chapter 3. Although the individual sub-dimensions do not yield models as strong as that of the summary scale (adjusted r-squares range from 0.18 to 0.33), the differences among the predictors provide evidence for a richer understanding of how people become civic or political animals.

Parental role modeling and socialization are both important but slightly different in their consequences: seeing a volunteer in the home is important in all three subdimensions of engagement, while talking politics in the home is apparently irrelevant for civic engagement but a significant predictor of political involvement. This may have contributed to lower levels of political engagement, since we know that, in comparison to older adults, fewer DotNets are being raised in political homes.

Religious attendance is a factor for civic engagement (individuals being drawn into various activities because of the activism of their church or synagogue). Interestingly, there is an inverse relationship between television viewing and civic activism: for young people, the more television one watches, the less involved one is in one's community and school. Finally, in the voice dimension, the factors that stand out are associated with social networking, which suggests that students who have been contacted by a group or association, have a lot of friends, or use the Internet with frequency are more likely to give expression to their political opinions than similarly situated students without these networks.

Finally, the irrelevance of many of our variables provides lessons as well. Importantly, almost every measure of coercion—service work requirements for grades or graduation—failed to meet standards of statistical significance. Instead, acquiring specific skills, discussing volunteer work or issues in an open classroom environment, or simply attending a school that arranged service work all lead to greater involvement.

A Note on College Students

We conducted a similar analysis of engagement among college students, which resulted in confirmation of the importance of various early socializers, and highlighted key attitudes that are associated with activism. We used the NYS, which included a series of questions asked of current college students that enabled us to create a summary measure of engagement that incorporates college-specific activities, similar to the high school index described earlier in this chapter. In this summary scale, we included all the broader measures of participation and media attentiveness, as well as attending a seminar or teach-in, belonging to political organizations in college, and paying attention to college student govern-

TABLE 5.12
Predicting Engagement among College Students

	Beta
College arranges volunteer work	.24
Discussed politics while growing up	.23
"I can influence government"	.22
"I can influence college"	.17
Perception that government has impact on daily life	.16
Course requirement to keep up on the news	.13
Issue mobilization	.11
Age	.10
Female	−.09
Attentiveness to government course requirement	.09
Household income	.07
Required to volunteer	.05
White	.04
Clear guidelines about right and wrong	.04
Interpersonal Trust	−.04
Enjoy college	.03
Mobilization	.03
Hispanic	−.02
Do things out of duty	.00

Note: Coefficients in boldface are statistically significant.
Source: NYS.

ment. The scale ranges from 0 to 22, with a mean of 8, a mode of 7, and a reliability of 0.72. The adjusted r-square for the model is 0.42.

As can be seen in table 5.12, there are some striking similarities between the factors that influence engagement among high school students and the influences on college students. The two most powerful predictors of engagement in college are parents (talking about politics at home) and schools (arranging for volunteer opportunities). Classes that require students to pay attention to politics and government also reap dividends; these students are more engaged than those who do not have such requirements.

A key difference between high school and college students, however, is the role of attitudes. For high school students, attitudes did little to distinguish between the involved and the uninvolved. Among college students, however, those who see the relevance of government for their daily lives and are fairly confident about their ability to affect both government in general and governance issues on campus are more engaged.

Conclusion

While our models do relatively well in overall explanatory power, no single factor stands out as especially important for predicting engagement. Instead, several characteristics in each model — stemming from the family, the schools, or perhaps even one's peers — collectively provide the explanatory power in the models. This suggests that there is no "silver bullet" antidote to apathy and disengagement, but also that widening the many narrow pathways can help more young people find their way to active citizenship and public life.

Families can be important role models. Engaged parents tend to raise engaged children. For some young people, schools can open the doors to civic and political life as well as teach specific civic skills. Individual teachers can play vital roles by encouraging students to talk openly and debate ideas. Religious institutions, policy organizations, and other groups can also invite young adults to participate in specific acts such as protesting, political campaigning, and community service. Together, these people and institutions can hold sway over the public participation of today's youth.

It is important to note here that much of the effort of schools is oriented around civic engagement, rather than political activities. Students are encouraged or required to volunteer in their community; and they have responded to these opportunities and pressures. While there are concerted and effective efforts to get students to pay attention and talk about the political world around them, there is less institutional effort aimed at getting young people *actively involved* in politics. This may be because school administrators want to avoid the appearance of taking sides in a political campaign. Perhaps leaders fear that students may find the process less fulfilling if their side "loses." Whatever the cause, the effect may be that young people are being trained in the habits of civic participation but are not learning the ropes of political activism — and it appears to be taking a toll.

Where Do Young People
Stand Politically?

A spate of headlines and press releases during the presidential election campaign of 2004 offered conflicting evidence about the political views of young people. At the start of the campaign, the Gallup Organization reported that Generation X had gone from "grunge to Gingrich" but noted a liberal tilt among DotNets (Carlson 2003). During fall 2004, the PRC found that "young voters displayed significantly more volatility in candidate preference than most other groups in the population" (Pew Research Center for the People and the Press 2004b). Harvard's Institute of Politics surveyed college students throughout the year leading up to the election and found a swing from support for Bush to a clear advantage for Democrat John Kerry (Harvard Institute of Politics 2003, 2004). On Election Day, voters aged 18–24 broke for Kerry by a margin of 56 percent to 43 percent, with those aged 25–29 dividing about evenly between the two candidates (51 percent Kerry, 49 percent Bush). The youngest cohort of voters was Kerry's strongest age group.

Members of the DotNet and Generation X cohorts grew up in different political climates, and these formative experiences have made a difference in their politics. Most of Generation X was socialized during a period of conservative reaction led by Ronald Reagan. Not surprisingly, there is a more conservative tint to the politics of Generation X. In contrast, most of the DotNets experienced the swing of the pendulum back to more liberal politics, including the election of Bill Clinton, the youngest president since John F. Kennedy. But the Clinton era was distinguished by a vigorous battle between left and right, with Republicans gaining the upper hand in Congress while ultimately losing important battles to the president over the scope and shape of government.

The result of the political back-and-forth experienced by youth over the past two decades, along with the political tumult of the 1990s, is a new generation of citizens whose views on issues do not conform easily to the existing political divides. In many respects they are more liberal than their immediate predecessors, but they also hold some views that cut across existing cleavages. Clashes over social issues and the American reaction to 9/11, which have defined U.S. politics in the past four years, have also shaped the way DotNets think about politics today.

A clearer understanding of the opinions and values of the DotNets gives us a view of potential changes in the political agenda that may occur when youth become more active and begin to gain significant political and economic power. Chapter 3 showed that young people are less active politically than their elders—and less active than their counterparts in previous cohorts. This means that their views on issues of the day may have a smaller impact on public policy. Elected officials feel less compelled to pay attention to a group that votes irregularly and does little to press its views on the system. But, even though they are less active now, by virtue of their large numbers and the natural progression of the life cycle, young people *will* become the leaders of tomorrow. While some of their opinions and orientations will change as they grow older and pass through other stages of the life cycle, some will not. Thus an understanding of their perspective today may give us a window through which to view our politics in twenty or thirty years when the DotNets of today will constitute a large voting bloc and will be leading the major institutions of business and government.

When we ask "Where do young people stand politically?" we are asking at least three different questions.

- The first asks for a description of the opinions of youth on key
  political issues, values, and orientations. For example, how
  many DotNets are Democrats and how many are Republicans?

- The second question is how young people compare with their elders. For example, are they more or less likely to think the war in Iraq was the right decision for the United States?

We can answer these first two questions together by looking at contemporary polling in the United States and comparing young people in the surveys to the rest of those polled.

- The third question is how young people today differ from their counterparts in the past, and how they are likely to change as they get older — moving through the life cycle. For example, do young people typically become more opposed to government spending as they themselves become more affluent and pay more taxes? What political values do they carry with them as they get older?

In this chapter we address these three questions by reviewing a wide range of current polling and several important collections of data that give us a window back through time.

Youth Today: Change with Continuity

There is no sign of a significant radical element in today's youth, no large segment likely to steer the country far to the left or right of where it has been going over the past several decades. Young people are committed to the same basic and often contradictory American values of democratic government, egalitarianism, and a free market economy as the rest of the public. Despite the growing fragmentation of the mass media and its audience, and the broadening array of political messages disseminated to the public, young and old come away from this cacophonous barrage with similar views of the political system, its leaders, and its institutions: that is to say, divided views (Pew Research Center for the People and the Press 2003a).

But youth bring some unusual combinations of views. A greatly oversimplified headline might read: *Youth are Social Libertarians Who Like Big Business and Big Government*. Yes, you read that right. Many young people hold views that seem contradictory in light of the way public opinion has typically divided in American politics since the 1930s. Compared with their elders, young people are more supportive of getting government out of the bedroom, out of the public schools, and out of the Social Security system but simultaneously *more* likely to approve of government's performance, more supportive of government regulation, public assistance to the poor, and national health insurance, *and* more likely to say that businesses have appropriate values. They are decidedly more socially tolerant and accepting of the racial and ethnic diversity with which they have grown up.

Even more clearly than among older cohorts, divisions among today's young citizens reflect the disputes that have been most salient in the recent past. Currently, the strongest correlates of partisan affiliation among the DotNets are views on the proper use of American military force and opinions on social and cultural issues. We will consider this observation in more detail at the conclusion of the chapter.

Partisanship and Politics

Some have claimed that youth are coming into the electorate more attached to the Republican Party than in the past. Are today's youth turning

TABLE 6.1
Party Identification

	DotNet %	GenX %	Boomer %	Dutiful %	Total %
Party ID					
Republican	26	30	30	32	30
Democrat	30	31	33	39	33
Independent	38	32	30	22	30
Other/Don't know	6	7	7	7	7
Total	100	100	100	100	100
With "leaners"					
Rep./lean Rep.	38	43	42	42	41
Dem./lean Dem.	49	45	47	48	47
Refused to lean	13	12	11	19	12
Total	100	100	100	100	100

Source: Pew Research Center Surveys conducted January 2004–April 2005.

Republican? In a word, no. Among *yesterday's* youth—GenXers and late Boomers—the number of Republicans equals the number of Democrats, perhaps reflecting the political dominance of Ronald Reagan as they passed through their formative years (table 6.1). But that tide has gone out, and at least for now, the Democrats have a small advantage among the youngest cohort of Americans. Among partisans and party "leaners"—

FIGURE 6.1
Party identification by age (5 year moving average).

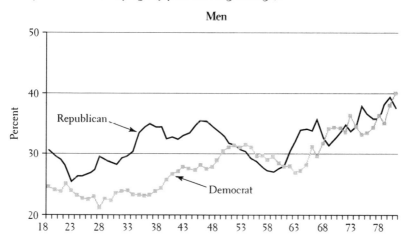

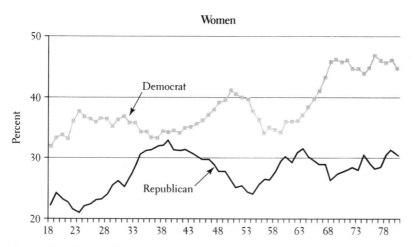

Source: Pew Research Center.

independents who are willing to express a preference between the parties — the Democrats have a decided advantage among DotNets but not among GenXers.

As has been true with young people for decades, the DotNets are less likely to call themselves Republicans or Democrats when asked about party affiliation (National Election Studies 1960–2000; Erikson and Tedin 2002). But like their elders, most of those initially reluctant to choose a party will say that they lean one way or the other when asked a follow-up question. The percentage of "true" independents is about the same across all age groups — about 1 in 10 (12 percent). And partisanship is not just an empty label to youth: a 2002 poll by the *Washington Post/Kaiser/Harvard* group (PKH) found more young people saying that there are important differences between the parties (65 percent yes, compared with 55 percent among those aged 55–64 and 50 percent among those 65 and older). This pattern belies the common notion that youth find the current political alignments irrelevant to issues that concern them.

These general age patterns in party affiliation hold for both men and women, but there is also a big gender gap, as there has been since the early 1980s. Women overall tilt Democratic by a margin of 38 percent to 28 percent, while men favor the Republican Party by a margin of 32 percent to 27 percent.[1] Women in every age group are more Democratic than Republican, with the largest gaps occurring among those aged 60 and older (see figure 6.1). But Democrats also have a big advantage

TABLE 6.2
Youth and the Vote, 2000 and 2004

| | 2000 | | | 2004 | |
| | Gore | Bush | Nader | Kerry | Bush |
Age	%	%	%	%	%
18–24	47	47	5	56	43
25–29	48	46	4	51	48
30–39	47	50	2	47	51
40–44	48	48	2	44	55
45–49	47	50	2	46	53
50–59	49	48	2	49	50
60–64	51	47	1	42	57
65–74	51	47	2	44	55
75+	50	48	2	54	45

Source: Exit polls by Voter News Service (2000), National Election Pool (2004).

among young women (ages 18–25) and Baby Boomers. Among men, Republicans match or outnumber Democrats among every age group.

Reflecting the small Democratic partisanship advantage among younger people, young people aged 18–24 were John Kerry's best age group in the election of 2004 (table 6.2). This group split evenly between Al Gore and George W. Bush in 2000, but gave Kerry a 56 percent to 43 percent advantage. Kerry also took a majority of the vote (51 percent) among those aged 25–29. Bush got 50 percent or more among every other age group except for those over the age of 75.

General Orientations about the Public and Private Sectors

Despite growing up in a strongly antigovernment popular culture, with regular exposure to politicians "running against government" when campaigning for office, most young people have surprisingly positive views of the federal government and approve of an expansive role for government in most spheres of its activity.

When asked to choose, a large majority of young people opt for a bigger government, or one that does more things, while other age groups are divided or tilt against activist government. In the PKH national telephone poll, a 69 percent majority of young people aged 18–29 opted for a bigger government providing more services. Among those aged 30–49,

TABLE 6.3
Scope of Government

In general, government grows bigger as it provides more services. If you had to choose, would you rather have a smaller government providing less services, or a bigger government providing more services?

| | AGE | | | | |
| | 18–29 | 30–49 | 50–64 | 65+ | Total |
Response	%	%	%	%	%
Smaller government	26	50	53	54	46
Bigger government	69	43	41	33	47
Don't know	5	7	7	14	7
Total	100	100	100	100	100

Source: *Washington Post* (2002).

only 43 percent wanted a bigger government (table 6.3). Many other polls tell the same story.[2] The Gallup poll found 50 percent of youth aged 18–29 saying they could trust the government in Washington to do what is right all or most of the time, while only 36 percent of respondents older than 30 thought this. And PRC questions about general orientations show similar results.

Enthusiasm for government among the DotNets is not all-encompassing. They are less supportive of traditional Social Security, with a majority expressing support for changes in the system that would allow investment of some payments in private stock funds. DotNets show an interesting traditionalist streak on church-state matters, exhibiting much greater support than other cohorts for government involvement in faith-based programs.

Despite the generally strong support for government, young people's attitudes about business are not especially negative and often are more positive than those of older Americans. As noted in chapter 4, only on the question of the benefits of regulation, which pits government against business, do we see more younger adults than older adults taking an antibusiness stance. But when government is not invoked, the DotNets are somewhat more positive about business than other age groups, with half (50 percent) agreeing that business generally strikes a fair balance

TABLE 6.4
Attitudes about Business

Responses	DotNet %	GenX %	Boomer %	Dutiful %	Total %
Business corporations generally strike a fair balance between making profits and serving the public interest					
Agree	50	44	34	39	40
Disagree	46	53	63	53	55
Don't know	4	3	3	8	5
Total	100	100	100	100	100
The strength of this country today is mostly based on the success of American business					
Agree	78	75	74	69	74
Disagree	20	21	23	25	22
Don't know	2	4	3	6	4
Total	100	100	100	100	100

Source: Pew Research Center 2002–2003.

between profits and the public interest; among Boomers, only 34 percent agree with this statement (table 6.4). Similarly, while big majorities agree that "the strength of this country today is mostly based on the success of American business," DotNets express the most agreement.

Attitudes about National Security

Young people traditionally present a paradox on national security issues. Despite being the vanguard of antiwar movements, they are also sometimes the most enthusiastic supporters of military engagement when the prospect is first raised. In many polls, youth were more favorable than older people to the idea of using military force to remove Saddam Hussein from power in Iraq. Similarly, they were more supportive of the war in Vietnam during its early years. Several Gallup polls in 1966 found more young than older people saying that it had not been a mistake to get involved in Vietnam. Yet they tend to display less consistency on these issues, and sometimes lead the formation of antiwar movements after hostilities begin. And compared with older cohorts, they have tended to be less supportive of the general notion of the use of military force, and to express lower levels of generalized patriotism (table 6.5). More broadly, they tend to have very low levels of knowledge about

TABLE 6.5
Opinions about the Use of Military Force

	Agree %	Disagree %	Don't know/ Refuse %	Total %
Best way to ensure peace is through military strength (July–August 2003)				
DotNet	46	54	0	100
Gen X	46	50	4	100
Boomer	55	42	3	100
Dutiful	62	35	3	100
U.S. made right decision in using force in Iraq (January–July 2005)				
DotNet	50	44	6	100
Gen X	53	42	5	100
Boomer	49	45	6	100
Dutiful	41	50	9	100

Source: Based on Pew Research Center Polls.

international issues, compared with other age cohorts. This may make them more susceptible to the winds of the moment.

Attitudes about Social Welfare Programs and Spending

Idealism and empathy for the poor and powerless are especially strong among younger people, and this translates into support for a social safety net, or at least for the principles behind such programs. While the public overall divides evenly on a question about government health insurance for the uninsured, a majority of youth in the PKH poll (57 percent of those aged 18–29) say that government should provide health insurance for the uninsured if it is able to spend more on health care; PRC's findings on a similar question echo this result. Pew Research Center polls also find young people more supportive of guaranteeing food and shelter to people who need it, and to helping those who are more needy, even if it means going deeper into debt; on both of these, youth are more liberal than their elders. And more generally, youth are more supportive of the idea of the government making an effort to reduce the gap between rich and poor in the United States.

But greater liberalism is not seen on every question of social welfare. Perhaps not surprisingly, the members of the youngest cohort in the National Election Studies surveys of 2000 and 2002 are not as supportive of increased spending on Social Security as older cohorts are (though a bare majority did support more spending, and few favor cutting spending). More significantly, the issue of Social Security privatization is one place where a libertarian, if not fully conservative, youth perspective is apparent. The 2002 PKH poll found 61 percent of young people (aged 18–24) supportive of a plan that would allow some investment of Social Security contributions in the stock market, and 55 percent of those aged 30–49 agreed; only 24 percent of people aged 65 and older were supportive (table 6.6). The same pattern was seen among voters in 2000. Voter News Service exit polling found 64 percent of youth aged 18–24, and 65 percent of those aged 25–29, supporting the idea of allowing private investment of Social Security taxes. Only among those 65 and older were as many as 50 percent opposed. And in the midst of President Bush's 2005 campaign to persuade Congress to change the system to allow private accounts, as public support slipped for the idea, a majority of young people remained in favor.

Part of the explanation for stronger support for a private investment option is that young people are much more likely than their elders to express confidence that they could make wise investment decisions with the money. Compared with only 25 percent among those 65 and older and 34 percent among people nearing retirement age (50–64), PKH found 54 percent of younger Americans very or somewhat confident of this. And, of course, there is the evident fact that youth don't yet feel the need for a retirement fund of any sort, a function of their place in the life cycle.

Another plausible explanation for young people's receptivity to Social Security privatization is the possibility that youth have less confidence that the program will actually be around when they reach retirement age. Something of an "urban legend" in the polling business holds that a survey showed young people more confident that alien life forms from outer space will be discovered than of actually receiving a Social Security check.[3] And while it is true that youth are less likely than older people

TABLE 6.6
Views of Social Security Privatization

	AGE				
	18–29 %	30–49 %	50–64 %	65 + %	Total %
Would you support or oppose a plan in which people who chose could invest some of the Social Security contributions in the stock market?					
Support	61	55	38	24	47
Oppose	32	42	58	67	47
Don't know	7	3	4	10	5
Total	100	100	100	100	100
How confident are you that you would make the right decisions if you were investing your future Social Security funds in the stock market? Would you feel . . .					
Very/somewhat confident	54	49	34	25	43
Not very/not at all confident	43	50	64	69	54
Don't know	3	1	1	5	2
Total	100	100	100	100	100

Source: Washingon Post (2002).

to think they'll benefit from the program, majorities still expect to receive benefits when they retire. A 2003 Fox News poll found 58 percent of those under 30 saying they anticipated getting benefits, while 36 percent thought they would not. By comparison, about three-quarters of those aged 44–64 expected to benefit.

Support for Environmental Protection

Young people have long been a strong constituency for regulation and spending to protect the environment, and that remains true today. Polling on the issue is complicated, since many questions about the subject elicit general sentiments of the "apple pie and motherhood" sort rather than considered judgments about trade-offs and competing values inherent in contemporary debates about environmental protection. Voter News Service's question on the 2000 exit polls discriminated very well on this question, yielding a virtually even split between voters who said it was more important to protect the environment and those who said it was more important to encourage economic growth. On this question, only among voters aged 18–24 did a majority side with the environment, 57 percent to 41 percent. All other age groups, including voters aged 25–29, split evenly or tilted slightly toward economic growth.

Social Issues and Values

Youth today both reflect and drive the growing liberalization of American social values. Compared with their elders, they are far more tolerant of homosexuality, more accepting of interracial dating, and less religious. But these generalizations have limits. Few American youth today are *irreligious*—compared with young people in most wealthy industrialized nations, most are remarkably religious. And on certain flashpoint issues—most notably abortion—they are no more liberal than the rest of the public, and there is no trend of growing liberalism. Moreover, on many issues they are more accepting of a porous wall between church and state.

Most DotNets are tolerant of homosexuals and oppose legal sanctions or restrictions on their rights (table 6.7). Majorities have a favorable opinion of lesbian women, and half are favorable toward gay men. An overwhelming majority oppose giving school boards the right to fire gay teachers, and a majority favor allowing gays and lesbians to enter into legal agreements that would give them many of the same rights as married couples. But even among DotNets, there is a division over gay marriage, with 47 percent in favor and 49 percent opposed. GenXers are similarly split (45 percent in favor and 46 percent opposed), and older cohorts are much more opposed.

The biggest battles over women's roles in society have been resolved, with large majorities disagreeing with the statement "Women should return to their traditional roles in society." But there are degrees of feeling on the subject, and young people — especially young women — have the strongest opinions. Among DotNets, 81 percent disagree with this statement, compared with only 53 percent among those 59 and older. Moreover, 62 percent of DotNets *completely* disagree, including 71 percent among DotNet women, far more than among other age cohorts. Similarly, 80 percent agree with the general statement "I have old-

TABLE 6.7
Homosexuality

	DotNet %	GenX %	Boomer %	Dutiful %	Total %
*School boards ought to have the right to fire teachers who are known homosexuals**					
Favor	25	29	34	48	35
Oppose	72	69	62	42	60
Don't know	3	2	4	10	5
Total	100	100	100	100	100
Do you strongly favor, favor, oppose, or strongly oppose allowing gays and lesbians to marry legally?†					
Favor	47	44	36	21	36
Oppose	49	45	52	65	53
Don't know	4	11	12	14	11
Total	100	100	100	100	100
*Favorable opinion of . . . ***					
Gay men	50	46	36	24	37
Lesbian women	56	48	37	25	39

*Source: Pew Research Center 2002–2003.
†Source: Pew Research Center July 2005.
**Source: Pew Research Center October 2003.

fashioned values about family and marriage," but only 65 percent of DotNets concur, including only 56 percent of DotNet women.

The subject of abortion does not conform to other trends in the general area of social issues—there has been no general trend of liberalization. The American public remains deeply divided on the topic, and individuals are divided within themselves, simultaneously believing that women should have control over their reproductive choices while also believing that fetuses need protection. Big majorities approve of abortion in cases of rape or incest, or to protect the health or life of the mother, but elective abortion is more controversial, and young people do not differ significantly from older people in their opinions about this. The General Social Survey has tracked attitudes on the issue since 1973, and currently finds only 42 percent of DotNets supportive of the right to abortion "on demand"—if a woman wants one for any reason (the same percentage as the overall public).

TABLE 6.8
Racial Attitudes

	AGE				
	18–29 %	30–49 %	50–64 %	65 + %	Total %
Do you support or oppose affirmative action programs that give preferences to blacks and other minorities?*					
Favor	49	38	31	31	38
Oppose	44	56	64	58	55
Don't know	7	6	5	12	7
Total	100	100	100	101	100
I think it's all right for blacks and whites to date each other.†					
Agree	91	84	77	57	76
Disagree	8	14	20	37	21
Don't know	1	2	3	6	3
Total	100	100	100	100	100
We have gone too far in pushing equal rights in this country.†					
Agree	34	44	49	56	47
Disagree	65	54	48	40	50
Don't know	1	2	3	4	3
Total	100	100	100	100	100

*Source: Washington Post (2002)
†Source: Pew Research Center 2002–2003.

On the subject of race, young people reflect the reality of growing up in an increasingly integrated and multiracial society, especially in their acceptance of blacks and whites dating each other (table 6.8). *All* cohorts in the population are more accepting of this today than in the recent past, but among DotNets, acceptance is nearly universal—91 percent—and Gen-Xers are not far behind (84 percent). Boomers (at 77 percent) are 20 points more likely than their elders to approve, but even among the oldest cohort, a majority now accepts the idea of interracial dating.

Yet, as American culture has become more racially tolerant socially, there is no comparable liberalization on the political front, with about half agreeing that "we have gone too far in pushing equal rights in this country," and majorities continuing to oppose the use of racial preferences to redress black-white inequality. But on both of these measures,

TABLE 6.9
Religion and Politics

	AGE				
	18–29 %	30–49 %	50–64 %	65 1 %	*Total* %
*Do you favor or oppose providing parents with tax money to help pay for their children to attend private or religious schools?**					
Favor	58	49	39	36	47
Oppose	38	47	57	54	49
Don't know	3	3	4	9	5
Total	99	99	100	99	101
*Do you favor or oppose allowing public schools to start each day with a prayer?**					
Favor	58	71	78	81	71
Oppose	37	25	17	14	24
Don't know	4	5	5	5	5
Total	99	101	100	100	100
Should churches and other houses of worship keep out of political matters or should they express their opinions on day-to-day social and political questions?†					
Keep out	42	41	44	53	45
Express views	53	56	52	40	50
Don't know	5	3	4	7	5
Total	100	100	100	100	100

Source: Washington Post (2002).
†*Source:* Pew Research Center July 2005.

young people are more liberal. More younger than older people support affirmative action with racial preferences (49 percent in the PKH poll, compared with 38 percent overall, and 39 percent in a different question on a Pew poll, compared with 26 percent overall). And nearly two-thirds of DotNets (65 percent) disagree that we have gone too far in pushing equal rights; 56 percent of older Americans (aged 59 and up) agree with this statement.

Religious belief and practice underlies many attitudes on social issues in the United States, and Protestants — especially those who consider themselves "born again" — tend to be conservative on social issues and to provide support for the Republican Party. Young people are less likely to be Protestants (46 percent versus 59 percent overall, though no less likely than other Protestants to say they are evangelical or born again) and slightly more likely than their elders to say they have no religion (14 percent for DotNets versus 9 percent overall). DotNets express less intensity in their religious convictions, with fewer saying they "completely agree" that prayer is an important part of their daily life (41 percent for DotNets, 52 percent overall) and fewer saying religion is an important part of their life (51 percent versus 61 percent overall). Though less religious than other Americans, by the standards of most industrial Western nations, DotNets are very religious.

On issues where religion and politics explicitly mix, the attitudes of young people are difficult to summarize (table 6.9). They are similar to other Americans in their tolerance of religious rhetoric by politicians and in their views on the appropriateness of churches expressing political views, more supportive of vouchers, and less likely to agree that public schools should start each day with a prayer (though a majority thinks it's okay).

Cohort Change over Time

Compared with older people, young people today have greater faith in government and far more tolerant views on race, gender roles, and homosexuality. Although they are less intensely religious, most are nevertheless quite religious, and just as accepting of the mixing of religion and politics as their elders — if not more so. They are more likely than other age cohorts to think that business has greater sway over their lives than government does, but also more likely to think that business strikes an appropriate balance between profit and the public interest. They are quicker to accept the use of military force overseas, but also quick to raise questions about the military involvement and the progress of its mission.

But how durable are these attitudes? How much of the generally liberal cast of youth will dissipate as the responsibilities of adult life press down upon them, and how much of it is truly generational . . . a marker of the times in which they were socialized? Can we see the future by looking at the young people of today? Judged by the norms among older Americans, the views of youth are distinctive mainly for their greater faith in government, support for welfare programs, social liberalism, probusiness attitudes, and skepticism about the great social insurance programs of the New Deal era. Are these distinctive opinions apt to persist?

Although the future is inevitably cloudy, we believe that youth attitudes on social issues signal lasting change, but that opinions on economic issues and the scope of government are more contingent, subject both to the inevitable changes that occur with passage through the life cycle and to external events and circumstances. It is entirely plausible that the political system will change to accommodate the social views of youth: one could reasonably predict that gay marriage will become a reality in the United States as cohorts willing to accept it eventually move into middle age and perhaps even more supportive ones follow them. But young people will probably be molded by the economic system as much as they mold it: youth like the modern welfare state now but are also open to alternatives that are currently anathema to many older Americans (such as the option to invest part of Social Security taxes in the stock market). Young people are notoriously uninterested in issues related to health care, so their views on Medicare reform and even national health insurance are not yet fully formed. Having not yet learned "what goes with what" in the current polarized partisan alignment, young people may be especially receptive to politicians who are willing to mix and match positions.

Gauging Cohort Change

To track these issues and gauge cohort change, we look at four sources of survey data that have asked comparable questions over a long period of time. The National Election Studies have interviewed national samples of Americans every two years since the 1950s, while the General Social Survey has conducted in-person interviews with large national samples roughly every two years since 1973. And the PRC has tracked American political values regularly since 1987. In addition, HERI has conducted annual surveys of entering college freshmen since 1966. Collectively, these data sources allow us to look at young people as they entered adulthood and to track samples of their cohorts over time as they got older.

General Orientations

Young people arrive at adulthood without strong predispositions against government and its purposes. They have imbibed smaller doses of the antigovernment rhetoric that accompanies modern political discourse, and although they are plenty cynical about politics and politicians, they are not reflexively opposed to what the modern liberal state tries to accomplish. Does this idealistic — some would say naive — view of government last?

This is a difficult question to answer because the target is moving. The last 12 years or so has witnessed an antigovernment revolt of greater scope than that seen during Ronald Reagan's presidency. The initial stage of the revolt, which occurred in 1994, was followed by a rebound in support for government. But along with the rehabilitation of government's image, the power of conservatives in general and the Republican Party in particular have grown. The result is that general satisfaction with government has increased, partly because its natural advocates on the Left have become energized on its behalf, and partly because conservatives believe that they have reined it in and put it to work on behalf of their interests (Pew Research Center for the People and the Press 2003a). Thus it is very difficult to sort out the meaning of trends in general attitudes about government among young people.

A common, if imprecise, measure of progovernment sentiment is ideological self-identification. Despite the fact that few political leaders embrace the liberal label (and that others use it as an epithet), it is somewhat surprising that the percentage of people who call themselves liberal (even if only "slightly liberal") has slipped only from 29 percent in 1974 to 25 percent in 2002 in the General Social Survey. Attachment to the conservative label has grown from 28 percent to 34 percent. The plurality remains in the middle. Yet young people are more likely than others to identify as liberal. Among voters surveyed by the National Election Pool on Election Day in 2004, 32 percent of those aged 18–24 said they were liberal, while 27 percent said they were conservative. Liberals also outnumbered conservatives among voters aged 25–29 (30 percent to 26 percent). Among all other age groups, conservatives were more numerous, reaching a two-to-one advantage among those aged 40–44 and those between 60 and 74 years old. (Moderates held the plurality in all age categories.)

Among college freshmen, the percentage accepting the liberal label fell precipitously from 1972, when liberals outnumbered conservatives by a margin of 41 percent to 15 percent, to 1984, when liberal and conservative were tied at 22 percent (figure 6.2). Through the rest of the Reagan and Bush I era, this parity continued. Since then, acceptance of the

FIGURE 6.2
Political ideology among freshmen.

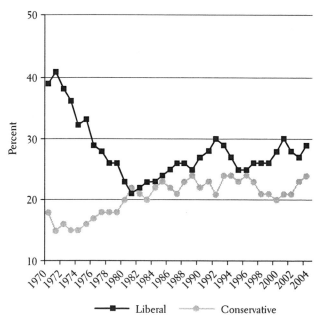

Source: UCLA Higher Education Research Institute.

liberal label has grown, with conservative affiliation bouncing up and down but staying below the levels of liberal identification.

Antigovernment sentiment has swung wildly since the 1980s, rising in the Gingrich tide of 1994 and subsiding since then. Comparing the late 1980s with the present, we find less agreement that government is wasteful and inefficient, with generational replacement responsible for most of this change. Pew Research Center surveys show an overall 10 point drop in this antigovernment sentiment between the late 1980s and recent surveys in 2002–2003 (table 6.10). Yet within cohorts, the change has been smaller and mixed in direction. Early GenXers became slightly more antigovernment (moving from 44 percent agreement in 1987–1988 to 49 percent in 2002–2003), while the World War II cohort became slightly less so (dropping from 70 percent to 64 percent). Boomers changed hardly at all.[4] The overall 10 point shift is driven largely by the departure of the oldest cohort in 1987–1988 (those born prior to 1918) and their replacement by the DotNets (and to a lesser extent, the GenXers), who were much more trusting of government (just 33 percent agreed that government is wasteful and inefficient).

Economics, Business, Regulation

As with general orientations about the scope of government, young people have taken more liberal positions on social welfare, regulation, and business than much of the rest of the public. But on these questions, the trend within cohorts has been mixed. On basic questions of social welfare

TABLE 6.10
Government Is Wasteful and Inefficient

Generation	1987–1988	2002–2003	Change
Born pre-1918	71%	—	—
WWII (1918–1945)	70%	64%	–6
Boomer (1946–1964)	62%	60%	–2
Gen X 1 (1965–1970)	44%	49%	+5
Gen X 2 (1971–1976)	—	47%	—
DotNet (1977–)	—	33%	—
Total	64%	54%	–10

Source: Pew Research Center Surveys.

programs and spending, support for activist government declines as people move through the life cycle. In National Election Survey polls, youth have tilted against the idea of government guaranteeing jobs and a good standard of living, and this conservative sentiment has grown within cohorts over time (even though there is no overall national trend in that direction). But on a measure of empathy for the poor, youth take a liberal stance and have grown more liberal since the late 1980s. And on the question of national health insurance, most youth support the idea, and this view has grown more popular among college freshmen since the mid-1980s (according to the UCLA surveys), though there was a dip in support in the aftermath of the failed Clinton effort to create a national health system in 1993–1994 (figure 6.3).

Compared with other cohorts, youth are more supportive of government efforts to equalize incomes, but the UCLA freshman survey found sharp declines in liberalism on this issue during the past decade. The percentage believing that the wealthy should pay a greater share of the taxes dropped dramatically beginning in the mid-1990s, from about 75

FIGURE 6.3
Support for national health insurance among freshmen.

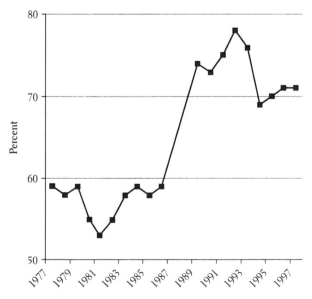

Source: UCLA Higher Education Research Institute.

percent during the 1970s to a low of about 50 percent, before rebounding slightly to 56 percent today (figure 6.4). The change is striking and may be accounted for, in part, by opposition to progressive taxation among Republican leaders in the 1990s. This view was typically presented indirectly, through opposition to capital gains taxes, inheritance taxes, and what were characterized as excessively high top rates.

On environmental issues, DotNets are more supportive of efforts to protect the environment, but their views are similar to those of Generation X when it arrived on the scene. Both are more supportive than other cohorts, but the Boomers are close behind. The UCLA freshman survey reflects a long downward trend in the percentage who say it's essential or very important to be involved in programs to clean up the environment, a measure that combines opinion on the issue with willingness to participate. This indicator was clearly reactive to the nature of the times: it hit a high of 42 percent when it was first asked in the

FIGURE 6.4
Opinion that wealthy people should pay a larger share of taxes (among freshmen).

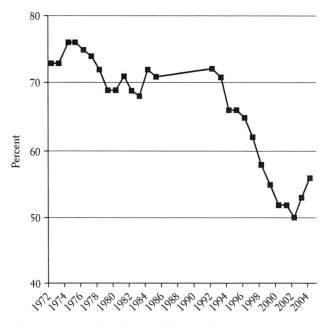

Source: UCLA Higher Education Research Institute.

early 1970s (at the birth of the modern environmental movement when the Environmental Protection Agency was established), declining quickly into the twenties by the 1980s, when Ronald Reagan was president, rising to the mid-thirties in the early 1990s, and then declining through the 1990s to only 17 percent in 2001.

The relatively probusiness attitudes of the DotNets appear to result from a combination of the probusiness nature of the times and the less judgmental quality of youth seen in evaluations of government—in essence, a combination of cohort and life cycle influences. Between 1987–1988 and 2002–2003, overall views about business profits became slightly more negative, perhaps reflecting the impact of Enron's collapse and other business scandals (table 6.11). Change within cohorts was slightly greater than the overall shift, with the World War II and Boomer cohorts shifting six points. Even with this somewhat negative overall judgment, DotNets arrived at adulthood as positive about business as GenXers were at the same point in their life cycle in 1987–1988.

Social Issues and Race

Much more than the political culture, the social culture touches young people and helps to shape their views. But the social culture has political import. On nearly every measure of social attitudes that touch on contemporary political issues—opinions about women's roles, homosexuality, race, guns, drugs, pornography—youth are more liberal than the rest of the country. On most of these (though not all), the trend within

TABLE 6.11
Business Strikes Fair Balance between Profit and Public Interest

Generation	1987–1988	2002–2003	Change
Born pre-1918	46%	—	—
WWII (1918–1945)	43%	37%	–6
Boomer (1946–1964)	40%	34%	–6
Gen X 1 (1965–1970)	49%	45%	–4
Gen X 2 (1971–1976)	—	42%	—
DotNet (1977–)	—	51%	—
Total	43%	40%	–3

Source: Pew Research Center Surveys.

cohorts over time has been in a liberal direction, as has the direction of the country as a whole.

Turning to specific issues, homosexuality occupies center stage in the culture wars today (to mix metaphors). The decision in late 2003 by the Massachusetts Supreme Court to require the state to recognize gay marriage galvanized advocates and opponents alike. The growing number of homosexual characters on television and in the movies has brought gay culture and perspectives to mass audiences. What to do about all of this is a deeply divisive issue in American politics. On the basic question of whether homosexual conduct should be prohibited, young people have become increasingly accepting over time, with just 30 percent of college freshmen in 2004 agreeing that homosexual relationships should be prohibited by law (figure 6.5). This was down from 50 percent in 1987, and had reached as low as 25 percent in 2002 before rising somewhat in the past two years. And indeed, majorities of the whole public — including

FIGURE 6.5
Opinion that homosexual relationships should be prohibited by law (among freshmen).

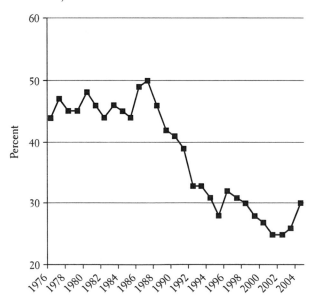

Source: UCLA Higher Education Research Institute.

evangelical Protestants — agree that society should not put any restrictions on the sexual conduct of consenting adults in private.[5]

A closer examination of the pattern of support for gay marriage across age groups in a 2003 poll suggests a distinct generational pattern, with breaks occurring among people currently in their mid-thirties and in their late fifties (figure 6.6). Individuals younger than about 35 are divided evenly on the question, while opposition is progressively more extensive among older Xers and the youngest Boomers. There is something of a plateau in opposition among Boomers — about 65 percent regardless of age within this cohort. Once we move past the Boomers, opposition is stronger among older respondents.

Perhaps the central issue in the culture wars for the past three decades has been abortion. This issue is marked by tremendous divisions in the society but also by great ambivalence within many individuals, who wrestle with strong but conflicting values in trying to determine what to think about it. According to the UCLA freshman surveys, support for legal abortion has been relatively stable among youth since the late 1970s, ranging from just under 55 percent to highs of 68 percent (figure 6.7). Support fell from very high levels in the early 1970s when the controversy over *Roe v. Wade* swirled through the society. The UCLA survey shows

FIGURE 6.6
Views on gay marriage, by age.

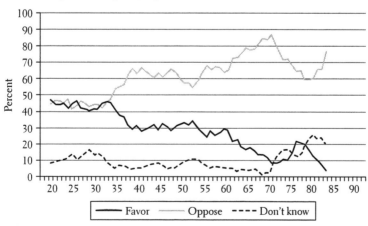

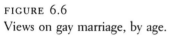

Source: Pew Research Center.

a surge in support during the early 1990s, followed by a return to the levels of the 1980s. Cohort trends from the National Election Studies suggest that DotNets, for all of their liberalism on most social issues, are not much different from Boomers and GenXers in their level of support for abortion under most circumstances.

National Security and Defense

The issue of national security has returned to the center of the political agenda. Although each cohort following the oldest has been less likely than the previous ones to agree that the best way to peace is through military strength, all cohorts except the oldest agreed more with this idea after September 11, 2001. DotNets and Gen Xers showed the greatest increase in agreement. But DotNets are still the least likely to agree, with about half agreeing, compared with over 60 percent for Boomers and Dutifuls. Similarly, the expression of patriotism is weaker in the DotNets,

FIGURE 6.7
Support for legal abortion among freshmen.

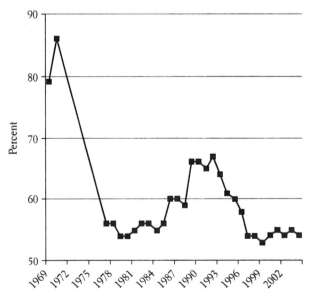

Source: UCLA Higher Education Research Institute.

but it grew markedly after 9/11 and stood at over 80 percent in 2003 (compared with over 90 percent for the other cohorts). And data from the Department of Defense's Youth Attitudes Tracking Survey in the late 1990s show that over 60 percent of young Americans said they would definitely not enlist in the military, up from only 40 percent during the 1970s, in the immediate aftermath of the Vietnam War (Morin 2001). It is still too early to gauge the impact of the war in Iraq on these attitudes among youth.

Conclusion

In every era, the idealism of youth interacts with the reality of the world they are joining. Government and politics can be tools for idealism, or channels for cynicism. American youth today face a political world in transition, wherein a national consensus on the value of government has broken down. At the same time, strong forces of modernism in the social world continue to undermine the hold of traditional values and hierarchies, a trend that youth have embraced and often led.

All of this suggests a loosening of the elemental ties of the New Deal coalition and its opposite. When the new party system was forged in the 1930s and 1940s, opinions about the scope of government, regulation of business, and the welfare state underlay the distinctions between the two major political parties. These considerations still motivate the Dutiful generation and, to a lesser extent, the Boomers. Issues related to race have political significance for all cohorts. But for the Boomers and especially for GenXers and DotNets, traditional values and religious commitment increasingly influence the choice of a political party (Campbell 2002). The DotNets' embrace of secular social values and their relatively lower levels of religious commitment played a role in the fact that they were Kerry's best age group in the 2004 presidential election.

Even more important in the 2004 election were views about the use of military force (Pew Research Center for the People and the Press 2005c). In several previous elections, values pertaining to war and peace had relatively little impact on partisanship or electoral choice. President Bush's response to 9/11, including the war in Iraq, polarized the nation and placed these issues at the center of the partisan divide. Values related to the use of military force were the strongest predictor of both party identification and presidential vote in 2004, but especially so among DotNets.

These changes do not necessarily signal an immediate partisan re-alignment or breakdown of the current structure of American politics. And despite the current advantage held by the Democrats among DotNets—especially among women—it is not obvious which, if either, party will benefit from generational changes in the values underlying the party system. Growing social liberalism on many issues—abortion is an important exception—certainly favors the Democratic Party. Skepticism about Social Security and progressive taxation, coupled with neutral or even friendly attitudes toward business, favor the Republican Party. The uncertainties regarding the war in Iraq and the efforts to prevent another terrorist attack make it impossible to speculate about their lasting impact on how the youngest generation orients itself to politics.

Although foreign and military values are more important in the partisan choices of youth today, tomorrow may find economic matters growing in importance. Baby Boomers are, for the most part, the parents of DotNets, and share some of the social values of the new cohort. Nevertheless, their economic interests may diverge significantly from those of the new generation of voters. Even as the vast numbers of Boomers move into their retirement years, nothing yet suggests that intergenerational economic competition will animate the politics of the near future, especially since youth currently rely more on social values than economic issues for their partisan choices. Nevertheless, the economic interests of the Boomers and DotNets are potentially opposed.

From this transition of alignments, it is entirely possible that a new politics will emerge. From the greater civic engagement of DotNets we will see more societal and governmental recognition of the nonprofit sector and its activities on behalf of the common good. The rise of the Internet as a tool for social organizing will make it easier for younger citizens and others without traditional political experience to raise their voices and join with other like-minded individuals.

Strong support for some type of national health insurance, even among people who usually say they don't need health insurance, augurs well for progress on this continuing societal conundrum—though not necessarily for any particular solution. But maintenance of social insurance for the elderly is apt to be a battleground. The inability of our current politics to engage in rational discussion on the issue is an ominous portent, and the demographics and the economics of the issue guarantee a showdown over the medium run.

The social liberalism of the DotNets suggests that the assimilation of immigrants from a vast range of nations and cultures will be met with greater understanding than in the past. Similarly, our current pitched battles over gay marriage are apt to fade into a low-level guerilla campaign as the electorate increasingly develops a live-and-let-live majority. But abortion—an issue on which much of the public remains conflicted and ambivalent—will continue to vex our politics, dependent upon the vagaries of Supreme Court nominations and White House incumbents. If *Roe* is overturned and some states move to ban all abortions, pro-choice forces will be energized. More generally, the religious dimension to our politics, so evident in the recent presidential elections, may grow in importance.

The successful politician of the next decades may look very different from those who dominate our politics today. They will not have to be more attractive, or more hip, to draw young voters. But it is clear that leaders who stress the longstanding issues that provide the foundation of the current party system may not fully appeal to today's youth. Politics in America, as well as citizenship, is in flux.

7

Civic Engagement, Political Engagement, and Generational Change

In the aftermath of the hotly contested 2004 presidential election, the press and the pundits devoted considerable attention to analyzing the meaning of the vote and its implications for the next four years. But many also took note of the fact that the American public reengaged in the political process at levels comparable to those of the early 1980s and close to that of the stimulating 1992 campaign, which featured two charismatic political newcomers, as well as the incumbent, George Bush. Interest in and attention to the 2004 campaign was exceptionally high, and voter turnout exceeded 60 percent of eligible citizens (Committee for the Study of the American Electorate 2005; Center for Information and Research on Civic Learning and Engagement 2005). Of particular note is that turnout among young voters, notoriously uninterested in campaigns and elections, increased by at least the same percentage as the rest of the population.

This increased engagement is a welcome turn of events for anyone concerned about the three-decade slide in electoral participation in the United States. But will it last? Throughout this book we have argued that we are witnessing a subtle but important remixing of the ways in which

U.S. citizens participate in public life. This new mix has privileged civic engagement over more traditional forms of political engagement such as voting, and focused on civil and corporate organizations rather than government institutions as the central arenas for public action. The reasons for this move away from traditional politics are myriad, but at heart they are structural, driven by three decades of political, economic, and sociocultural change. We have further argued that while these systemic changes have affected all citizens, their impact has been greatest on those who have come of age in recent years, since these more recent cohorts have no alternative experiences against which to contrast the *Zeitgeist* of the late twentieth and early twenty-first centuries.

If, as we believe, this altered view about how one engages the public sphere is a generational characteristic rather than simply something that will fade with age, the implications for the nature of democratic politics in the twenty-first century are profound. This is so because new generations, once influenced by the nature of the times, become the driving force for change as they move into positions of authority. Transferrals of political power from one group to another are often the most significant moments in a nation. Such transitions can happen in a variety of ways — from the results of a peaceful and orderly election, to coups, civil wars and, as recently in Iraq, outside military intervention. In most cases, however, we can identify a moment at which the transition occurs, whether that be the ceremonial swearing-in of a new president or the official recognition of a new government by other nations.

However, political transitions also happen in less obvious and more evolutionary but no less fundamental ways. Generational change is one such transition. After all, what could be more potentially revolutionary than the inevitable replacement of *every leader and adult citizen* in a nation? And yet that is what happens every half-century or so. Of course, this change is gradual and relatively unsystematic. Nonetheless, one of the great leaps of faith we make as social beings is the hope that what is best about our current society will be available to, preserved, and improved upon by our children and grandchildren.

Perhaps because of the stakes involved, a great deal of attention is often paid to comparing one generation to another. More often than not, these comparisons paint less than flattering pictures of youth, beginning implicitly or explicitly with the question "What's wrong with kids today?" Whether the topic is lifestyles (hair length, clothes, music, sex) or more "serious" issues (educational performance, crime, drug use, economic competitiveness, or public service), young people are almost always seen as falling short of the standards set by earlier generations, and presumed to be directly or indirectly contributing to the decline of some aspect of our culture, society, and polity.

Such comparisons—if done in more than offhanded and self-serving ways—are complicated by four factors, however. First, it is difficult to disentangle what elements of the attitudes, opinions, and behaviors of young people are the result of simply *being* young and what are more permanent generational characteristics that will remain as they age. Second, it is difficult to determine the extent to which differences, whether driven by age or generation, are the *result* of already occurring changes in our society (e.g., fewer young people read newspapers because they were born into a world already dominated by television and the Internet) or rather the *cause* (e.g., newspapers are losing their importance because fewer and fewer young people are reading them). Third, it is often difficult to make meaningful comparisons across generations because of the poor quality of data or the lack of data upon which to base these comparisons. Fourth, and perhaps most important, it is difficult to say which changes are in fact "a problem" and which are changes that at worst simply give rise to "different" attitudes and behaviors, and at best, make for more reasonable, effective, and adaptive responses to the world that the new generations have inherited.

In this book we have tried to understand the changing nature of democratic engagement in the United States by comparing the civic and political engagement of the four age cohorts that currently make up the U.S. population. In doing so we have also tried to be sensitive to the complicating factors just discussed. We believe this research provides a comprehensive and systematic portrait of civic and political engagement in early twenty-first-century America, how it has changed, and the role of generational differences in this change. And while we do not claim that our research provides a definitive answer to how this generational replacement will affect the short- and longer-term contours of American democracy, we believe that it provides some important glimpses into the direction in which we are headed, raises some important questions about what we still need to know, makes some useful suggestions about what we might do as a society to preserve what is best about our democracy and what is best about the civic and political engagement of today's youth, and offers some possible avenues for improving those areas where we fall short of the democratic ideal.

Civic and Political Engagement in Contemporary America: An Age-Based Portrait

Looked at as a whole, the patterns of civic and political engagement uncovered in our research tell a familiar story. As can be seen in table 7.1, nearly half (48 percent) of the adult population can be characterized as disengaged from both the civic and political realm.[1] Those who do participate are slightly more likely to participate in traditional politics (20 percent) than in civic activities (16 percent). And about one in seven adults (16 percent) engage with some frequency in both civic and more directly political activities. This overall portrait does not tell the full story, however. As with any study based upon the analysis of cross-sectional survey data, the findings presented throughout this book are complex, incomplete, and sometimes difficult to interpret. Nonetheless, several patterns emerge that point to significant and interpretable differences between the two oldest cohorts on the one hand and the two youngest ones on the other. These differences, if they continue, eventually will produce an overall mixture of civic and political engagement among Americans as a whole that is quite different—in both good and bad ways—from what we currently see.

First and foremost, simple claims that today's youth (i.e., members

TABLE 7.1
Profile of Engagement across the Generations

	DotNet %	GenX %	Boomer %	Dutiful %	Total %
Disengaged	57	53	42	43	48
Political specialist	15	13	19	31	20
Civic specialist	17	21	19	9	16
Dual activist	11	13	20	16	16
Total	100	100	100	100	100

Source: NCES1.

of Generation X and, especially, the DotNet generation) are apathetic and disengaged from *civic* life are simply wrong. On many of our indicators of this dimension of engagement (e.g., voluntarism or charitable activities), young adults look as or more involved than older Americans. Given that participation tends to increase with age, young people's current levels of civic involvement strikes us as impressive and promising for the future. This finding is a challenge both to the common stereotype of Xers as a generation of slackers and to more systematic analyses such as that of Robert Putnam (2000), which lays much of the blame for recent declines in social capital at the feet of America's youth.[2]

Second, to the extent that recent generations *are* less engaged than older Americans or earlier generations of young Americans, this is most evident in the area of "traditional politics." Today's youth are less likely to engage in activities such as voting, most other forms of involvement in campaigns and elections, contacting public officials, identifying with the major political parties, or joining or being active in other explicitly political organizations. They are also less likely to express interest in politics and public affairs, to follow such issues in the media, or to be knowledgeable about them. They are less likely to believe that citizenship entails traditional obligations such as voting, paying attention to government decisions or contacting a public official. And, for DotNets, they are more likely to believe that the private sector of businesses and corporations has greater influence on their lives than does government. When it comes to more civic (e.g., one-on-one voluntary or charitable activities) or economic-based (e.g., boycotting and buycotting) forms of public engagement, young people hold their own against older ones, though even in this realm they do not see these activities as "obligations" of citizenship or as explicitly "political" activities. Such a pattern is consistent with our reading (chapter 2) of the environment in which recent generations were socialized, with its emphasis on the inherent superiority of markets over politics, the seemingly unending string of political scandals, and the general denigrating of government as the problem rather than the solution to society's ills. It is arguably also consistent with an honest appraisal regarding where power increasingly lies in the contemporary world (i.e, in the economic and private spheres rather than the governmental and political ones), a point we return to (and dispute) later in this chapter. And it is consistent with the view that, despite increased participation in the unusually intense and close 2004 election, the future of democratic citizenship in the United States is likely to be more civic than political.

Third, younger Americans hold a complicated, sometimes inconsistent mix of attitudes toward the social and political system of which they are a part. On the one hand, their impression of "politics" is dominated by negative images of partisan bickering, corruption, lying, and a sense that politics is boring, confusing, and a realm that is for people (such as the rich and powerful) other than themselves. Consistent with Putnam's (2000) argument regarding the generational roots of declining social capital, they (and DotNets in particular) also are much more likely than older citizens to believe others can not be trusted or would take advantage of them if given the chance. On the other hand, there is some evidence that while still generally negative in their orientation toward politics, the youngest cohort is *less* cynical than older cohorts, including members of Generation X. And despite their lower level of involvement in traditional politics, both GenXers and, especially, DotNets are more likely than older Americans to believe that government should do more to solve problems, that government regulation of business is necessary, and even (for DotNets) that government generally does a better job than it gets credit for. This complicated set of orientations suggests to us that the worldview of younger Americans is still very much in formation. Equally uncertain is how this worldview will connect to their future engagement — and thus the future of citizen engagement in the United States more broadly — in public life.

Fourth, while younger Americans share many of the political and social opinions of older ones, they bring a number of distinct views to the table, making it important that their voices be heard. Characterizing this mixture of views in traditional terms is not easy, however. America's youth are more likely than older citizens to call themselves liberal, but their stands on specific issues are more complex than this simple label suggests. For example, while (in the spring of 2004) they were more likely than older Americans to disagree that military strength is the best way to ensure peace, to want to bring U.S. troops home from Iraq as soon as possible, or to believe that the United Nations should have the most say in establishing a new government in Iraq, they have also been among the strongest supporters of the war in Iraq. Younger Americans are more likely to support social welfare issues such as government provision of health insurance to the uninsured, guaranteed food and shelter to those in need, and government efforts to reduce the gap between rich and poor. But they are less likely to support increased spending on Social Security and more likely to support privatization of the Social Security system. They are more likely than older Americans to choose protecting the environment over encouraging economic growth as a priority. And, again compared to older Americans, they are far more tolerant of homosexuality and gay marriage, more supportive of women's equality, more accepting of interracial dating, and less religiously observant. Yet they are no more supportive of abortion than older Americans and are more likely to support the use of tax money to help parents pay for sending children to private or religious schools.

Our conclusion is less that younger Americans represent a distinct and consistent ideological block than that there are enough differences on enough important issues between them and older Americans to suggest that their presence or absence in public debate on such issues matters. At a minimum, were younger Americans to participate in numbers more proportionate to their percentage of the adult population, the frequency, tenor, and perhaps even the policy outcomes of debates over issues such as those just mentioned would be different. Candidates, public officials, political parties, and the news media would need to take the concerns and views of younger people more seriously. And, more speculatively, should the collective stands of DotNets in particular continue to resist our traditional notions of liberal and conservative or of Democrat and Republican as they age, it may well be that the parties will need to rethink their current ideological alignments, leading to a fundamental reshaping of the political landscape. The likelihood, pace, and direction of such a realignment would depend, however, on whether and how young people engage in politics as they age.

How Political Is Civic Activity?
How Political Are Civic Activists?

The central conclusion of this book is that the current and future contours of citizen participation in the United States are changing, largely because members of different generations differ not only in their willingness or ability to participate but also in the types of activities they perform, and that these choices often cluster, even if imperfectly, between involvement in the civic and political realms. More specifically, we have presented evidence that compared to older Americans, younger Americans are reasonably well engaged in civic life, but significantly less engaged in politics. Further, we have argued (and will argue more fully later in this chapter) that while civic engagement is an important and valuable component of citizenship, engagement in more traditional forms of politics matters because government and what it does matters. True, the last two decades have featured increasing discussion over the degree to which the private and nonprofit sectors can and should take over social welfare activities that the government has performed since the creation of the modern welfare state in the 1930s and 1940s. Nonetheless, one is hard pressed to think of any aspect of our daily lives — the food we eat, the clothes we wear and the cars we drive, the quality of the air we breathe and the water we drink, the jobs we hold and the houses we live in, the quality and quantity of education we obtain, our personal and collective health and safety, our nation's place in the world, even whom we can marry — that is not affected and often even determined by the actions and inaction of government. To the extent that this view is correct, the relative underrepresentation of today's younger Americans in the explicitly political realm is a current and future concern — especially given the distinctiveness of some of their issue stands — both for themselves and for the polity as a whole.

Consider, for example, our finding that only 16 percent of Americans are "dual activists" who engage significantly in both the civic and political realms. At a minimum, this finding suggests that only a small portion of the public are comfortable moving back and forth between these two forms of public life. It also suggests that large numbers of Americans (36 percent) are "specialists" who restrict their public engagement to either political (20 percent) or civic (16 percent) involvement. Further, we found that the percentage of dual activists, specialists, and unengaged citizens varies by generation. For example, given their relatively good performance in volunteering, working with others on community problems, fund raising, and group membership, it is not surprising to find that 17 percent of DotNets qualify as "civic specialists," a percentage that is comparable to that found in the population as a whole (16 percent), and much higher than that demonstrated by the oldest cohort of citizens (9 percent). They are underrepresented, however, among "political specialists" (15 percent among DotNets, 20 percent overall, and 31 percent among Dutifuls) and "dual activists" (11 percent among DotNets, 16 percent in the general population and Dutifuls, and 20 percent among Boomers) and overrepresented among the "disengaged" (57 versus 48 percent overall, 43 percent among Dutifuls, and 42 percent among Boomers).

GenXers demonstrate a pattern of opting for civic over political engagement that is similar to that of the DotNets, though more exaggerated. A greater percentage of this cohort (21 percent) qualify as civic specialists, and a smaller percentage qualify as political specialists (13 percent), than any of the other three generations. They are also less likely than Boomers or Dutifuls (though slightly more likely than DotNets) to be dual activists, and more likely than either of the two older cohorts to be disengaged from either form of public involvement.

The comparatively low percentage of DotNets and GenXers who are dual activists or political specialists provides evidence that members of these most recent generations are disconnected from more explicitly political life. But the specific implications of these findings depend in part on whether the civic versus political distinction is a meaningful one. How separate *are* the political and civic realms? Can engagement in civic life be viewed as politics by other means? That is, does participation in activities not directly aimed at public officials or government (for example, working with others to solve a community problem) produce changes in the behavior of such public officials or in the actions of government? Does or can engagement in civic activities lead to more traditional political engagement? That is, does participation in civic life (for example, volunteering at a soup kitchen) lead to more directly political action (for example, voting for a candidate whose platform includes the issue of poverty or homelessness)?

There is little consensus on the answers to these questions in the literature. On the one hand, some scholars argue that civic activities such as volunteering for nonprofit service organizations or supporting charitable causes have little to do with politics or policy, do little to encourage more avowedly political participation, and may even serve as *substitutes* for such political activity, displacing the essential work citizens need to do to keep a democracy healthy (Delli Carpini 2000; Hepburn 2001; Mattson 2000; Myers-Lipton 1998; National Association of Secretaries of State 1999; Wade 1996). On the other hand, others have argued that civic engagement can be political, at least under certain circumstances. As Burns, Schlozman, and Verba put it, "voluntary activity in both the religious and secular domains outside of politics intersects with politics in many ways" (2001: 58). They go on to say that this intersection occurs when the goals of civic organizations coincide with political goals, or the objects of the activity include the public sector, or the organizations pursue explicitly political means to attain their goals. Fiorina also sees the relationship between these two spheres of public life as context dependent, writing that civic engagement can be "highly political, entirely nonpolitical, and anything in between" (2002: 515).

This debate is not limited to scholars, finding its way into discussions among practitioners regarding, for example, the strengths and weaknesses of school-based programs such as service learning (Barber 1984; Boyte and Farr 2000; Gibson 2001; Kahne and Westheimer 1996; Niemi 2000). Much like the academic community, practitioners disagree on whether and under what conditions participation at an early age in programs that encourage *civic* engagement such as voluntary community service will lead to more explicitly *political* engagement such as voting, joining political organizations, or contacting public officials later in life.

Our earlier findings regarding the relationship between service learning and engagement (chapter 6) suggest that under certain conditions (i.e., when service is directly tied to classroom discussion about the underlying issues) it can lead to greater civic *and* political engagement. But what about the relationship between civic and political engagement more broadly? Understanding this relationship is particularly important to assessing the causes and implications of young people's apparent rejection of traditional politics. It is possible, for example, that DotNets' participation in the civic world is an intentional effort to affect politics and policy through other avenues—that is, a rejection of the *means* of politics and policy but not the *ends*. This would suggest a very different future from what would exist if their civic involvement was unrelated, in intention or impact, from politics and policy.

One way to ascertain the interplay of civics and politics is to determine if citizens themselves see a political component to their civic activities. To explore this issue, in our spring 2002 national survey we asked people who volunteered to tell us the main reason for their work: to address a social or political problem, to help people, or some other reason. We asked about volunteering in five different arenas—religious, environmental, civic or community, youth, political, or some other. In four of the five arenas, a relatively small percentage said their motivation was to address a social or political problem (see table 7.2). Indeed, even among those who volunteered for a political or electoral group, less than a majority (46 percent) chose this response. Across the five categories, only 21 percent said they volunteered to address a social or political problem. The percentage was higher among regular volunteers (looking only at groups other than political organizations) — 24 percent — but still fell well below even a plurality.

These results suggest that for most people, volunteer work is not consciously motivated by political concerns. But we feared that the wording of our question might have tilted the table toward a socially desirable response — helping others — and away from the political. To test this possibility, as well as to explore the perceived relationship between civic and political engagement in greater detail, we took a closer look at volunteering in a survey of New Jersey residents in 2003.[3] In this survey we asked volunteers a more straightforward question as to whether they regarded their participation as an attempt to address a social or political problem or not.[4]

One in five adults said they volunteered on a regular basis (just slightly below national estimates). As can be seen in table 7.3, of these, nearly half said that they thought of their volunteer work as an effort to address a social or political problem, more than double the percentage who saw such a connection when given the alternative option of "helping

TABLE 7.2
Main Motivation for Volunteer Work

Type of volunteer work	Political/ Social %	Help Others %	Other Reason %	Don't Know/ Refuse %	Total
Religious	4	71	24	1	100
Political/electoral	46	29	25	0	100
Environmental	22	45	32	1	100
Civic or comm.	11	77	12	0	100
Youth	8	75	17	0	100
Other	13	60	27	0	100
All types	21	85	33		

Source: NCES1.

others" in our national survey. In addition, while only 18 percent thought that the problem was something that government, rather than people in the community, should be addressing, another 17 percent volunteered that it was the responsibility of both the government and the community. Thus 35 percent felt that government had some role to play. And about one-fourth said that they had taken the step of contacting a government official about something related to their volunteer work in the past 12 months. When combined, fully 44 percent connected their volunteer work to the political world, either by seeing it as something that government should address or by having contacted a government official about it.

Another important form of civic engagement is informal collaboration with others in one's community to solve problems. About a fifth of New Jersey residents (22 percent, comparable to the national average of 18 percent in fall 2002) said they had engaged in such an activity during the past 12 months. Over two-thirds of these individuals said they thought of this as an effort to address a social or political problem. About one in five said it was something government should address rather than a problem for people in the community, and an additional 16 percent volunteered that both the government and the community were responsible

TABLE 7.3
Political Relevance of Volunteering and Community Problem Solving

Volunteer activity	
See work as effort to address social or political problem (percentages based on those who volunteered in the last year)	49%
Believe government should address	35%
Contacted government official as part of volunteer work	24%
Either believe government should address or contacted official	44%
Community problem solving	
See work as effort to address social or political problem (percentages based on those who worked to solve a community problem in the last year)	68%
Believe government should address	38%
Contacted government official as part of volunteer work	39%
Either believe government should address or contacted official	57%
See political relevance of either volunteer or community problem solving work (among those doing either)	50%

Source: *Star-Ledger*/Eagleton-Rutgers Poll No. 143, April 24–May 4, 2003.

(for a total of 38 percent who saw government as relevant to the issue). And, tellingly, 39 percent had contacted a government official as a part of their work. Taking into account those who had either contacted an official or said the government had a role to play in the issue, 57 percent of these civic activists made a political connection to their community work.

When we consider both volunteering and collective community problem solving together, half of those active in these civic realms connect this work to the political world through at least one of these two explicitly political channels (i.e., seeing the problem being addressed as the responsibility of government and/or contacting a public official about the problem). What should we make of this finding? One the one hand, it suggests that a substantial portion of what we have labeled "civic" involvement is explicitly or implicitly viewed by those who do it as politically relevant, either substituting for or supplementing something that government should be doing as well. Three considerations limit this more optimistic conclusion, however. First, an equally large portion of those engaged in civic activities such as volunteering or working with others *do not see* a connection to politics or government. Second, while many of those who volunteer (49 percent) or work with others to solve a community problem (68 percent) see their involvement as addressing a social or political problem, many fewer (24 and 39 percent, respectively) actually *act* in an explicitly political way, at least as measured by contacting a public official. And third, all of these findings apply only to the approximately one in five citizens who report that they volunteer regularly (18 percent) or work with others to solve a community problem (22 percent). Thus, for the vast majority of citizens, civic engagement is neither a pathway to nor substitute for political engagement, because they either do not participate regularly in the former or because they do not see or act on a connection in the latter. In the end, this suggests that the connections between civic and political engagement that we do find are more instructive in pointing to the *potential* for forging such links than their actual existence among citizens today.

Thus far we have looked at the way citizens as a whole view the connection between politics and their civic participation. But do younger Americans—DotNets and GenXers—see this relationship differently? Apparently not. In both our national and our New Jersey surveys, there were no significant differences between younger and older respondents in perceptions that their civic activities were addressing social or political problems, that the problems they were working on were something government should be addressing, or that they were issues about which they had contacted government officials. In short, younger Americans appear no less likely (though also no more likely) than their elders to see a political component to their civic involvement, a finding that bodes well for the future of democratic politics in the United States.

We can offer two final pieces of evidence regarding the complex connection between civic and political action. Earlier (chapter 3) we described two additional "dimensions" of public participation—"public voice" and "cognitive engagement"—beyond what we described as "political" and "civic" engagement. The former captured a collection of ways citizens could express their opinions to the media, the private sector, and government, while the latter captured the degree to which citizens cared about and followed public affairs and politics. Civic specialists were generally as likely as political specialists to publicly express their opinions (an inherently political act) through activities such as boycotting, petitions, contacting officials, and so forth (see table 7.4). And, tellingly, dual activists (those who engaged in both civic and political activities) were significantly more likely than either of the "specialists" to express their opinions through these various outlets of "public voice." This relationship—civic specialists as likely to express an opinion as political special-

TABLE 7.4
Expressions of Public Voice in the Previous 12 Months

	All %	Disengaged %	Electoral specialist %	Civic specialist %	Dual activist %
Boycotted	38	30	39	42	55
Buycotted	35	27	37	37	52
Written petition	22	12	24	26	48
E-mail petition	12	7	12	17	24
Contacted official	18	9	18	17	45
Talk show	8	3	10	8	21
Contacted media	10	4	9	15	26
Protested	4	3	3	5	10
Canvassed	3	1	2	3	10
3 or more of these	24	11	28	26	58

Source: NCES1.

ists, and dual activists more likely than either—can be seen even more clearly when considering multiple expressions of public voice. Just 11 percent of the disengaged have done three or more of these activities; among dual activists, 58 percent have done so.

These findings add to our sense that for a portion of citizens, civic involvement is connected to politics, at least as captured by our measures of "public voice." They also suggest, however, that citizens are most likely to express their voices when they are already active in *both* the civic and the traditional political realms. We believe this is an important observation, because it reinforces the notion that the most effective type of citizenship is one that combines civic and political engagement, and that the most effective citizen is one who is comfortable and active in both worlds. A somewhat less promising conclusion regarding the political relevance of civic participation emerges when we look at its connection to "cognitive engagement." Once again, we find that dual activists are the most cognitively engaged, adding to our sense that the combination of civic and political involvement is the hallmark of "good" citizenship. However, it is also clear that civic specialists, while more cognitively engaged in politics than citizens who do not regularly participate in any way, are less cognitively engaged than political specialists. Making the safe assumption that a cognitively engaged citizenry is desirable, this last finding is an important reminder that while civic participation may be connected to politics in some ways, there are limits to this connection, and it would be a mistake to assume that it can substitute for more explicitly political engagement.

Clearly the analyses presented in this section do not fully answer the question with which we began: How political is civic activity? Nonetheless, taken as a whole, we can draw seven conclusions. First, the line between civic and political engagement is blurry at best, with as many as half of those engaged in civic activities seeing or treating their actions as political. Second, this line is also a porous one, with many of the citizens we have characterized as civic specialists also expressing their public voice in other arguably political, if not always or obviously electoral or government-focused ways. And third, dual activists are the most likely to also engage in other means of expressing their political voices and in being cognitively involved in politics and public affairs. These first three conclusions suggest that civic engagement in general and the apparent tendency of many younger Americans to choose civic over explicitly political forms of participation may not be as dire as we and others have suggested. In addition, they suggest that, in the proper context, civic engagement can be a pathway to political engagement. And they suggest that citizens who are facile with *both* civic and political forms of engagement are also the most likely to express their opinions and be cognitively involved in politics and public affairs, adding to our sense that "good" citizenship in the twenty-first century requires and benefits from both forms of engagement.

This more optimistic interpretation must be tempered by our final four conclusions, however. First, it remains the case that despite these blurry and porous boundaries, the vast majority of citizens are either disengaged from all forms of public life or specialize in either civic or political forms of engagement. Second, half or more of those who are civically engaged show no signs of connecting this engagement to politics and government. Third, only a small percentage of Americans are explicitly engaged in politics, either as specialists or dual activists. And fourth, it remains the case that more younger Americans than older ones are disengaged from any form of participation, and fewer are likely to be either political specialists or dual activists. In short, while civic engagement may also be political in a sense, and may even lead to certain kinds of political engagement, there remain numerous reasons to be concerned about the relative lack of direct involvement in the political realm of Americans in general, and younger generations in particular.

Looking into the Future: The Relative Importance of Life Cycle and Generational Effects

Disentangling the relationship between civic and political involvement is crucial to understanding the short– and long–term implications of the research presented in this book. But so, too, is disentangling the relative roles of life cycle and generational effects on age-based differences in engagement. As discussed in chapter 1, *if* such differences result from consistent changes associated with one's age, then one might reasonably expect that as GenXers and DotNets age, they will increasingly resemble today's older Americans in their civic and political attitudes, opinions, and actions. For example, one might expect that as they age, today's youth could become slightly less engaged in civic acts such as volunteering for a charitable or social cause, but become more engaged in following public affairs and voting. If, however, more ingrained generational differences are at work, then the age-based changes in the contributions of the various groups' attitudes, opinions, and behaviors that we have documented are likely to remain (though this is not inevitable, as we discuss later in this chapter), potentially leading to important differences in how citizens interact with the public realm and, ultimately, what the public realm looks like. For example, over time, rates of news viewing and voting would decline, while civic activities might increase slightly. Conclusions regarding the relative impact of life cycle and generational effects would also affect the ways in which we might, as a nation, try to address concerns such as declining participation in traditional politics.

We readily admit that definitively determining the relative impact of these two age-based processes on the patterns of engagement is beyond our ability. This is true in part because of the absence of measures over time of many of the attitudes, opinions, and behaviors we have examined, in part because of inherent methodological difficulties in disentangling such effects, and in part because, at least for the youngest age cohort, the process of developing a generational character is still very much in play. Nonetheless, we believe we can say some things about this issue. Before doing so, however, it is important to note that even if the differences we have documented are due mostly or entirely to life cycle effects, *they would still be important*. We say this for two reasons. First, the relatively low levels of participation in traditional politics by young people, coupled with age-based differences in opinions on major issues, means that the distinct public voice of this sizable portion of the population is being muted. In short, young people's interests are not being fully represented. This relative underrepresentation of young people in traditional politics has implications not only for them but also for the rest of the population. The priorities of government, the specific solutions chosen to address these priorities, even the leaders who represent us are likely different today from what they would be if young people participated more than they currently do (consider here our simulation in chapter 1 suggesting that if young adults had voted at levels comparable to their percentages in the population, the outcomes of recent elections might well have been different).

Second, even if young people's civic and political involvement is likely to mimic that of older generations as they age, this is hardly a ringing endorsement for the health of our democracy. As many observers have noted, civic and especially political engagement in the United States has generally fallen short of what one might hope in a democracy, especially over the past 30 years (Putnam 2000). Knowing that young people are traditionally less likely than older people to participate in elections, or are more likely to engage in one-on-one volunteering, does not mean that these patterns are inevitable. And even if they are, it may still be possible to increase *overall* levels of participation even if young people remain *relatively* more or less engaged than older ones. In short, knowing that life cycle effects are important can help us discover how best to increase participation in the future, rather than resigning us to accept existing levels or patterns as immutable.

That said, we have several reasons to suspect that differences in civic and political participation between younger and older Americans result from more than just differences in age. In some cases (for example, for voting or most forms of news use) the gap between the two younger cohorts and the two older cohorts are too large to explain away by the effects of aging alone. In other cases (for example, views on politics and government) the gap between DotNets and GenXers is too large to attribute to the relatively small differences in their respective ages. In still other cases (for example, generational identity or participation in consumer activism) the patterns across the four cohorts are distinct enough to undermine any sense of gradual and consistent change as one ages. And in other cases (for example, opinions about race, gender, or homosexuality) differences between young and old clearly represent a sea change in attitudes that cannot be attributed to growing conservatism as one ages. Finally, where our data have allowed us to look at cohorts over time (most directly in chapters 4 and 5), these more systematic analyses strongly point to lasting generational differences. No one of these patterns is definitive, but taken as a whole they suggest that at least some significant portion of the unique views and behaviors of younger Americans that we have documented is likely to last as they age, and thus to influence the nature of democratic engagement for decades to come.

Shaping the Future: Pathways to Civic and Political Engagement

Suggesting that the age-based patterns of civic and political engagement summarized earlier in this chapter and detailed more fully throughout this book result from some combination of life cycle and generational effects is illuminating, but what leads to these effects? In the broadest sense, we believe they can be explained in part by the political, economic, and social environments (detailed in chapter 2) in which the post–Baby Boom generations were raised. As shown in chapter 6, our analyses regarding the pathways to civic and political engagement are largely consistent with prior research in this area. People, regardless of their age or generation, are more likely to participate in public life if they have the motivations, skills, resources, and opportunities to do so. To the extent that young people of any generation are encouraged and assisted to develop these motivations, skills, resources, and opportunities — through family discussions and parental modeling, formal and informal school programs, outreach by nonprofit and political organizations, the media, and the like — they are more likely to respond by becoming engaged. To the extent that such encouragement and assistance emphasizes one aspect of public life (for example, voluntary activity) over another (for example, voting), one would expect to see this reflected in the attitudes and behaviors of the young. And to the extent that such encouragement and assistance is absent or is declining across the board, one would expect to see similar declines in the relative and absolute involvement in all kinds of engagement.

On the basis of this simple approach, we can, at least to some extent, interpret the age-based patterns we have uncovered. Raised in an environment that largely denigrated government and sang the praises of market populism and individual solutions to collective problems, it is little wonder that younger generations would choose civic and economic over more traditionally political forms of engagement. This tendency has been reinforced by school programs that encourage (and sometimes even require) nonpolitical service, while shying away from anything that even hints of partisan politics. It has also been reinforced by a media environment that simultaneously sends messages about the irrelevance and corruption of politics while ignoring the interests and inputs of young people. And it has been reinforced by political organizations that largely ignore both the interests and the potential participation of young people — that simply fail to ask young people to become involved. In short, young people's civic and political engagement is a reflection not of apathy or content but of the world they have inherited. It is a reflection of *us* as we really are.

The story is not all bad, of course. As we have seen, young people are remarkably open to issues of social and racial diversity. They care about many public issues. They are concerned about issues of justice and equity. They are involved in a wide range of civic activities. They see an important role for government. They understand their economic power and are willing to use it for social causes. In all these ways, "the kids are all right" (or "alright," in the Who's version). Nonetheless, in both relative and absolute numbers, too many young people — tomorrow's majority — are either disengaged entirely from public life or more specifically from the traditional world of politics.

Where does this leave us? Acknowledging that the concluding chapter of this generational saga has yet to be written, and that unforeseen events can alter the patterns we have uncovered, we believe that absent a conscious, collective, and systematic effort to provide young Americans with the motivation, skills, and opportunities to participate in politics, we will continue to see a slow but steady exodus from this realm of the public sphere. While dramatic events or particularly compelling campaigns (such as that in 2004) may lead to sporadic increases in voter turnout, over time these rates will continue to decline, as will participation in other aspects of campaigns and elections. Attention to and interest in public affairs, politics, and government will further erode. Solutions to our public concerns will increasingly be sought through the private and nonprofit sectors. Citizens will increasingly define public engagement in terms of their churches, clubs, and acts of individual good will rather than through elections, parties, and government policy. These trends may be subtle, but their impact will be profound, challenging the very definition of a representative democracy led by a government of, by, and for the people. And future generations, raised in such an environment, will inherit this view of the world, and so add to this gradual triumph of "the new civics" over "traditional politics" as the definition of the public sphere and their place in it.

It need not be this way, however. True, much of what leads to a generation's political worldview — economic boons and busts, war, scandal, technological change, and so forth—is outside of anyone's easy or direct control. Nonetheless, throughout this book we have pointed to a variety of replicable ways in which younger Americans can and have been socialized to think and act politically. Of these, four are of particular note. First, what happens in the family matters. Young people raised in families that discuss and follow politics, and that provide adult models of civic and political behavior, are more likely to demonstrate these traits themselves. Second, what happens in schools matters. Increases in voluntary activity among young adults is directly attributable to the greater attention paid to this form of public involvement in schools, largely through the service learning movement. There is no reason to think that a similar effort, focused more explicitly on forms of political engagement, could not be equally successful.

Third, what civic and political organizations do matters. One of the greatest predictors of public involvement is whether or not someone has been asked to participate. Unfortunately, there has been a decline in the number of civic and especially political organizations that seek out the direct involvement of their members and constituents (Putnam 2000; Skocpol 2003), and of those that do, there is a noticeable tendency to ignore young people in these requests. But what is clear is that if they are asked, people—including young people—will participate, even in traditional politics such as voting (Green and Gerber 2004). This was tangibly demonstrated in the 2004 election, where preliminary evidence suggests that in the ten "battleground states" where intensive voter registration and get-out-the-vote efforts by nonprofits, advocacy groups, and the political parties—many aimed directly at young people—dramatically increased turnout among 18- to 29-year-olds, as compared to recent elections, and all but eliminated the age gap in voting (Center for Information and Research on Civic Learning and Engagement 2005). And fourth, what the media do matters. There is a clear relationship between following public affairs in the media and being civically and politically engaged. But too often the media presents information in ways and on topics that hold little appeal to citizens in general and younger citizens in particular. There is nothing inherent in providing news that requires this disconnect, however. Making news more interesting, relevant, understandable, and actionable would surely increase its audience, and in doing so increase the number of citizens—young and old—who participate in public life and who see the relevance of politics (Patterson 1993;

Patterson 2002; Rosen 1999). The growing number of media available to people (from cable and satellite to the Internet) coupled with the ability to target particular demographic groups, while posing the threat of audience fragmentation, also provide the opportunity to offer different segments of the population news and other kinds of public affairs information that is of relevance and interest to them.

We make no claims that making the necessary transformations in families, schools, civic, and political organizations or the media would be easy or even likely. To the contrary, if the past is any guide, one would be hard pressed to conclude anything but that current trends in the depoliticization of American citizenry will continue unabated as today's youth become tomorrow's adults. But neither should one assume that the kinds of changes hinted at in this chapter are "utopian." Indeed, many promising efforts in each of these areas already exist. For example, nonprofits such as Kids Voting, the League of Women Voters and the American Association of Retired People have introduced programs designed to encourage parents, siblings, and friends to discuss politics with young people and introduce them to the experience of voting. High school and college-based initiatives such as "Student Voices," "Project 540," "Public Work," "Freedom's Answer," "First Vote," and Campus Compact's "Raise Your Voice" have collectively integrated a more political notion of service learning and a more experiential version of civic education into the curriculum and after-school activities of literally thousands of schools across the country. Groups such as the Youth Vote Coalition, Rock the Vote, and the New Voters Project have organized grassroots and on-line, youth-focused voter registration and get-out-the-vote drives, and even the two major parties are increasing their attention and resources devoted to young voters as a potential "swing group." As noted earlier, these efforts appear to have been remarkably successful in 2004. And media outlets from the *New York Times* to MTV are experimenting with ways to package the news so that it resonates with and educates young people (for example, both the *Chicago Sun-Times* and the *Chicago Tribune* have recently launched newspapers aimed at those under the age of 30).

The short- and long-term impact of these and hundreds of other efforts to increase the political involvement of young Americans remains, for the most part, uncertain and circumstantial, though there are notable exceptions, such as the field experiments conducted by Green and Gerber (Green and Gerber 2004) that convincingly demonstrate significant increases in youth voter turnout as a result of nonpartisan, peer-to-peer canvassing and telephone contacts (see also research collected, conducted and sponsored by the Center for Information and Research on Civic Learning and Engagement [CIRCLE]). And clearly even when added together, the scope of existing programs and initiatives pales in comparison to what would be needed to reverse at least two generations of political disengagement. Nonetheless, while both more research and a wider reach are needed, the mere existence of such efforts, along with evidence that the service learning movement itself is increasingly focused on the need to more directly integrate politics into its mission (see, for example, the Carnegie Corporation's publication *The Civic Mission of the Schools*, 2003), suggests that change, while perhaps not likely, *is* possible. Ideally, this change would develop a new generation of citizens who see the importance of both civic and political engagement, and the connection between the two.

Conclusions

As a liberal democracy, the United States combines a dependence on both governmental and civil institutions to address public issues of the day. Governmental institutions include the legislative, executive, and judicial branches of local, state, and federal government, as well as the various service agencies and organizations that interact daily with citizens. Civil institutions include families, religious organizations, neighborhood associations and clubs, schools, foundations, and nonprofit organizations. Given this state of affairs, citizens need to be able to engage in the institutions and process of government *and* of civil society, since both are authoritative determiners of how goods, services, and values are allocated in a society. Because government matters, participation in civil society — through contributing to charitable causes, volunteering in one's local community, joining civic associations, and the like — cannot substitute for voting, working for a party or candidate, or contacting one's elected official about a policy concern. At the same time, because civil institutions matter, participation in the electoral and policy process can not substitute for engaging in this aspect of our society. There may be times and circumstances in which one type of engagement is preferable to another, but over time and across groups, both are crucial. In short, each is a necessary but not a sufficient requisite if citizens are to have an authoritative and equal voice in the democratic process.

The importance of both the civic and political spheres and the connection between the two was made starkly evident by the terrorist attacks of 9/11 and their aftermath. The attacks triggered an awakening of citizens' civic spirit. Donations of time, money, clothing, and blood poured into the nonprofit community, as Americans from across the nation responded to the suffering in New York, Washington, and Pennsylvania as they would to a neighbor in the midst of a crisis. This outpouring of voluntary assistance was both tangible (i.e., it provided needed resources to address a real problem) and symbolic (i.e., it helped with the grief, shock, and mourning, produced a sense of national solidarity, and partially renewed our national reservoir of social capital). In short, America's "civic side" was in full and marvelous display.

But civic spirit alone could not address this "problem." A consummate political event, the attacks were spawned by years of foreign policy decisions and indecision, and triggered numerous government actions, beginning with the actions of local fire and police departments (and of local, state, and national emergency relief agencies), and carrying over to major changes in our privacy laws, a growing national deficit, ongoing investigations regarding the failures of our national security apparatus, the greatest reorganization of the federal government in history, and two wars, one of which (against Iraq) was questionably related to the new "war on terrorism" and has led to a precipitous decline in America's standing in the world.

In light of this momentous chain of events, citizens' *political* response strikes us as potentially more important than their civic response. And what was this response? Interest in politics and public affairs appeared to rise for the first time in decades among college freshmen, trust in government spiked, and news readership and viewing increased briefly. Formal and informal discussion of the issues of terrorism, civil rights, national security, and war increased (Jacobs, Delli Carpini, and Cook 2004). Thousands of citizens on both sides of various issues signed petitions, made phone calls, and took part in demonstrations, protests, and rallies.

And yet despite this, one is left with the feeling that public input had little if any impact on the actual actions of government, serving more as a backdrop to events than a driving force for them. For example, despite majority opinion opposing U.S. military intervention in Iraq or only favoring such intervention with U.N. support, the United States intervened militarily (only *after* this intervention did a majority support the action, a classic rally-around-the-flag effect). Voter turnout in state and local elections in 2001 and congressional elections in 2002 showed little to no signs of increase, and few races centered or turned on issues related to 9/11 and subsequent events. Turnout in the 2004 presidential caucuses and primaries, while initially higher (both in general and among younger citizens) than normal, quickly returned to typically low levels. Despite the substantial spike in turnout in the 2004 general election, more attention was devoted in media coverage of the campaign to Bush's and Kerry's respective military records during the Vietnam War than to the war in Iraq or the state of the economy, arguably two of the three (along with the war on terror) central issues of the presidential campaign. In the end, according to exit poll data, while majorities of voters felt the war in Iraq was "going badly" (52 percent) and that the national economy was doing "not good or poorly" (52 percent), only a third selected one of these two issues as the most important to their vote choice.[5] Six weeks after the election, with nearly 60 percent of Americans reporting that they were "dissatisfied" with the way things were going in the country, only a third reported that they were following the situation in Iraq "very closely," and only 16 percent said they were following the debate over intelligence reform (the major issue regarding the war on terror) "very closely" (Pew Research Center for the People and the Press 2004a). In short, given the stakes involved, most Americans' political responses (as opposed to America's), were arguably less forceful, engaged, or consequential than their civic ones.

Perhaps the chain of events beginning on September 11, 2001, and including the 2004 presidential election will yet mark a watershed, drawing more Americans more consistently into political life, and even serving as a defining moment for the political identity of DotNets. Only time will tell. But the evidence presented in this book suggests that such a political reawakening will require overcoming the impact of decades of forces that have worked to push two generations away from traditional politics. Three years after the terrorist attacks and in the midst of an increasingly expensive and controversial war, younger Americans remain less engaged in traditional politics and public affairs than their elders.

Fortunately, however, our research and that of others suggests that this need not remain the case. Ten years of service learning initiatives make clear that given the opportunity and incentives, youth participation in civic life can be increased. Explicitly civic forms of engagement have identifiable if sometimes tenuous ties to more traditional politics, connections that can be made stronger through more explicit efforts to connect service to politics and policy. Consumer politics (i.e., boycotting and buycotting) appears to be a potentially rich and undertapped vehicle for organizing and mobilizing younger Americans. Research on efforts to increase youth voting through grassroots contacting clearly demonstrates that such efforts can be successful (Green and Gerber 2004). The 2004 Howard Dean presidential campaign, and efforts made by both parties and numerous other groups in the 2004 general election, showed that the right message, sent through the right media and aimed directly at young people, can bring heretofore "nonpolitical" youth into the system. In short, given the motivation, skills, resources, and opportunities, young people are ready and willing to add more politics into their still evolving repertoire of public sphere activities, not in place of their civic and economic involvement but in harmonious combination with it. Providing this motivation and these skills, resources, and opportunities is the challenge — not just for young people themselves, but for those of us who claim to care about them, and about the future of our democracy.

Appendix

Research Design (Chapter 3)

Data for this book were collected during a two-year project funded by the Pew Charitable Trusts. The research had two principal goals: (1) to develop a reliable but concise set of indicators of civic and political engagement, with a special focus on youth aged 15–25; and (2) to assess the civic and political health of the nation.[1] To accomplish these aims we employed a five-stage research design, moving from qualitative to quantitative.

Stage 1: Expert Panels

We began our field work in the spring of 2001 by convening two "expert panels" of those who either work with active youth on a daily basis or who study their political predispositions and behavior. Our intention was to start tabula rasa: we knew little about how young people were active in the civic and political life of the country, and wished to be blinded by no presumptions. The extant literature, to us, seemed to be bound too heavily to the past traditions of political science that focused largely on voting behavior, and we were concerned about reification. Thus we chose a bottom-up approach. That is, rather than asking about how young people participated in normal political and civic activities, we asked what young people were doing, and then wondered whether these activities could be considered civic or political (see appendix table 1 for sample questions used in the panels).

Our expert panelists came from all walks of engagement life. They included representatives from political parties, labor unions, nonprofits, racial and ethnic-oriented groups, voting- and school-based civic organizations, among others. The discussion guide we started with was open-ended. Simply put, we asked specialists working in the field of youth civic engagement to tell us what they thought was on the minds of young people, what their values were, what sense they made of the wider world,

APPENDIX TABLE 1
Expert Panel Discussion Questions

• **Activities and interests of young people**
  What kinds of political activities do young people participate in?
  What are the biggest challenges to youth involvement in politics and civic life?
  Where is the most hope and promise for youth involvement?
• **The post–Baby Boomer generation(s)**
  Do young people today participate less than or differently from others?
  How do young people today differ from older generations; what are the reasons?
  Is there a difference between Generation X and the latest wave of young adults and teens?
  Is the current young group a "generation"? What shared experiences make them so?
• **Political information and attitudes**
  Where do young people get their information about politics? What do they know?
  Describe how young people think about politics: as evil, irrelevant, or inaccessible?
  Do they believe they can influence politics; do they want to influence politics?
  Do volunteers in nonpolitical work see a link between their activities and politics?
• **Basic values**
  How do young people define "community"? Is it a place, or a set of interests?
  Are the young people you work with connected to any particular community?
  What core values do you think they have; and where are they learning these lessons?
• **Guidance for our work**
  When we study youth, civic, and political engagement, what should we consider?
  Are there measures of political engagement among young people that have been overlooked, or that we won't find through surveys? Where else should we look?
  How could we help you better assess the effectiveness of your work?

---

how they would describe young people in terms of personality and in their commitment to civic and political life, and what they did in terms of actions. The results of these two expert panels framed the questions we set out to explore in the second phase of our research. The following list shows the names of those who participated in our panel discussions, along with their affiliation at the time of their participation.

Mallory Barg	AmeriCorps
Rick Battistoni	Providence College
Amy Cohen	Corporation for National Service
Julia Cohen	Youth Vote 2000
Marco Davis	National Council of La Raza
Steve Culbertson	Youth Service America
Alison Byrne Fields	Rock the Vote
Ivan Frishberg	Public Interest Research Group
William A. Galston	University of Maryland
Vina Nguyen Ha	Korean Youth and Community Center and Southern Californians for Youth
Sandy Horwitt	National Association of Secretaries of State
Adrienne King-McCorkle	National Coalition on Black Civic Participation
Kimberly Roberts	AFL-CIO
Peter Schurman	MoveOn.org
Stephanie Seidel	Bread for the World
Susan Blad Seldin	College Democrats
Vicki Shabo	Lake Snell Perry and Associates
Robert Sherman	Surdna Foundation
Diane Ty	YouthNOISE
Mara Vanderslice	RESULTS
Lisa Wernick	College Republican National Committee

Stage 2: Focus Groups

We took what we had learned from our discussions with those on our expert panels as the raw fodder for the development of a discussion guide we could use in focus groups we conducted with young people, and also groups in other age ranges. As described, we had stratified the world into four generational groups, based upon prior research and the objectives of the study. We conducted 11 focus groups during May and June of 2001, in four distinct regions of the country—the West (northern California: three groups), Midwest (Chicago: three groups), South (North Carolina: two groups), and Northeast (New Jersey: three groups)—to talk to people of all ages about politicians, government, citizenship, the kinds of problems they face in their communities, and a variety of other relevant topics in order to figure out what people think about politics and citizen engagement. Almost every one of the groups was stratified by age into one of the four groups we have described, with a greater number of groups being conducted with DotNets and GenXers. We also conducted a number of specialty groups, including one group comprising mainly young African Americans in North Carolina. Following the initial round of our focus groups, we revisited some of our DotNet and Generation X focus group participants after the 9/11 terrorist attacks in order to see what, if any, impact a national tragedy such as this had on their perception of government and politics. And finally, we conducted two additional focus groups following our national telephone survey in order to gauge the validity of our engagement typology, as described in detail in chapter 3.

While we modified the discussion guides used in each of these original four-site groups as we learned from one group to the next, each group covered a similar terrain. We started by asking in open-ended fashion what life was like in each of the communities we were in, followed by a discussion of what group participants may have done to participate in civic or community life. When this topic was exhausted, we asked what participants thought about what makes "a good citizen" and whether there were obligations of citizenship, and if so, what people believed them to be. We then moved the discussion into views of politics, often beginning this section by asking participants to "write down the first word that comes to mind when I say the word . . ." and then probing with the nouns "politics" and "government" among others. In most groups this led us into a discussion of (the importance of) "voting" as a form of participation. The last segments of the groups included a generational discussion, encompassing both what young people are like these days, and how each age group thought they might be different than those who have come before and after them, depending on relevance to the particular group sitting around the table.

Stage 3: Questionnaire Pretesting and Internet Sample of Youth

Stage 3 of the research design encompassed two main activities. First, we ran a series of question wording experiments to test the most reliable and valid ways of measuring sets of behaviors and attitudes. These experiments on question wording focused on how to minimize socially desirable responses, the time frame over which behaviors could reliably be recalled, and alternative ways of either formulating questions or framing response categories for respondent choice.[2] We were fortunate to have access to statewide surveys in both New Jersey and Virginia in the fall of 2001, where each state was holding its gubernatorial election, for testing.

Second, we realized from the conduct of focus groups with young people that there was a gap in our knowledge of their world, which we wanted to close before going into the field with a final instrument. Even after the focus groups, we felt we knew less than we would like about young people in general, and about their school-based experiences in particular. To glean additional insight into these areas, we commissioned Knowledge Networks (KN) to conduct the NYS. Knowledge Networks conducts web-based surveys with a true probability sample design by providing Internet access to randomly selected households.

Between January 29, 2002, and February 25, 2002, Knowledge Networks administered a survey to youth aged 15 to 25 about the activities they are engaged in, either by themselves or with others. The NYS was administered to a total of 1,166 KN panel members in two waves of data collection. An e-mail reminder was sent to nonresponders three days after the survey was fielded. An additional e-mail reminder was sent to the final 800 nonresponders on February 12, 2002. The research subjects completed the self-administered survey using an Internet appliance provided by Knowledge Networks. The median time for a participant to complete the survey was 18 minutes.

There were three study groups that were stratified by education status. The subsamples included (1) persons currently in high school; (2) those currently in college or graduated from college; and (3) all others who did not fit the previous group descriptions between the ages of 15 and 25. To determine group status, an in-field screening question was used. The completion rate was slightly lower for the high school sample (62.5 percent versus 65.7 percent).

Stage 4: National Civic Engagement Survey I

The primary data we rely on in this book come from NCES1, which was conducted between April 4 and May 20, 2002. We employed Schulman, Ronca, and Bucavalas, Inc., to conduct a nationally representative telephone survey of respondents aged 15 and older. Owing to our focus on youth, DotNets and GenXers were oversampled (N = 1001 and 1000, respectively). We rounded out our sample by interviewing 604 Baby Boomers and 602 Dutifuls. Thus, our sample contains both a cross-section of all respondents aged 15 and older at the time of the survey and a disproportionately large sample of our two youngest cohorts. We weighted according to the proper educational, gender, racial, and ethnic characteristics of the general population based on census data. We also included a weight to ensure the accurate proportional representation of the four age cohorts.

For the cross-section, interviewers asked to speak with the person in the household aged 15 and older with the most recent birthday. Parents or guardians were asked for permission to speak with respondents not of legal age in order to provide informed consent. Similar procedures were used for selecting respondents for the two youth oversamples. We first filled our quota for the DotNet demographic by asking to speak with the person in the household between the ages of 15 and 25 with the most recent birthday. Parental consent was obtained before proceeding to speak with the respondent. Once the DotNet quota was filled and the person on the phone said there were GenXers in the household, interviewers asked to speak with that person between the ages of 26 and 37 with the most recent birthday.

Stage 5: Validation, Verification, and Supplementation — National Civic Engagement Survey II

In order to test the stability and reliability of certain measures, we conducted a second national survey shortly after the 2002 election. The NCES2 obtained telephone interviews with a nationally representative sample of 1,400 adults living in continental United States telephone households. The interviews were conducted in English by Princeton Data Source and Schulman, Ronca, and Bucuvalas from November 14 to November 20, 2002.[3]

As many as 10 attempts were made to contact every sampled telephone number. Calls were staggered over times of day and days of the week to maximize the chance of making contact with potential respondents. Each household received at least one daytime call in an attempt to find someone at home. In each contacted household, interviewers asked to speak with the youngest male currently at home. If no male was available, interviewers asked to speak with the oldest female at home. This systematic respondent selection technique has been shown to produce samples that closely mirror the population in terms of age and gender.

The interviewed sample of all adults was weighted by form to match national parameters for sex, age, education, race, Hispanic origin, and region (U.S. Census definitions). These parameters came from a special analysis of the March 2001 Current Population Survey (CPS), which included all households in the continental United States that had a telephone.

The contact, cooperation, completion, and response rates for the NCES2 are as follows.

- Contact rate — the proportion of working numbers where a request for interview was made: 64 percent
- Cooperation rate — the proportion of contacted numbers where a consent for interview was at least initially obtained, versus those refused: 55 percent
- Completion rate — the proportion of initially cooperating and eligible interviews that were completed: 96 percent
- Response rate: 33 percent

Factor Analysis for Electoral, Civic, and Voice
Dimensions of Engagement

Appendix table 2 presents results from a factor analysis using Varimax rotation that demonstrates how we arrived at our three dimensions of behavior. The list of variables excludes two items that tapped behaviors that were very similar to two other items in the list: "boycotting" and signing electronic petitions. Similarly, two types of fund raising for charity were combined into a single indicator. The factor analysis was thus conducted on 16, rather than 19, separate indicators.

Voting and Nonvoting (Chapter 4)
General Problems in Measuring Registration and Voting in Surveys

The questions *How many are registered?* and *How many vote?* would seem to be straightforward questions. And they are. It is the answers that are a little curvy. And so before we move to estimates, we wish to begin this section with a few caveats of measurement and definition.

APPENDIX TABLE 2

Factor Analysis for Electoral, Civic, and Voice Dimensions of Engagement

	Electoral	Civic	Voice
Regular volunteer for a nonpolitical organization	.75		
Community problem solving	.69		
Active membership in a group or organization	.65		
Raise money for charity	.48		
Display campaign buttons, stickers, etc.		.73	
Contribute money to a political organization or candidate		.62	
Vote regularly		.55	
Persuade others politically		.55	
Volunteer for a political organization or candidate		.47	
Protest			.60
Boycott			.56
Sign a written petition			.52
Call into radio talk show			.50
Contact elected official			.47
Contact print media			.42
Canvass			.31

Caution 1: Social Desirability

It is always difficult to estimate the incidence of behaviors when they are known to have a socially desirable patina in the political culture. The icon of "voting" no doubt has continued currency in which a good citizen is supposed to trade, making estimates from a public opinion survey or set of surveys subject to inflation. No doubt, error is disproportionately one way. There remain more pressures for a respondent to tell an interviewer that he or she does do something that is valued by the dominant cultural norm than there are reverse incentives for the same respondent to report not having engaged in a behavior when she or he has in fact done so.

But are cultural pressures for a socially desirable response constant for our age groupings? Do DotNets feel the same pressures as Dutifuls to overreport socially desirable behaviors, given that fewer of them report engaging in the behavior? If so, a comparative analysis of registration and voting spanning our ages—from DotNets to Xers to Boomers to Dutifuls—would find a consistency of overreporting, and one could have faith in the relative differences between age groups, even if one was not sure of the absolute level. However, should we believe that this norm applies with unequal force to the different age groups, we would expect less pressure for the culturally desirable responses of being registered and having voted among the younger age groups, for whom the norms have not been fully inculcated or taken root. In this case, we would expect observed differences between generations to overstate the actual differences in the population. All the data we present are based on citizen response to opinion surveys that, while we know them to overreport socially desirable behavior, may also be subject to an interaction effect between such acts and cohorts the magnitude of which we can only guess. So we have a first caveat emptor with regard to social desirability.

Caution 2: Different Modes, Different Estimates

As practitioners, we well understand that survey methods interact with survey findings. While we believe that a mixed-mode approach is a source of strength in the long run, it may also produce some inconsistencies in the short. Here some of our estimates are from self-administered Internet samples; others are from telephone surveys. Differences in modes, response rates, and field houses used to collect data all may introduce sources of variation in estimates of behaviors.

Caution 3: Different Bases, Different Statements

There has been some debate lately about the difference between the voting *age* population (VAP) and the voting *eligible* population (VEP) as a measure of turnout. In computations of the former, the number of those actually voting is put over the denominator of all those over 17 years of age; in the latter, the denominator is a lower figure corrected by estimates of the number ineligible to vote for a variety of reasons such as noncitizenship or institutionalization.[4] Given that a higher number of younger residents may be immigrants, failure to adjust the VAP (those who are eligible to vote and who comprise the sampling frame for participation in surveys) to the VEP might artificially overstate the differences in electoral activity between the two younger and older generations.

Roadmap to Our Measures: Data Sources and Questions Asked

Unfortunately, we do not have all the data we would like to address these questions. The main telephone survey (NCES1) was not designed with this purpose in mind. However, we were able to insert questions exploring the motives behind nonparticipation on two subsequent surveys. Each data set has limitations, although they are somewhat offsetting. Together, however, they afford us the opening of a small window into the world of noninvolvement among today's youth.

We included a number of questions on the second telephone survey (NCES2) examining those who chose not to participate in the electoral arena. We asked all respondents if they were eligible and then if they were registered to vote. If so, they were asked how frequently they voted in elections and if they had voted in the national elections of 2002, which took place just two weeks before the survey was fielded. Those not registered[5] were read a list of seven closed-ended reasons why they had not done so, and asked to indicate whether each was a *major* reason why not, a *minor* reason, or *not a reason* at all. Registered voters who sat out the election were asked to respond to the same seven items as possible reasons why they might not have voted. This data set has the advantage of being tied to asking motivations about a specific, recently occurring election, but it has the disadvantage of being relatively shallow in its base of respondents. The NCES2 survey was not stratified by age cohort, giving us smaller samples of DotNets and GenXers to work with than we would have liked.

The National Conference of State Legislatures (NCSL) survey conducted in the summer of 2003 offsets these features. Because it over-sampled DotNets, it has a fairly robust respondent base of young adults.[6] But the dependent variable of electoral participation is keyed not to a specific election but to whether people reported having voted in "all," "most," "some," or "not many or no" elections. Nonparticipants were presented with nine reasons and asked to check off all those why they were not registered or did not always vote, as appropriate.

It is worth noting that because the two surveys have different "voting" questions acting as filters to define nonparticipants, they let differential numbers through this screen. However, we think this is not an important concern for two reasons. First, even though done through different modes and at slightly different times, the NCES2 (telephone) and NCSL (Internet) surveys produced virtually identical estimates of registered voters, the one question that was the same on both surveys (see appendix table 3). Second, as demonstrated by the virtually parallel lines in the

APPENDIX TABLE 3
Registered to Vote: NCES2 and
NCSL Estimates

	NCES2	NCSL
DotNets	64%	64%
GenXers	76%	79%
Boomers	84%	84%
Dutifuls	88%	90%

Source: NCES2 and NCSL.

adjacent figure in their relationship to the generational cohorts, the screens functioned quite consistently between the two samples (appendix figure 1). The percentages indicate the proportion of each group classified as nonparticipants.

As noted, the results from the NCSL analysis, presented in appendix table 4, are largely confirming. In this case, we have had to contrast DotNets with "all others" to achieve even a minimum sample size in the "other category," even though including Xers with the older two groups minimizes "DotNet–Other" differences.

While more reasons for not voting are given in responses to the NCSL survey — both as a function of asking about more items in this self-administered survey and asking only for "reasons" as opposed to "major reasons" — we note the same patterns in the data as we described in the text of chapter 4. First, DotNets are less able to articulate any reason for not voting in all elections. Second, fewer nonparticipating DotNets give purposive reasons for not voting, such as being alienated, being turned off by politics or the negative character of politics, and not seeing a difference between candidates they are asked to choose between. They are much more likely than older respondents to feel they don't have enough information to cast an informed vote, and somewhat more likely to say they do not vote for reasons of convenience. Finally, an important

APPENDIX FIGURE 1
Percentage identified as nonparticipant in NCES2 and NCSL.

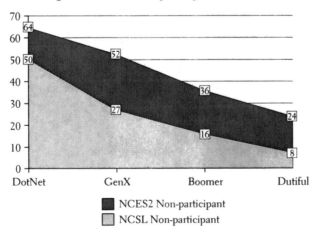

observation is that very few DotNets (or others for that matter) say they do not vote because they think they can make more of a difference by volunteering in their communities. All in all, it is very hard to find a clear answer to the question of why young citizens are disproportionately absent from the electoral realm. Neither in the Internet or telephone survey did we find a key to open the door of nonvoting by looking through the self-reports of motivation. There is certainly as much in these data to suggest the problem may be a lack of relevancy as there is to suggest a rejection of politics. Perhaps simply not having a good enough reason *to* participate is also a good enough reason *not* to.

APPENDIX TABLE 4
Reasons for Not Voting in the NCSL Survey

	DotNets	All Others
*Reasons for not registering/not voting**		
I'm not interested in politics	35%	41%
I'm not informed enough to make a decision	39%	27%
I am turned off by the process/negative political advertising	27%	43%
I dislike politics and government/I don't trust politics	27%	35%
It's hard to get reliable information about the candidates	24%	27%
I don't have time/I'm often away/It's inconvenient	22%	18%
My one vote isn't going to make much of a difference	16%	18%
I can make more of a difference by volunteering in my local community	14%	12%
There's often no difference between the two candidates	13%	34%
None of the above	26%	13%
Number of these nine reasons given by respondents		
0 reasons	28%	12%
1 reason	26%	31%
2 reasons	13%	15%
3 or more reasons	33%	41%
Mean number of reasons	2%	2.4%
Total number of cases	214	100

*Multiple responses accepted; entries are expressed as percentages.
Source: NCSL.

Notes

Chapter 1

1. These are the results of a "what if" simulation we ran for the 16 states in which the losing candidate received at least 47 percent of the vote. We adjusted the turnout for four age ranges, 18–29, 30–44, 45–59, and 60-plus, so that their proportion of the vote was set to their incidence in the population (from census figures) rather than the distribution of actual turnout on election day (from Voter News Service estimates). The division of the vote for each candidate in each age group was held constant from the Voter News Service election day exit poll. Gore would have won Florida, where those between 18 and 29 years of age divided their vote 55 percent for Gore to 40 percent for Bush. Unfortunately for Gore, while those under 30 years of age made up 19 percent of the state's population, they comprised a slimmer 15 percent of those going to the polls on election day. Even this small turnout differential between those eligible to vote and those actually voting would have switched the outcome of Florida.

Chapter 2

1. Loeb (1994) challenges the emphasis that Strauss and Howe (1993) place on the significance of the rise in divorce rates for Xers, citing scholarship that indicates that not all children suffer as a result of their parents' divorce. How-

ever, one could argue that even if the individual effects of divorce are, fortunately, less drastic than Strauss and Howe suggest, the increased prevalence of divorce in American society does send a message of institutional disintegration.

2. See, for example, the report prepared for the Kettering Foundation by the Harwood Group entitled *College Students Talk Politics* (1993).

3. Although clearly an overstatement for those with an understanding of American history and an appreciation for the 25 percent unemployment figures that confronted young people in the 1930s, the economic "disadvantages" of this generation are starkest when compared to those of their immediate predecessors (and to early expectations).

4. Indeed, some argue that the phenomenon of more Xers attending college is another indicator of poor secondary education, in that high schools no longer provided adequate training. Others argue that this is reflective of changes in the labor market. Either explanation (or both together) suggests that for Xers, a high school diploma was no longer adequate preparation for earning a living wage in the workforce.

5. Edmondson (1992).

6. Note that Skocpol and Fiorina (1999a) document the increasing professionalization of politics, arguing that organizations today don't want members to be active, they only want their money.

7. According to the College Board, the average math SAT score of those entering college classes in 2003 was 518, the highest since 1967; the average verbal score was 508, the highest score since 1986 (up from a low of 499 in 1994).

Chapter 3

1. While such behaviors have been duly noted by political scientists, no consensus exists on how best to categorize them. For example, Verba and Nie saw contacting officials as occupying its own dimension (1972), while Barnes and Kaase (1979) assigned demonstrations, petitions, and boycotts to the category "unconventional participation," despite the relatively high incidence of the latter two.

2. See the appendix for more detail on the composition of the focus groups.

3. Some, such as canvassing, protesting, or working as a volunteer for someone seeking elected office, are rare but not so rare that a large survey will miss them.

4. We did not include cognitive engagement in this analysis because we wanted to focus on participatory behaviors intended to affect the political or civic world. The individual measures of cognitive engagement do cohere into a common factor.

5. We do not include voter registration among our 19 indicators because it is unavailable to part of our youngest cohort (we do include intention to vote for these individuals).

6. This self-reported percentage may be somewhat inflated—according to the post–2000 election Current Population Survey, approximately 70 percent of U.S. adult citizens are registered to vote. The Federal Election Commission reports, on the basis of population estimates and reported voter registration totals from each state (the latter are also widely acknowledged to be somewhat inflated), that 76 percent of the voting age population is registered.

7. A person's estimate of his or her regularity of voting may be preferable to reported turnout in any given election. Compared with many other Western nations, the United States holds more elections and makes voting more difficult (via registration requirements, holding elections on workdays, and the like). The low turnout for any given election may yield a somewhat misleading conclusion regarding citizen disengagement.

8. With the possible exception of voting, none of the items in our index is, of itself, a *necessary* behavior for engaged citizenship. Instead, the behaviors are simply *indicators* of latent constructs of engagement. As with all measurement, more indicators mean better (i.e., more reliable) measurement.

The question, of course, is how many activities are needed to cross the threshold. Setting a standard of only one activity would mean that 78 percent of the population would be judged to be active in one or both dimensions; this seems too high, given all we know about citizen engagement in public life. Similarly, requiring three activities would mean that only about one-fourth of the public could be considered active in one or both dimensions. This is more plausible than the 78 percent figure, especially to the pessimists among us, but it also seems too low, given that off-year voter turnout—a fairly stringent indicator of electoral engagement—exceeds this figure. When considering both the civic and electoral dimensions, surely more than a quarter of the public is engaged in public life. Thus, the standard of two or more activities in each dimension seems defensible.

We also considered the case of people who do one thing in each of the two core dimensions. These individuals constitute about 9 percent of the adult population, and fall between the disengaged and the specialist groups in other measures of activism. For the sake of parsimony, we ultimately decided not to treat them as a distinct group.

9. Items within each dimension were combined into a scale using factor analysis, and the factor scores for each individual were then averaged for each age category. These averages are plotted in the figures as a "moving average."

10. Researchers at the Higher Education Research Institute at UCLA have

documented significant fall-off in civic engagement during the postcollege years. See Vogelgesang and Astin (2005).

11. DotNets not yet old enough to have voted are somewhat more sanguine about their prospects as voters: 44 percent say expect that they will always vote.

12. The HERI surveys have many virtues, but it should also be noted that they are limited to the population of four-year college students, which is changing. Many more young people are going to four-year colleges today, compared with the 1960s and 1970s. Consequently, this population is more heterogeneous and perhaps less elite socially and economically now than it was in the early years of the survey. One result of this is that surveys based on four-year college students may understate the strength of the trend toward greater civic engagement among all youth, and relatedly may overstate the extent of political disengagement, despite the fact that it remains, in some respects, an elite survey.

13. "Buycott" is a term used by both the Left and Right. A search using Google shows that buycotting is encouraged for causes as different as Dixie Chicks records, local gun stores, and American-made automobiles.

Chapter 4

1. This national survey was conducted with a nationwide sample of 1,500 young people between 15 and 25 years of age in January 2002. Figures reported here are based on those 18 and older only.

2. A full discussion of these issues for those specialists in voting behavior may be found in the appendix, which also includes a full description of procedures used in constructing nonvoting measures.

3. The results from the NCSL analysis are presented in the appendix.

4. We also asked a general lifestyle (nonpolitical context) question about the role of duty versus choice, and found no cohort differences. There was little intergenerational difference in the agreement with the statements "I do things out of duty, because I'm supposed to" or "I do things only when I want to do them."

5. This survey, conducted in the summer of 2003, included 632 DotNets, 159 GenXers, 255 Boomers, and 240 Dutifuls. Data used in analysis are weighted back to proportional representation of the four age groups within the U.S. population at the time of the survey.

6. The final row of each item in table 4.2 shows percentages with "don't know" responses omitted.

7. Items were randomized upon administration

8. Unfortunately, we have data on this item only for DotNets.

9. We conducted a principal component factor analysis of these 17 dichotomous items, with a varimax rotation and pairwise deletion of missing data.

10. The survey was conducted with a random sample of 1,002 New Jersey residents 18 years and older between April 24 and May 4, 2003. Details for poll 143 can be found at the Rutgers University Web site hosting data collected by the *Star-Ledger*/Eagleton-Rutgers Poll: http://slerp.rutgers.edu.

11. The "community" question read: "Thinking about the problems you see in your community, how much difference do you believe YOU can personally make in working to solve problems you see—a great deal of difference, some difference, a little difference, or no difference at all?" The "efficacy" question read: "People like me don't have any say about what the government does." (Agree/Disagree). The first is from the NCES1; the second from a survey conducted in August 2003 by the PRC.

Chapter 5

1. This is reinforced by the work of Highton and Wolfinger (2001), who found that although the adult-roles theory partially explains lower levels of turnout among youth, it falls far short of explaining the full gap between young and old.

2. Since the factors that motivate participation are the same for all age groups, most of the analysis in this chapter is based on the full sample, not just young people.

3. The field is rich with research on citizen engagement. We list here just a few of the more notable works in recent years: Rosenstone and Hansen (1993), Verba, Schlozman, and Brady (1995); Nie, Junn, and Stehlik-Barry (1996); and Burns, Schlozman, and Verba (2001).

4. Missing from our list of "initial characteristics" is income, a common socioeconomic status indicator. Indeed, we found sizable differences in citizen engagement between people in higher versus lower income households. For example, those with annual incomes in excess of $65,000 are almost three times as likely to have donated to a candidate, party, or other organization that supports candidates as those who report incomes of less than $30,000 a year (23 percent versus 8 percent, respectively). However, we chose to exclude income from our model because (1) a correlation analysis comparing the relationship of a host of possible precursors to the various dimensions of engagement showed that household income is among those that are only weakly related; (2) we believe education—a later step in our model—is a sufficient indicator for socioeconomic status; and (3) there was a significant amount of missing data in this indicator.

5. Minority status comprises two variables—one that indicates whether a respondent is a person of color, and another that accounts for nonnative birth in the United States.

6. For a thorough analysis of the conditions under which education promotes citizen engagement, see Nie, Junn, and Stehlik-Barry (1996).

7. Of course, television is also an information medium. It's possible that watching more of it may expose people to societal problems and thus spur their involvement in order to change what they heard about or saw on television. But this is unlikely, since the array of things to watch on the tube are largely designed to entertain, not inform.

8. See, for instance, Brehm and Rahn (1997) and Putnam (2000).

9. The difference between Nets and older citizen narrows but remains significant when we include a related question regarding civic duty. Thirty–two percent of GenXers, Boomers, and Dutifuls endorsed "It is my responsibility to get involved to make things better for society" and "Being a good citizen means having some special obligations," compared to only 21 percent of Nets.

10. Of course, attention to news and political knowledge are both important resources for participation and forms of engagement in and of themselves.

11. For a thorough analysis of the importance of mobilization for citizen engagement, see Rosenstone and Hansen (1993).

12. Maximum likelihood estimation was used to approximate the effect of each set of variables on the various types of citizen engagement. Standardized coefficients are presented in each subsequent table.

13. See, for instance, Verba, Schlozman, and Brady (1995); Youniss, Mc-Lellan, and Yates (1997); Astin, Sax, and Avalos (1999); Wilson (2000); Conway and Damico (2001); Flanagan and Faison (2001); Perry and Katula (2001); and Kirlin (2002). Interestingly, scholars have documented that the connection between high school activities and later civic involvement is not linear—activists in high school are more likely than their less active counterparts to be involved as adults, but only after a "sleeper" period in which they are relatively disconnected from civic life (Jennings and Stoker 2001).

14. See, for instance, Galston (2001). One recent study that does address this question has documented a positive relationship between open classroom discussions and higher levels of civic knowledge as a teenager and greater propensity to vote as an adult (Torney-Purta, Lehmann, Oswald, and Schulz 2001).

15. As with many studies about the role of schools in the political socialization of teenagers and adults, the decentralized nature of education in America poses particular difficulties. Our measures of institutional support, for example, can document whether or not students are provided with an opportunity to discuss their service work in a classroom setting, but it cannot tell us about the nature of that discussion, the skill with which a teacher facilitates talk, or

even the number of students enrolled in the class. Despite these obstacles, a major advantage of these two data sets is their large sample size, which allows us to analyze differences among groups within this age cohort; the surveys were also very extensive, providing a wide range of measures of political, civic, and school-level engagement of young people today.

16. A school requirement for volunteer work might not specify the year in which the work had to be done; thus it is not illogical that some students faced with this requirement did not actually volunteer this year.

17. See, for instance, Verba, Schlozman, and Brady (1995).

18. The variable for participation in high school organizations is a scale from 0 to 3 that indicates whether a respondent is involved in no organizations, one organization, two organizations, or three or more organizations.

19. To test the impact of this assumption on our analysis, we experimented with several alternatives. First, we moved the attentiveness measure to the other side of the equation, making it a predictor variable instead of part of the dependent variable. There was no real difference in our overall ability to explain the variance (the r square was essentially unchanged), although including it slightly altered the statistical significance of some of the other independent variables. When we removed the variable from our analysis altogether (as both a predictor and an outcome), we explained less of the variance (lower r square) and had a slightly different mix of statistical significance for a few variables. None of these changes greatly affected the substance of our conclusions, however, and we remain convinced by the theoretical rationale for its inclusion in the dependent variable.

20. Specifically, we used the following measures: working with others to solve a community problem, attending a local government or neighborhood meeting, participating in a walk, run, or bike ride for charity, volunteering for groups (coded as none, one, two, or more), contacting a government official, participating in a boycott, signing an e-mail petition, following news of politics and government, talking about the news, talking about political news, serving as an officer or representative or working on a campaign for student government, self-reported level of attention to student government, the number of organizations involved in and out of high school (with sports excluded—an option that was not available for the NCES1).

21. See, for example, Burns, Schlozman, and Verba (2001).

Chapter 6

1. Based on PRC polls conducted August 2003–April 2004.
2. The 2000 National Election Studies' standard seven-point scale on gov-

ernment spending and services found 51 percent of the youngest cohort (aged 18–22) and 48 percent of those aged 23–30 favoring expanded services, compared with 39 percent for the sample as a whole.

3. A survey conducted on behalf of the Third Millennium showed that only 28 percent of people aged 18–34 think Social Security will exist when they retire; 46 percent think UFOs exist.

4. For the sake of clarity, the box omits data from 1994, when all cohorts manifested stronger antigovernment sentiment. This "period effect" moderated after 1994.

5. The PRC October 2003 poll (Pew Research Center 2003b).

Chapter 7

1. Keep in mind that our operating definition of "disengagement" is reporting having done fewer than two of the civic or political acts included in our surveys over the past year.

2. Putnam does acknowledge that voluntary activity has increased among younger Americans, though unlike our own data, his suggest that even in this arena they lag behind the age cohort we label the Dutifuls. And consistent with Putnam's argument, we find that younger Americans are less engaged in traditional politics than older cohorts, and less trusting of their fellow citizens. Nonetheless, the overall thrust of Putnam's thesis—that generational replacement is driving a large portion of the overall decline in social capital in the United States—misses what we believe is a more complex and mixed story of young people's involvement in public life.

3. The overall incidence of volunteer work within the past year among New Jersey residents (35 percent) was comparable to what we found for the U.S. public at large (39 percent in fall 2002), giving us some confidence that our findings from the New Jersey sample would have relevance beyond this single state.

4. We also asked whether their work involved something the government should address or whether it was something for people in the community to address on their own. And we asked whether, in the past 12 months, they had contacted a government official as a part of this work. We asked this series of follow-up questions about volunteering, as well as about a related form of civic involvement—working with others to solve a community problem.

5. Tellingly, 75 to 80 percent of those selecting these issues voted for the challenger, John Kerry. Nineteen percent of voters selected the war on terror as the most important issue, 86 percent of whom voted for President Bush, helping to give him his slight margin of victory in 2004.

Appendix

1. A public report that details our initial findings and the index of civic and political engagement can be found at the Web site: www.civicyouth.org (Keeter et al. 2002b).

2. For a description of what we found in our experiments, see Keeter, Zukin, Andolina, and Jenkins (2002).

3. In the course of analyzing the data collected during the main wave of data gathering, a number of subsequent methodological and substantive questions arose, as is always the case. We wished to explore the reliability of a particular set of civic engagement behaviors that would form the core of an index and were concerned about the possibility of a "house effect" in estimates of a particularly important variable measuring the rate of volunteering. Our desire to explore field house effects stemmed principally from what we observed regarding the measurement of volunteer activity. The identical question asked in a survey conducted by the PRC not long after we completed our spring survey yielded an estimate of volunteer activity of 55 percent. This was in stark comparison to our spring estimate of 33 percent. Adding to our puzzlement were estimates gleaned from an omnibus survey that asked the same question in August 2002. Regardless of where the question was placed within the survey, around 4 in 10 (43 or 44 percent) respondents reported volunteer activity in the previous 12 months. Thus, because we had some evidence to disconfirm our theory that where the question was placed relative to others in the questionnaire affected estimates of volunteer activity, we turned our attention to the possibility that differences between field houses might explain the findings.

In order to establish the reliability of our core indicators of engagement as measured in our original survey and assess house effects in regard to volunteer activity, we conducted two identical and simultaneously administered telephone surveys using different field houses in the fall of 2002. Schulman, Ronca, and Bucuvalas, Inc., the field house that collected our original data, was used again in order to validate findings from our original survey. Princeton Data Services was the other company chosen to validate our findings from our original survey findings, as well as account for the possible influence of field house effects on the measurement of volunteer activity. Each field house surveyed a total of 700 respondents. A reduced version of the spring instrument was used by both field houses. Questions measuring the core indicators of engagement remained in their original sequence.

A full accounting of what we found regarding field house effects is addressed in Zukin, Jenkins, Andolina, and Keeter (2003).

4. See McDonald and Popkin (2001).

5. Those not eligible to be registered have been excluded from this analysis.

Thus this examination of nonparticipation is based on those who could have participated but chose not to do so.

6. While starting with 632 DotNets, this number is reduced to 456 once those ineligible to participate have been excluded. Again, the analysis in this section excludes those not eligible for reasons of age, citizenship, or institutionalization from the base of nonparticipants.

Bibliography

AIDS Project Los Angeles. 2003. "Timeline of the Epidemic." Available at: http://www.apla.org/facts/timeline.html. Accessed December 31, 2005.

Astin, A. W., Linda J. Sax, and J. Avalos. 1999. "The Long-Term Effects of Voluntarism during the Undergraduate Years." *Review of Higher Education* 21, 2: 187–202.

Barber, Benjamin R. 1984. *Strong Democracy: Participatory Politics for a New Age*. Berkeley: University of California Press.

Barker, Lucius J., Mack Jones, and Katherine Tate. 1994. *African Americans and the American Political System*. Englewood Cliffs, N.J.: Prentice Hall.

Barnes, Samuel H., and Max Kaase. 1979. *Political Action: An Eight Nation Study*. Beverly Hills, Calif.: Sage.

Boyte, Harry C., and James Farr. 2000. "The Work of Citizenship and the Problem of Service-Learning." *Campus Compact Reader* 1: 4–10.

Brady, Henry E. 1999. "Political Participation." In *Measures of Political Attitudes*, ed. John P. Robinson, Phillip R. Shaver, and Lawrence S. Wrightsman. New York: Academic Press.

Brehm, John, and Wendy Rahn. 1997. "Individual-level Evidence for the Causes and Consequences of Social Capital." *American Journal of Political Science* 41: 99–1023.

Brokaw, Tom. 1998. *The Greatest Generation*. New York: Random House.

Brooks, David. 2001. "Organization Kid." *Atlantic Monthly*, April, 40–46, 48–54.

Bureau of the Public Debt. 2001. "Historical Debt Outstanding—Annual 1950–

2000." Available at: http://www.publicdebt.treas.gov/opd/opdhisto4.htm. Accessed December 31, 2005.

Burns, Nancy, Kay Lehman Schlozman, and Sidney Verba. 2001. *The Private Roots of Public Action : Gender, Equality, and Political Participation*. Cambridge, Mass.: Harvard University Press.

Campbell, David E. 2002. "The Young and the Realigning: A Test of the Socialization Theory of Realignment." *Public Opinion Quarterly* 66: 209–234.

Caplow, Theodore, Louis Hicks, and Ben J. Wattenberg. 2000. *The First Measured Century: An Illustrated Guide to Trends in America, 1900–2000*. Washington, D.C.: AEI Press.

Carlson, Darren K. 2003. "GenXers Go from Grunge to Gingrich." Gallup Organization: http://poll.gallup.com/content/default.aspx?ci=9133. Accessed December 31, 2005.

Carnegie Corporation. 2003. "The Civic Mission of Schools." Carnegie Corporation of New York and Center for Information and Research on Civic Learning and Engagement: http://www.civicmissionofschools.org/. Accessed December 31, 2005.

Center for Information and Research on Civic Learning and Engagement. 2005. "Census Data Shows Youth Voter Turnout Surged More Than among Any Other Age Group." May 26, 2005: http://civicyouth.org/PopUps/ReleaseCPS04_Youth.pdf. Accessed December 31, 2005.

Chakravarty, Subrata N., and Katherine Weisman. 1988. "Consuming Our Children?" *Forbes* 142: 222–232.

Cohen, Jason, and Michael Krugman. 1994. *Generation Ecch! The Backlash Starts Here*. New York: Simon and Schuster.

Cohen, Michael Lee. 1993. *The Twenty-something American Dream: A Cross-Country Quest for a Generation*. New York: Dutton.

Committee for the Study of the American Electorate. 2005. "Turnout Exceeds Optimistic Expectations; More Than 122 Million Vote; Highest Turnout in Thirty-Eight Years." Washington, D.C.

Conger, John Janeway. 1988. "Hostages to Fortune, Youth, Values, and the Public Interest." *American Psychologist* 43: 291–300.

Conway, M. Margaret, and Alfonso J. Damico. 2001. "Building Blocks: The Relationship between High School and Adult Associational Life." Paper presented at the annual meeting of the American Political Science Association, San Francisco, August 30–September 2.

Council for Excellence in Government. 2004. "A Matter of Trust: Americans and Their Government, 1958–2004."Available at: http://excelgov.org/. Accessed December 31, 2005.

Crimmins, Eileen M., Richard A. Easterlin, and Yashuiko Saito. 1991. "What Young Adults Want." *American Demographics* 13: 23–33.

Cutler, Blayne. 1980. "Up the Down Staircase." *American Demographics* 11: 32–37.

Dahl, Robert Alan. 1989. *Democracy and Its Critics*. New Haven, Ct.: Yale University Press.

Delli Carpini, Michael X. 1986. *Stability and Change*. New York: New York University Press.

———. 1989. "Generations and Sociopolitical Change." In *Political Learning in Adulthood: A Sourcebook of Theory and Research*, ed. Roberta S. Sigel. Chicago: University of Chicago Press.

———. 2000. *The Youth Engagement Initiative: A Six-Year Plan for Increasing the Amount and Quality of Young Americans' Involvement in Public Life*. Philadelphia: Pew Charitable Trusts.

Dunn, William. 1992. "Hanging Out with American Youth." *American Demographics* 14: 24–33.

Easterlin, Richard A., and Eileen M. Crimmins. 1991. "Private Materialism, Personal Self-Fulfillment, Family Life, and Public Interest: The Nature, Effects, and Causes of Recent Changes in the Values of American Youth." *Public Opinion Quarterly* 55, 4: 499–533.

Erikson, Robert S., and Kent L. Tedin. 2002. *American Public Opinion: Its Origin, Contents, and Impact*. 6th ed. New York: Longman.

Fiorina, Morris P. 2002. "Parties, Participation, and Representation in America: Old Theories Face New Realities." In *Political Science: The State of the Discipline*, ed. Ira Milner Katznelson. New York: Norton.

Flanagan, Constance A., and Nakesha Faison. 2001. "Youth Civic Development Implications of Research for Social Policy and Programs." *Social Policy Report* 14: 3–14.

Freyman, Russ, and Brent McGoldrick. 2000. "They Pretend to Talk to Us, We Pretend to Vote: Candidates and Young Adults in Campaign 2000 and Beyond." Washington, D.C.: Third Millennium Project.

Galston, William A. 2001. "Political Knowledge, Political Engagement, and Civic Education." *Annual Review of Political Science* 4: 217–234.

Gerbner, George and Larry Gross. 1976. "Living with Television: The Violence Profile." *Journal of Communication* 26: 173–199.

Gibson, Cynthia. 2001. *From Inspiration to Participation: A Review of Perspectives on Youth Civic Engagement*. Berkeley, Calif.: Grantmaker Forum on Community and National Service.

Green, Donald P. 2004. "The Effects of Election Day Voter Mobilization Campaign Targeting Young Voters." Center for Information and Research on Civic Learning and Engagement: http://civicyouth.org/PopUps/WorkingPapers/WP21Green.pdf. Accessed December 31, 2005.

Green, Donald P., and Alan S. Gerber. 2004. *Get Out the Vote! How to Increase Voter Turnout*. Washington, D.C.: Brookings Institution Press.

Gurin, Patricia, Shirley Hatchett, and James S. Jackson. 1989. *Hope and Independence: Blacks' Response to Electoral and Party Politics*. New York: Russell Sage.

Halberstam, David. 1999. *Playing for Keeps: Michael Jordan and the World He Made*. New York: Random House.

Hanson, Russell L. 1985. *The Democratic Imagination in America: Conversations with Our Past*. Princeton, N.J.: Princeton University Press.

Harvard Institute of Politics. 2003. "New Poll Finds America's College Students Politically Conflicted, but Leaning in Favor of President Bush." October 20: http://www.iop.harvard.edu/pdfs/survey/fall_2003.pdf. Accessed December 31, 2005.

———. 2004. "College Students Plan to Vote in Record Numbers, Kerry Builds on Lead, Harvard Poll Finds." October 21: http://www.iop.harvard.edu/pdfs/newsroom/survey_fall_2004.pdf. Accessed December 31, 2005.

Hepburn, Mary A., ed. 2001. *Service-Learning and Civic Education in the Schools: What Does Recent Research Tell Us?* Bloomington: Indiana University Press.

Highton, Benjamin, and Raymond E. Wolfinger. 2001. "The First Seven Years of the Political Life Cycle." *American Journal of Political Science* 45: 202–209.

Holtz, Geoffrey T. 1995. *Welcome to the Jungle: The Why behind Generation X*. New York: St. Martin's Press.

Howe, Neil, and William Strauss. 2000. *Millennials Rising: The Next Great Generation*. New York: Random House.

Infoplease. 2001. "Abortions and Abortion Rates." Family Education Network: http://www.infoplease.com/ipa/A0005099.html. Accessed December 31, 2005.

Jacobs, Lawrence, Michael X. Delli Carpini, and Fay Lomax Cook. 2004. "How Do Americans Deliberate?" Paper presented at the annual meeting of the Midwest Political Science Association, Chicago, Ill., April 15–18.

Jenkins, Krista. 2003. "Exploring the Paradoxical Relationship between Feminist Consciousness and Participation." Ph.D. diss., Rutgers University.

Jennings, M. Kent, and Richard M. Niemi. 1981. *Generations and Politics*. Princeton, N.J.: Princeton University Press.

Jennings, M. Kent, and Laura Stoker. 2001. "Generations and Civic Engagement: A Longitudinal Multiple-Generation Analysis." Paper presented at the annual meeting of the American Political Science Association, San Francisco, Calif., August 30–September 2.

Johnson, Roy. 1988. "The Jordan Effect." *Fortune*, June 22, 124–131.

Kahne, Joseph, and Joel Westheimer. 1996. "In the Service of What? The Politics of Service Learning." *Phi Delta Kappan* 77: 593–599.

Keeter, Scott, Cliff Zukin, Molly Andolina, and Krista Jenkins. 2002a. "Improving the Measurement of Political Participation." Paper presented at the annual meeting of the Midwest Political Science Association, Chicago, Ill., April 25–28.

———. 2002b. "The Civic and Political Health of the Nation: A Generational Portrait." Available at: http://civicyouth.org/research/products/youth_index.htm. Accessed December 31, 2005.

Kettering Foundation. 1993. "College Students Talk Politics." Bethesda, Md.: Harwood Group.

Kirlin, Mary. 2002. "Civic Skills Building: The Missing Component in Service Programs?" *PS* 35: 571–576.

Levine, Peter, and Hugo Mark Lopez. 2002. "Youth Voter Turnout Has Declined, by Any Measure." Center for Information and Research on Civic Learning and Engagement: http://www.civicyouth.org/research/products/Measuring_Youth_Voter_Turnout.pdf. Accessed December 31, 2005.

Lipsky, David, and Alexander Abrams. 1994. *Late Bloomers*. New York: Random House.

Loeb, Paul Rogat. 1994. *Generation at the Crossroads: Apathy and Action on the American Campus*. New Brunswick, N.J.: Rutgers University Press.

Mannheim, Karl. 1952. *The Problem of Generations*. London: Routledge.

Mattson, Kevin. 2000. *Higher Education and Civic Renewal: A Report for the Carnegie Corporation of New York*. New York: Carnegie Corporation.

McDonald, Michael, and Samuel Popkin. 2001. "The Myth of the Vanishing Voter." *American Political Science Review* 95: 963–974.

Meacham, Jon. 1995. "The Truth about Twenty-Somethings." *Washington Monthly* 27: 21–26.

Meredith, Geoffrey, and Charles Shewe. 1994. "The Power of Cohorts." *American Demographics* 16: 22–31.

Miller, Arthur, Patricia Gurin, and Oksana Malanchuk. 1981. "Group Consciousness and Political Participation." *American Journal of Political Science* 25: 494–511.

Morin, Richard. 2001. "Gen Y Goes AWOL." *Washington Post*, April 9. B05.

Morone, James A. 1990. *The Democratic Wish: Popular Participation and the Limits of American Government*. New York: Basic Books.

Myers-Lipton, Scott J. 1998. "Effect of a Comprehensive Service-Learning Program on College Students' Civic Responsibility." *Teaching Sociology* 26: 243–258.

National Association of Secretaries of State. 1999. *New Millenium Project–Part 1: American Youth Attitudes on Politics, Citizenship, Government, and Voting*. Washington, D.C.: National Association of Secretaries of State.

National Commission on Civic Renewal. 1998. "A Nation of Spectators: How Civic Disengagement Weakens America and What We Can Do About It." College Park, Md.

National Election Pool (ABC News, Associated Press, CBS News, CNN, Fox News, NBC News) and Edison Media Research and Mitofsky International, November 2, 2004. iPOLL Databank, The Roper Center for Public Opinion Research, University of Connecticut: http://www.ropercenter.uconn.edu/ipoll.html.

National Election Studies. 1960–2000. Center for Political Studies, University of Michigan: http://www.electionstudies.org/nesguide/nesguide.htm.

Nie, Norman H., Jane Junn, and Kenneth Stehlik-Barry. 1996. *Education and Democratic Citizenship in America*. Chicago: University of Chicago Press.

Niemi, Richard M. 2000. *Trends in Political Science as They Relate to Pre-College Curriculum and Teaching*. Woods Hole, Mass.: Social Science Education Consortium.

Pateman, Carole. 1970. *Participation and Democratic Theory*. Cambridge: Cambridge University Press.

Patterson, Thomas E. 1993. *Out of Order*. New York: Knopf.

———. 2002. *The Vanishing Voter: Public Involvement in an Age of Uncertainty*. New York: Knopf.

Perry, James C., and Michael C. Katula. 2001. "Does Service Affect Citizenship?" *Administration and Society* 33: 330–365.

Pew Research Center for the People and the Press. 1992. "Campaign '92: Survey 7, Generation Divide." July 8: http://people-press.org/reports/display.php3?ReportID=19920708. Accessed December 31, 2005.

———. 1994. "The New Political Landscape." September 21: http://people-press.org/reports/display.php3?ReportID=19940921. Accessed December 31, 2005.

———. 1998. "Deconstructing Distrust: How Americans View Government." March 10: http://people-press.org/reports/display.php3?ReportID=95. Accessed December 31, 2005.

———. 1999. "Retro Politics: The Political Typology, Version 3.0." November 11: http://people-press.org/reports/display.php3?ReportID=50. Accessed December 31, 2005.

———. 2003a. "The 2004 Political Landscape: Evenly Divided and Increasingly Polarized." November 5: http://people-press.org/reports/display.php3?ReportID=196. Accessed December 31, 2005.

———. 2003b. "Religious Beliefs Underpin Opposition to Homosexuality." November 18: http://people-press.org/reports/display.php3?ReportID=197. Accessed December 31, 2005.

———. 2004a. "Public Opinion Little Changed by Presidential Election." December 20: http://people-press.org/reports/display.php3?ReportID=234. Accessed December 31, 2005.

———. 2004b. "Young People More Engaged, More Uncertain." September 30: http://people-press.org/commentary/display.php3?AnalysisID=99. Accessed December 31, 2005.

———. 2005a. "Beyond Red versus Blue." May 10: http://people-press.org/reports/display.php3?ReportID=242. Accessed December 31, 2005.

———. 2005b. "Public More Critical of Press, but Goodwill Persists." June 26, 2005: http://people-press.org/reports/display.php3?ReportID=248. Accessed December 31, 2005.

———. 2005c. "Trends 2005." January 24. http://pewresearch.org/trends/. Accessed December 31, 2005.

Project for Excellence in Journalism. 2005. "The State of the News Media, 2005." Available at: http://www.stateofthenewsmedia.org/2005/index.asp. Accessed December 31, 2005.

Putnam, Robert D. 2000. *Bowling Alone: The Collapse and Revival of American Community*. New York: Simon and Schuster.

Putnam, Robert D., Robert Leonardi, and Raffaella Y. Nanetti. 1993. *Making Democracy Work: Civic Traditions in Modern Italy*. Princeton, N.J.: Princeton University Press.

Rahn, Wendy. 1998. "Generations and National Identity: A Data Essay." Communication in the Future of Democracy Workshop, Annenberg Center, Washington, D.C.

Rahn, Wendy, and John Transue. 1998. "Social Trust and Value Change: The Decline of Social Capital in American Youth, 1976–1995." *Political Psychology* 19: 545–565.

Rosen, Jay. 1999. *What Are Journalists For?* New Haven: Yale University Press.

Rosenstone, Steven J., and John Mark Hansen. 1993. *Mobilization, Participation, and Democracy in America*. New York: Macmillan.

Russkoff, Douglas, ed. 1994. *The Gen X Reader*. New York: Ballantine Books.

Schattschneider, E. E. 1942. *Party Government*. New York: Farrar and Rinehart.

Schattschneider, E. E. 1960. *The Semisovereign People: A Realist's View of Democracy in America*. New York: Holt, Rinehart, and Winston.

Sears, David O., ed. 1975. "Political Socialization." In *Handbook of Political Science*. Reading, Mass.: Addison-Wesley.

Skocpol, Theda. 1999. "How Americans Became Civic." In *Civic Engagement in American Democracy*, ed. Theda Skocpol and Morris P. Fiorina. Washington, D.C.: Brookings Institution Press.

————. 2003. *Diminished Democracy: From Membership to Management in American Civic Life*. Norman: University of Oklahoma Press.

Skocpol, Theda, and Morris P. Fiorina. 1999a. "Making Sense of the Civic Engagement Debate." In *Civic Engagement in American Democracy*, ed. Theda Skocpol and Morris P. Fiorina. Washington, D.C.: Brookings Institution Press.

————, eds. 1999b. *Civic Engagement in American Democracy*. Washington, D.C.: Brookings Institution Press.

Strauss, William, and Neil Howe. 1991. "The Cycle of Generations." *American Demographics* 13: 25–33.

————. 1993. *Thirteenth Gen: Abort, Ignore, Retry, Fail?* New York: Random House.

Tate, Katherine. 1993. *From Protest to Politics: The New Black Voters in American Elections*. Cambridge, Mass: Harvard University Press.

Tocqueville, Alexis de. 2001. *Democracy in America*. New York: Signet.

Tolleson-Rinehart, Sue. 1992. *Gender Consciousness and Politics*. New York: Routledge.

Torney-Purta, Judith, Rainer Lehmann, Hans Oswald, and Wolfram Schulz. 2001. *Citizenship and Education in Twenty-Eight Countries: Civic Knowledge and Engagement at Age Fourteen*. Amsterdam: International Association for the Evaluation of Educational Achievement.

United States Census. 2003. "Estimated Median Age at First Marriage, by Sex: 1890 to Present." Washington, D.C.

U.S. Dept. of Education. 1983. "A Nation at Risk: The Imperative for Education Reform." Washington, D.C., National Commission on Excellence in Education.

Uslaner, Eric. 2000. "Producing and Consuming Trust." *Political Science Quarterly* 115: 569–590.

Verba, Sidney, and Norman H. Nie. 1972. *Participation in America*. Chicago: University of Chicago Press.

Verba, Sidney, Kay Lehman Schlozman, and Henry E. Brady. 1995. *Voice and Equality: Civic Voluntarism in American Politics*. Cambridge, Mass.: Harvard University Press.

Vogelgesang, Lori J., and Alexander W. Astin. 2005, April. *Post College Civic Engagement among Graduates*. HERI research report number 2. Los Angeles: University of California.

Voter News Service survey by ABC News, CBS News, NBC News, Fox News, CNN, Associated Press and Voter News Service, November 7, 2000. iPOLL Databank, The Roper Center for Public Opinion Research, University of Connecticut: http://www.ropercenter.uconn.edu/ipoll.html.

Wade, R. Saxe. 1996. "Community Service-Learning in the Social Studies:

Historical Roots, Empirical Evident, Critical Issues." *Theory and Research in Social Education* 24: 332–359.

Washington Post, Henry J. Kaiser Family Foundation, August 2-September 1, 2002. iPOLL Databank, The Roper Center for Public Opinion Research, University of Connecticut: http://www.ropercenter.uconn.edu/ipoll.html. Accessed December 31, 2005.

Whitmie, Richard. 1996. "Experts Are Baffled: Why Are Social Barometers Suddenly Improving?" Gannett News Service.

Wilson, John. 2000. "Volunteering." *Annual Review of Sociology* 26: 215–240.

Youniss, James, Jeffrey A. McLellan, and Miranda Yates. 1997. "What We Know about Engendering Civic Identity." *American Behavioral Scientist* 40: 620–632.

Zukin, Cliff. 1997. Generation X and the News. Washington, D.C., Radio and Television News Directors Foundation: http://www.rtnda.org/resources/genx/. Accessed December 31, 2005.

Zukin, Cliff, Krista Jenkins, Molly Andolina, and Scott Keeter. 2003. "Test and Retest: Analyzing Survey Research Challenges to Measuring Civic and Political Behavior." Paper presented at the annual meeting of the American Association for Public Opinion Research, Nashville, Tennessee, May 15–18.

Index

Clinton, Bill, 14, 108–9, 156
  political scandals of, 40, 114
Cognitive engagement, 81–85, 198
  civic engagement and, 65–66
  by generation, 81–83, 82t
  media as source for, 81–83
  political engagement and, 65–66
  "public voice" v., 54–56
Cohen, Amy, 213
Cohen, Julie, 213
Community service, 229n11
  activism and, 50
  civic engagement and, 72
  volunteerism and, 196–97
Consumer activism. *See also* Political
    consumerism
  boycotts as, 80t
  "buycotting" as, 62, 77–79, 80t, 81,
    228n13
  DotNets as, 47–48
  political, 62, 77–81
  as "public voice," 75
Corporation for National Service, 213
Corporations
  DotNets and, perception of, 162t, 177,
    189
  governmental influence by, 117
  life impact by, 117t
  profit v. public interest within, 177t
Council for Excellence in Government,
    90–91
CPS (Current Population Survey), 217
  registered voters in, 227n6
Culbertson, Steve, 213
"Culture wars," 25
  abortion as part of, 179, 183
Current Population Survey. *See* CPS

Davis, Marco, 213
Dean, Howard, 210
Democracy, thin, 9
Democratic Party
  age demographics for, 6, 160–61
  gender demographics for, 160
"Disengagement," 232n1
  civic engagement v., 63
Divorce, GenXers and, 24–25, 225n1
DotNets, 12, 15, 18, 36–48
  abortion rates and, 37

abortion views of, 37, 168, 180f
AIDS and, 38
on citizenship, 98–99
civic engagement of, 67t
consumer identity of, 47–48
corporations and, perception of, 162t,
    177, 189
crime rates and, 37
cultural influences on, 21–22
demographics for, 15, 37
economic opportunities for, 37, 39–40
educational activism of, 39
ethnic diversity among, 158
on gender roles, 167
"generational identity" for, 94, 119
GenXers v., 20, 44–45
globalism and, 42, 46
homosexuality and, views on, 166–67
on interpersonal trust, 104, 119
liberalism of, 182–83
media influences on, 41–43
on national health insurance, 175f,
    182
nationalism of, 42
optimism of, 36–37
patriotism among, 180
political capital of, 137, 156
political engagement of, 40–46, 67t,
    69t, 122, 162
on political parties, 110f, 112t
pregnancy rates and, 37
racial tolerance among, 168–69, 204
religious tolerance among, 170
in Republican Party, 158–59
"soccer moms" and, 37
Social Security programs and, 158
social values of, 166–70, 177–80, 204
socialization of, 21
voter turnout projections, 156
voting demographics of, 68
"Dual activists," 64, 192, 198–99
  by generation, 193
Dutifuls, 14
  on citizenship, 97–98
  civic engagement of, 67t
  demographics for, 14
  government perceptions of, 29
  as "greatest generation," 14
  political engagement of, 67t, 69t

NYS (National Youth Survey)
  civic engagement as focus of, 55
  demographics of, 55, 139
  interpersonal trust as part of, 107t
  KN and, 215

Partisanship, political engagement and,
    130
Persian Gulf War. See Gulf War
Pew Charitable Trusts, viii, ix, 55, 211
Pew Research Center. See PRC
PKH (Washington Post/Kaiser/Harvard)
    group, 160–61, 164
Political capital, 129t
  civic engagement and, 128–29
  of DotNets, 137, 156
  "public voice" and, influence on, 136
Political consumerism, 62, 77–81
  by generation, 77–78
  goals of, 77–78
Political engagement. See also Elections;
    Elections, presidential; "Political
    specialists"; Volunteerism; Voter
    turnout; Voting
  activities for, 60f
  age as factor for, 6, 7f, 122, 188–91
  of Baby Boomers, 30, 67t, 69t
  civic activism and, 194, 198–200
  civic v., 5–10, 51–52, 113t
  cognitive engagement and, 65–66
  consumers and, 62, 77–81
  cultural influence on, 10
  definition of, 6
  of DotNets, 40–46, 67t, 69t, 122, 162
  of Dutifuls, 67t, 69t
  within educational institutions, 84f,
    139–41, 139–44, 230n15
  by educational level, 84f
  efficacy of, 118–19
  family influence on, 123, 205
  financial contributions and, by
    generation, 69, 71f
  by generation, 85t, 188t
  generational change as factor for, 186–
    87, 202
  of GenXers, 34–35, 67t, 69t
  media influence on, 205
  participation in, 10, 134t
  partisanship in, 130
  "political specialists," 65

"public voice" and, 65–66
  service learning and, 194
  volunteerism v., 193, 196t
  voter registration and, 59
  voting as part of, 6
Political parties
  age demographics among, 159f
  decline in number of, 10
  Democratic Party, 6, 160–61
  gender and, 160
  identification, by generation, 158t, 173,
    173f
  public views of, by DotNets, 110f, 112f
  Republican Party, 158–60, 172
"Political specialists," 65
  "civic" v., 199
  by generation, 193
Politicians, public views of, by
    generation, 109t
PRC (Pew Research Center), 55, 164, 172
  political engagement surveys by, 84,
    174
Pregnancy rates, DotNets and, 37
"Project 540," 206
Public engagement. See Civic
    engagement
Public Interest Research Group, 213
"Public voice," 75–77, 198
  civic engagement and, 65–66, 65t, 151
  cognitive engagement v., 54–56
  consumer activism as, 75
  expressions of, 76t, 135t, 198t
  by generation, 77
  political capital's influence on, 136
  political engagement and, 65–66, 65t
  purpose of, 54
"Public Work," 206
Putnam, Robert, 10, 52, 189
  Bowling Alone, 52
  cooperative activity for, 51
  expressive behaviors for, 51

Race. See also Minorities
  civic engagement and, 125
  DotNets' views on, 168–69, 204
  "generational identity" and, 97
  tolerance, by age, 168t
"Raise Your Voice," 206
Reagan, Ronald, 15, 27, 108, 172
  GenXers under, 155–56, 159

Vietnam War, 23
  Baby Boomers and, influence on, 14, 18, 30
  generational influences of, 19
  in media, 19
Vina Nguyen Ha, 213
Volunteerism
  by age, 8f, 232n2
  by Baby Boomers, 7
  community service and, 196–97
  within educational institutions, 75, 138–41, 144–45, 144t, 231n6
  by generation, 7, 74
  motivations for, 194–95, 195t
  for organizations, 61
  political engagement v., 193, 196t
  in U.S., rates of, 61
Voter News Service, 166, 225n1
Voter registration
  in CPS, 227n6
  in NCES2, by generation, 221t
  in NCSL, by generation, 221t, 222f
  political engagement and, 59
Voter turnout
  DotNets and, projections, 156
  for elections, increase in, 5
  factors for, 91
  "generation gap" and, effect on, 10, 90–94
  in NCES2, 90–91
  trends in (1972–2004), 6f, 70t, 185
  for 2004 election, 185
  for 2002 election, by generation, 93t, 209
  VAP for, 220
  VEP for, 220
  for youth, decline in, 3–4, 90–93
Voting. See also Voter registration; Voter turnout
  civic engagement v., 4
  coalitions for, 206
  educational programs for, 206

  measuring surveys for, 218–20
  in NES, 61
  nonprofit organizations for, 206
  in political engagement, 6
  registration for, 59, 221t, 222f, 227n6
  social desirability of, 219
Voting age population. See VAP
Voting coalitions
  New Voters Project, 206
  Rock the Vote, 206
  Youth Vote Coalition, 206
Voting eligible population. See VEP

Wars
  "culture," 25, 179, 183
  Gulf War, 15, 18–19, 23, 28
  Iraq War, 17–18, 209
  Korean War, 22
  Vietnam War, 14
  WWII, 14, 18–19, 22
Washington Post/Kaiser/Harvard group. See PKH
Watergate, 14, 23
Wernick, Lisa, 213
White, Ryan, 24–25
World Trade Organization, protests against, 42–43
WWII (World War II), 14, 18, 22
  "Baby Boom" after, 22
  in media, 19

Youth. See also NYS (National Youth Survey)
  activism among, 138
  media directed, 206
  voter turnout declining for, 3–4, 90–93
Youth Attitudes Tracking Survey, 181
Youth Service America, 213
Youth Vote Coalition, 206
Youth Vote 2000, 213
YouthNOISE, 213

CPSIA information can be obtained at www.ICGtesting.com
Printed in the USA
LVOW07s0817130915

453902LV00001B/4/P

9 780195 183177